BORN
AT THE
RIGHT
TIME

BORN
AT THE
RIGHT
TIME

a memoir

Ray Connolly

Find out more about the author at
www.rayconnolly.co.uk
mail@rayconnolly.co.uk

Malignon

The Rhythm of Life (co-writer of series)

PLAYS FOR RADIO

An Easy Game to Play
Lost Fortnight
Tim Merryman's Days of Clover (series)
Unimaginable
I Saw Her Standing There (short story)
God Bless Our Love
'Sorry, Boys, You Failed The Audition'
Devoted

For Plum

Author's Note

This is a book about what made me and made many of the people mentioned in it. Most of us were either war babies or baby boomers who grew up and made our careers during decades of extraordinarily rapid change.

It is also, in part, a book about popular music and some of the musicians and songwriters who created it. Because, whether we like it or not, music has accompanied all of us during most of our lives.

And then there's Plum, my friend and then my girlfriend, who became my wife and mother to our children, Louise, Dominic and Kieron. It's a book about her and them, too.

INTENSIVE CARE UNIT, CHELSEA &
WESTMINSTER HOSPITAL
JULY 2020
DAY 102

RAY: I had a lucky life until now. I was lucky to get into an excellent university, lucky to get a job that I was good at, and then lucky to have a decent career. I was lucky, too, to marry the only girl I ever loved and to have had a long and happy marriage, and to have three wonderful children… Then I got Covid.

DOCTOR: Ray, you're still lucky.

RAY: I am?

DOCTOR: Yes. You survived.

Prologue

Not many journalists were ever given the opportunity to talk privately to Elvis Presley, and then to write about it. I did, but I don't know of any others. It was July,1969, and Elvis had just begun a season in Las Vegas, singing before a live audience for the first time in eight years. I'll tell you how I got to meet him, what he said and what his performance was like, on another page. But for now, just believe me when I say that, for this young journalist, it was, at the time, the most exciting moment of his working life.

A day or so later, I set off back to London, stopping off in New York on my way. Bob Dylan was soon to appear in Britain at the Isle of Wight pop festival, so, I phoned his manager, Al Grossman, hoping to arrange an interview for when Dylan was in London. To my surprise, I was immediately asked to come over to the manager's office, and, when I arrived, even more surprised when he suggested that I interview Dylan on the phone there and then.

'Call Bobby and ask him if he can talk to this reporter from London,' Al Grossman shouted to his secretary.

Within minutes, Bob Dylan (or should I now think of him as Bobby) was on the line. Normally, my interviews were, to some extent, planned, but this one had been sprung on me. So, while I collected my thoughts, I told Dylan that I'd just been to see Elvis.

'Really!' Dylan exclaimed. 'I read the review of the show in *The New York Times*. Was he good? Really good? Who was in the band? Were the Jordanaires with him? And Scotty Moore on lead guitar? No? What did he sing? Did he do "That's All Right, Mama", "Mystery Train" and the Sun Records stuff?'

The Elvis questions poured out of him. Bobby Dylan was interviewing me.

A couple of days later I was back in London and had occasion to phone John Lennon. So, I told him. 'I've just been to see Elvis.'

'Elvis! *Yes?* Was he good? What did he sing? Was Scotty Moore with him? Were the Jordanaires there? Did he do his early songs? "That's All Right", "Don't Be Cruel", "Hound Dog"? Then John Lennon ran through other early Elvis hits, asking, almost word for word, the same questions that Dylan had wanted answering.

I realised something with those phone calls. No matter how famous a star might become, he is always a fan of someone who went before. And, at that moment, when it came to Elvis, as far as Dylan and Lennon were concerned, they weren't world famous; and I wasn't a journalist. All three of us were, in our own minds, still the fifteen-year-old Elvis fans we once had been.

1.

'Deeply regret to inform you…'

My father was thirty-three when he was lost at sea during the Second World War. I was three years old. My only memory of him, indeed my earliest memory of anything, is of a day in the summer of 1944 when he returned home from the United States and opened his suitcase on the carpet in our dining room. Under his starched, white Royal Navy shirts were two chocolate bars, one for my sister, Sylvia, and another for me. I can't remember anything else about him.

Unlike my father, I was born at the right time. When the Royal Navy vessel on which he was billeted sank in the Western Approaches in October 1944, he would probably have known little, if anything, about the Education Act that had recently been passed by Parliament, and which would make higher education possible for his children; while the National Health Service was still three years from being set up. Both of those reforms were fundamental in shaping my life and the lives of millions of others, making our times and expectations completely different from his. Mine was a fortunate generation. His wasn't. But our luck didn't come without the efforts of those who laid the foundations upon which our lives were to be built.

Decades of technological, chemical, industrial, educational and medical advancement since the Second World War have brought changes to our world that my father couldn't have imagined; and piggybacking on many of those changes, have been the worlds of culture, media and entertainment. Television now brings us worldwide news, football from everywhere, reports of wars and revolutions, droughts and forest fires, movies, quiz shows, cartoons, sex, chefs, comedians… just about every possible human activity. My father possibly never knew what a television was. He would almost certainly never have seen a TV programme.

He liked music, I've been told, but he couldn't have imagined that one day music of all kinds, from all countries and in all shapes, would be available at the touch of a button. Music can now be in every room in our homes, in our cars, and in every bar, shop, lift and dentist's surgery. It is a constant in our lives. That would not have been the case at any previous time in history.

My father would have been a boy when, while learning to play the piano by ear, the invention of radio took music beyond the concert halls, theatres, pubs and marching bands. It would have been an exciting time. I've been told that he liked popular songs. What he couldn't have foreseen would be a world that was filled with those songs, a place where songwriters are now among the richest people in the nation, a country in which whistling a merry tune has been replaced by wearing earbuds. For good or bad, music and entertainment are part of the world we now live in. And it's a world around which I've built my life.

It wasn't, however, the world my mother lived in when, on returning home with her two children from staying with my Auntie Beatrice in Manchester in the Spring of 1945, she realised that she had accidentally left her handbag containing her keys on the train. Unable to get into our house, she asked the daughter of a neighbour to climb through an unlocked kitchen window and let us in.

This the girl did, but on pulling open the front door, she found something on the mat. It was a thick, manilla envelope from the Admiralty. Inside was my father's wallet, which had been recovered when his body had been washed up on a beach in Brittany. In it, my mother discovered, were sea-stained, studio-taken photographs of my sister, Sylvia, as a little girl, and me, as a toddler, together with a slip of blue paper, on one side of which were details of my mother's bust, waist and hip measurements, and, on the other, two song titles, 'You'll Never Know' and 'You Are My Sunshine'. They were wartime favourites, for which, presumably, my father had intended to buy the music when the opportunity arose. My parents owned a piano, but my mother didn't play by ear, and they didn't have a gramophone.

The arrival of the wallet was, my mother would remember, the moment at which any lingering dreams of a miracle departed. The initial telegram, sent months earlier, had simply read: *'DEEPLY REGRET TO INFORM YOU THAT YOUR HUSBAND JOHN CONNOLLY ORDNANCE ARTIFICIER D/MX 90406 HAS BEEN REPORTED MISSING PRESUMED KILLED ON WAR SERVICE'.* The return of the wallet now meant that my father's body had been found, and any vague hope of some administrative mistake, or an overlooked rescue, was gone. At thirty, my mother had become a war widow with two small children to bring up. My father was one of the 383,700 British servicemen in the Second World War who never came home.

We burned Hitler on a bonfire a few months later. At least, I thought we did. I'd stood at our sitting room window and watched as a huge tree in a field across our road was cut down in teeming rain. Then, a few evenings later, we were taken in a coach to a playing field to watch as a bonfire was lit under a mountain of logs and bushes.

'Can you see Hitler up there at the top, Raymond?' a neighbour asked me, pointing to a stuffed guy in a chair as the flames reached him.

I could, but I didn't understand. It was VE Day. The only thing this four-year-old knew about Hitler was that he was a very bad man, whom, I'd been told, was already dead. So how could they now be burning him alive?

That pretty much encapsulates my memories of World War II. It would be fifty years before I visited my father's grave, that of the only British serviceman in the cemetery in Servel, a little French village in Brittany, and learned, thanks to a documentary for the BBC, what my father had been doing in the Atlantic Ocean in 1944. Only after that, did I discover how he'd spent some months while in the Royal Navy, at a US Army base in Asbury Park, New Jersey, where he taught young American soldiers how to maintain the engines they would be using when they arrived in Europe for the invasion. And that he and a colleague would, every Saturday night, visit a piano bar where my father would leaf through the sheet music and make requests to the pianist. 'He seemed to know every song there was,' the colleague would one day tell me.

There was a song that had been written before the war, and which he would have known well and probably listened to in that Asbury Park piano bar. And it seems to me to have perfectly fitted those times. Built around the phrase 'I'll be seeing you', it turned a jaunty goodbye into a sad reflection on separation and loss. It summed up my mother's situation and that of so many others in 1945, when people were happy that the war was over, but who had no soldier to welcome home. 'I'll be seeing you with every lovely summer's day, in everything that's light and gay, I'll always think of you that way…I'll be looking at the moon, but I'll be seeing you.'

I never knew my dad. Like the memories of so many others, he was metaphorically canonised after his death. My mother didn't often talk about him, other than to say he liked to play the piano at parties, and to remember that 'before the war' he'd planted the spreading bramble of little pink roses at the end of our garden. 'John would have known how to prune them,' she would sometimes say sadly. My sister and I were too young to enquire too deeply about him.

'*Before the war!*' That was the phrase we heard so much as children, a suggestion of a time when things had been looking good for this young couple, who, after meeting at a church dance, had saved for years to put a deposit down on one of the bright, brand new semi-detached houses that were being built in the fields outside the towns in the inter-war period. They'd just about settled into 53 Clarkes Crescent, Eccleston, St Helens, bought some furniture and a radio, laid the lawns, front and back, had their first baby and were thinking about another when the war began and their dream ended.

They both came from working class families, my paternal grandfather being the son of an Irish shoemaker from County Galway. It was said, he'd driven a Liverpool tram when he'd first come to England, then settled into a rented back street cottage in St Helens, with a job in a bottle factory and a lifetime reading the *News Chronicle.* He never once went back to Ireland, or saw his parents again, all his brothers and sisters having emigrated to America, apart from one who went to Australia. His wife, my grandmother, a daily communicant when I knew her, on whose mantelpiece Palm Sunday was commemorated all the year round alongside a framed picture of the Sacred Heart of Jesus, was a second-generation Irish immigrant. A marriage certificate from 1875, which I've recently seen, showed that neither of her Irish parents had been able to read or write, both marking their wedding assent with an 'x'. So, my father was brought up in probably the poorest home I've even been in, before, on leaving school at fifteen, he studied engineering at night school. The future would be better.

My mother's background wasn't much more promising, just a rung or two higher up the social scale. In a story of Victorian melodrama, her mother, my Grandma, had been abandoned as a child when her own mother had died in childbirth and her father had remarried. By the age of thirteen she was in service. Meeting an itinerant violinist, Grandma was married at 17, having eight children before her fiddling husband ran off to manage a theatre in Southsea with a new woman, with whom he had two more daughters. Despite the desertion, I never heard her utter one word of reproach about her husband. The nearest she came to it was when, in her late seventies, I asked her if she would like to live her life again.

'Not my life,' she replied quietly. I didn't realise the sad significance of her reply at the time. Not *her* life. At least her daughters were able to give her a happy and comfortable old age.

Whether I inherited an interest in music from my father or my mother's father I can't say or know if it's even genetically possible. What I do know is that I recall most of the major moments in my life through music; popular music mainly. Like an aide memoire, songs have always lingered as an accompaniment to events at the back of my mind. Play me a few bars of 'You Are My Sunshine' and tears from childhood invariably spring; give me a line or two of the Beach Boys harmonies on 'God Only Knows' and I'm listening to Alan Freeman on *Pick Of The Pops* with the girl who would become my wife, a twenty year old Plum, one Sunday afternoon on her father's boat on Ullswater in 1966; while the Fine Young Cannibals' 'Good Thing' puts me in a record shop in Harare, Zimbabwe, with my son, Dominic, during his gap year.

This isn't unusual. Most of us will relive a moment of our lives when prompted by a musical trigger. My good fortune has been that for many years as a journalist, then as a film and TV writer, I've found myself interviewing and meeting some of the most successful musicians and songwriters in the world, then sometimes using their work to add colour to my screenplays and mood to my novels. What was a craze as a boy, then a teenage obsession, became my job, and, eventually, simply part of who I am.

And when, at the age of 79, I was put in an induced coma and, unconscious for weeks, was struggling to breathe as Covid laid waste my body, the nurses asked Plum which records they should play me in the hope that favourite music might help my recovery. Weeks later, I'm told that, with my eyes still closed, unable to speak and unaware that I was being watched, or even knowing where I was, I appeared to turn a critical corner in my illness. Del Shannon's

'Runaway' was being played, and my dry lips began to mutely mouth the lyrics of the song, while my fingers played an imaginary piping organ in the record's instrumental break.

You never miss what you never had, and I don't think I ever consciously missed my father. I was brought up by women and always felt comfortable with women. I still do and 53 Clarkes Crescent, Eccleston, was a good place to start life. A pleasant suburban road, there were cows in the meadow a hundred yards away, and it was only a short walk in our best clothes to a wooded Carmelite convent for mass on Sundays. How did my mother afford to keep her house with no husband to support the family? By taking a clerical job a couple of miles' bicycle ride from where we lived. When she'd been at school, she'd wanted to be a teacher, but, as further education had been out of the question, her first job had been in a St Helens shop selling women's dresses. By the time she reached her forties, and I was in my mid-teens, it would turn out to have been good training for a second career when she opened her own dress shop. In the meantime, her mother came to live with us. Grandma, who would sometimes hum the tunes that her husband had played on his violin, would stay, until, at 83, she died one Easter holiday while I was home from university.

Kneeling at her side as she read to me the 'Rupert Bear' picture serial every day in the *Daily Express* is my abiding memory of her. I learned to read by following the words as she read them. 'Just William' and the 'Famous Five' books, which we would borrow from the library, came next. By the time I could be bothered to read for myself, and she could get back to her Agatha Christies, she had received a sound knowledge of the habits of middle-class, postwar children who went to boarding schools and drank ginger beer.

When she wasn't reading to me, Grandma would sit with me as we listened together to E. M. Pardoe's 'Bunkle Butts In' on *Children's Hour*. Violet Carson (who later became known as Ena Sharples in *Coronation Street*) was the producer; and Billie Whitelaw was the teenage girl playing Bunkle, the eleven-year-old boy in the serial. Naturally, I had assumed Billie to be a boy, but when I met Billie Whitelaw at a party in later life, she remembered Bunkle as just another role in a busy schoolgirl career. To her he'd been a job: to me he'd been a hero, a dramatised version of myself, the first fictional character with whom I identified.

I didn't realise it then, but the Bunkle series also introduced me to composer Edward Elgar, whose 'Chanson de Matin' had been chosen as the series' incidental music. There was real class in radio theme music in those days. That was the thing about the BBC. It might, I now know, have been stuffy and paternalistic, but with no rival radio stations to compete for listeners, and no commercial breaks, the producers took seriously their mission to educate as well as to inform and entertain. By way of the Home Service and the Light Programme, a growing child could get a good grounding in popular literature and music. With its mélange of light classics and pop songs, from Kathleen Ferrier's 'Blow the Wind Southerly' to a Puccini aria and 'There'll Be Bluebirds Over The White Cliffs of Dover', *Two-Way Family Favourites* governed Sunday lunchtimes, as Jean Metcalfe in London and Cliff Michelmore in Germany played requests for British soldiers still stationed in post-war Germany. We never listened to the Third Programme, the forerunner of Radio 3. That would have been considered highbrow in our house. But it was there for those who wanted it. In so many ways, the BBC was helping lay out some of the building blocks that would help build our world into a place better than it had been... 'before the war'.

2.

'The King stammers, too, you know, Raymond'

I was never the top of the class in my primary school. Top four or five out of thirty odd, I suppose. My sister, two years older, was much cleverer than I was. I wrote, I was told, good little compositions, but arithmetic was, and would remain, my stumbling point, even at an elementary level. And while Sylvia was dutiful in practicing her piano scales, I gave up on lessons after weeks of struggling with 'Handel's Largo'. I've wished ever since that I'd paid more attention to my quavers and semi-quavers, or that I'd had a piano teacher who might have suggested perhaps making something up for myself. But that wasn't the way the piano was taught then.

For me, the best parts of education were the Holy Days of Obligation, when we Catholics got extra days off school to celebrate the feasts of various saints, a perk that the Church of England children didn't have. We had to go to mass at first, of course, but, after that, it was a holiday. So, I always felt that we were specially privileged to be part of 'the One, True, Holy and Apostolic Church', as the Catechism taught us. Another part of me might have felt that a Holy Day of Obligation was a bit like playing truant without guilt, which, I suppose, is what my mother did one sunny Ascension Thursday, when, very unlike her, she took a day off work to take us on a picnic.

The venue for the picnic was somewhere she must have known since her own childhood and involved a bus ride, then a walk through a bluebell wood. I'd never seen so many bluebells before. It was magical. Then we sat on top of an open hill, that people around there called Billinge Lump, a young war widow and her two children, looking out across the West Lancashire plain, drinking orange squash and eating bread and jam.

My first ambition was to become a farmer, or, more accurately, to own a horse like Daisy. Daisy pulled the milk float that went up our road six days a week. The milkman at the reins was called Joe, a kind and sunny man, probably aged about 30, who adopted me as a minder for Daisy while he was delivering his bottles and jugged quarts. When I was riding with him, high on the float, I felt very important. Eventually, when I was nine, he would take me back to his farm, sit me behind the wheel of his tractor and ask me to steer slowly down the field while he was perched on the back planting, I don't know what…turnips or cabbages, perhaps.

He was, I suppose, the only man to ever take a fatherly interest in me, and he would let me hold the reins as Daisy trotted along the road while he sang 'Galway Bay' and 'I'll Take You Home Again, Kathleen'. When I got older, and began to know about these things, I realised he must have been a Bing Crosby fan.

Then one day he got married and went to live with his wife in a cottage that was almost tucked under the high stone walls of Lord Derby's Knowsley Park estate. In half-term holidays, I would go to the farm and accompany his sister-in-law as she took milk to the hall and its stables, Lord Derby being apparently a keen horseracing man. I'd never seen anywhere as vast and grand as Knowsley Hall. It was a palace. I know now that the estate covers 2,500 acres, which is seven times the size of London's Hyde Park. And I remember feeling that we were entering a different country when we went through its massive iron Victorian gates into its woods and avenues of horse-chestnut trees, where conkers lay like gold nuggets in hundreds on the grass, and where one day three fallow deer dashed in front of our milk float.

I was reminded of those days a few years ago. Attending a talk in London by the American singer Natalie Merchant, I was surprised when she told how she'd just come back from staying at Knowsley Park, which she'd visited because Edward Lear had once stayed there, and she had adapted one of his poems as a song. 'Does anyone here know Knowsley Park?' she asked the audience.

'I do,' I said, tentatively putting up my hand.

'Oh, really? Are you part of the Lord Derby family?' she asked.

'Not really,' I murmured. 'I delivered the milk.'

Eventually, Joe's wife had a baby, and I spent one Saturday helping him put up a wire-netting fence for his chickens, after which we went inside for some tea as his wife breast-fed her baby. I'd never seen a woman breast-feed before, so, when I got home, I told my mother.

She didn't say anything, but her expression said that she wasn't at all happy that a 'good Catholic boy' like me should ever have witnessed such a thing.

It really was a different age.

'The King stammers, too, you know,' adults would say kindly. Yes, I did know, as did every other stammering child at that time.

I've been told that I didn't stammer when I first started to talk, that it arrived at about the age of five, and then got progressively worse throughout my childhood. Perhaps it should have got me down, but I really don't think it did, though it must have worried my mother. All kinds of methods were tried to 'cure' me. Some teachers in my primary school suggested I clap my hands between each word; another, later, said I should go up to the blackboard and write on it the words I couldn't say. Usually, though, most teachers just pretended that I wasn't there, rarely asking me to read out in class, and I didn't draw attention to myself by putting my hand up to answer a question. Stammerers don't.

I was eventually sent for elocution lessons, in the hope that this might help. It didn't. The only result was that I probably ended up talking a bit posher than the other children in my class. I still stammered, but perhaps my stammer had become a little more up-market.

We forget nowadays how close we all might be to death, but that became very clear to me when, at eight, and, just before Christmas, 1948, my sister, Sylvia, caught diphtheria, which was then an infectious, life-threatening disease. She was ten, and in my bedroom, where I sometimes pretended to be a priest celebrating mass, I would lie awake reciting Hail Marys for her and singing 'Silent night, holy night,' in my little boy soprano voice. I don't suppose it did her any good, but it probably helped me.

For my mother, just four years after losing her husband, it must have been terrifying. Sylvia was in an isolation ward, so the closest my mother could get to her was to watch her from behind a glass pane. I had to go into isolation, too, in case I was a carrier. So, in a personal lockdown, not allowed to go to school or talk to any other children, it was a lonely and frightening run-up to Christmas, as my mother and Grandma decorated the house and put up the cards.

On Christmas Eve I was sent off to bed early, probably with the usual joke that Father Christmas wouldn't come if I didn't go to sleep. At eight, I obviously didn't believe it, but I did go to sleep, and he did come. In the morning there was a sock and a pillowcase at the end of my bed. In the sock were the usual Brazil nuts, chocolate and maybe an orange, and in the pillowcase a new pair of pyjamas and a Dinky car. There was also a Christmas card on which was a note: 'There's something else for you downstairs in the hall.'

Having no idea of what to expect, I went downstairs, unaware that my mother had heard me get up and was following me. In the hall, there was indeed something under a blanket. Reaching out, I lifted the blanket, then stepped back into my mother's arms in shock. A gleaming, brand new, shining Philips boy's bicycle was propped against the wall. 'Happy Christmas,' my mother said.

It's impossible now to convey my astonishment at that moment. This was post-war Britain. To get a bike for Christmas, a *new* bike, wasn't so much unexpected as beyond expectations. No-one I knew had a new bike. Not in 1948. We might have been living in a bicycle culture, but that meant old, rusting, much repaired bikes that had been made before the war. This was a shining new steed of a bike. It was like being given a Ferrari for Christmas.

Naturally, I couldn't wait to get outside and cycle up and down the road on Christmas Day. But, over the years, I've often wondered how my mother could possibly have afforded to buy it.

'I just did,' she would explain. 'With Sylvia being in hospital, and you not allowed to go out, I had to make Christmas special for you.'

It was more than special.

Sylvia came home from hospital just before Easter, and she was sitting in the dining room when I got back from school for my lunch. Apparently, the three tests she'd done that morning had all been negative, so she was free to leave. I was so surprised, I was embarrassed, and didn't know what to say to her. I'd got used to being an only child. Now we were a family again.

Not every family was so lucky. The son of my mother's best friend died later that year from tetanus poisoning. He was called

Gerald, and he was twelve. My father's only brother had died a year earlier from peritonitis. With modern drugs and medical help now available to all of us, we've forgotten how delicate was the thread protecting us not so very long ago.

The first dog I owned I christened Gyp. I got him as a puppy from Joe's farm. He was black and white and he bit people. Not us, just the neighbours. But, in the end, they said he had to go. Sylvia brought our next dog home from school one day. It had been given a boy's name, Tony. But, on closer observation, my Grandma, who knew about these things, noticed that it was a female dog, so we changed the spelling of her name to Toni.

She was a pretty, little thing, a terrier, mongrel type, I suppose, and we loved her. Then one day a naughty, big white dog from down the road took a shine to her and the two became very friendly indeed. Luckily, I understood a thing or two about what dogs did with each other, Hugh, a clever boy in my class having explained. So, when Grandma poured a bucket of cold water over the shameless pair, I quickly remonstrated.

'Don't do that, Grandma,' I said. 'She's going to have a puppy and he's giving her a blood transfusion.'

Grandma laughed and laughed all day about that. I didn't know why. My friend Hugh later went to be a priest.

As with everyone in those days, cinema was a real treat, and my mother would take Sylvia and me into town to see the MGM musicals that she liked. *The Great Caruso* and *The Student Prince*, both of which starred Mario Lanza singing popular Italian arias, were her favourites. Mine were Westerns, especially *Broken Arrow*, with James Stewart, which at ten led me to my first attempt at writing a screenplay. It was in a notebook with a shiny blue cover that I bought especially for the job. I must have written at least a page and a half when I summoned my school friends, Bobby Yates, Norman Ryan and Valentine McDermott to a nearby wood for a rehearsal. I was, obviously, going to play the James Stewart part, as well as being the auteur writer-director and producer, and they were my non-speaking Apache Indian tribe. That was as far as I'd got.

A more ambitious project followed the General Election in 1951, an end-of-term exercise in improvisation that I devised for the same group of friends. This time they had lines to say, which didn't go very well when Bobby froze as he forgot his one line, 'Vote Conservative'.

The war seemed to me to be long over, when the nation celebrated the Festival Of Britain on London's South Bank. It was 1951 and an exciting time. We were moving into a new era. 'Modern' was the buzz word of the time. Everything had to be new and modern, including us. And, not to be outdone, Liverpool held its own pageant on the River Mersey. Normally we couldn't have gone, Liverpool being ten miles away. But a very kind family from across the road invited us to go with them, which meant that three adults and four children all squeezed into their little car.

Our neighbours had presumably been told that we would get a better view from the far side of the river, so it was quite an adventure as I went through the Mersey Tunnel for the first time. I still looked for the fish, although I knew I wouldn't see them. I'm sure the evening was very exciting, as tugs and ferry boats festooned with fairy lights paraded up and down the river, but that isn't what I mostly remember. To fill the gaps between the firework displays, at their little Mersey *son et lumiere,* the organisers laid on musical interludes, by playing over the loudspeakers the only two records it seemed they had. They were jaunty, singalongs, Guy Mitchell's 'My Truly Truly Fair' and 'The Roving Kind', and their flipsides, all played again and again. I thought they were wonderful.

Hearing those handclaps and choruses and accompanying French horns, as rockets shot up into the sky and cascaded across the water, was for me a life-changing moment. That night, at the age of 10, I became a pop music fan.

The most worrying time in any child's home in 1952 was when the results of the scholarship came through the letterbox. Known later as the 11-Plus, the scholarship was the examination that could magically change life's expectations. Pass it, and the doors opened to a brighter future, a grammar school, followed maybe by college or university, then possibly a profession, certainly a white-collar job. Fail it, and an educational scrapheap, known then as a secondary modern school, awaited. It shouldn't have been like that, and it hadn't been intended that it would be so life determining. But, for too many children, that's what it was.

To be honest, I thought I'd done pretty-well in the scholarship, but when my mother opened the letter, it turned out I hadn't. I'd failed. As I've said, I couldn't do sums. There's a word for it now. It's called dyscalculia. In my day, they had a simpler word. Dunce.

No matter how hard my mother probably tried, nothing could have hidden her disappointment in my failure. There was just one hope left for me. The St Helens Catholic Grammar School, where she had hoped to send me, had another private exam for fee paying boys. I took that, and, after my mother paid a pleading visit to the headmaster, I was accepted. I can only hope that the fees were modest for the son of a war widow.

3.

'K-K-Katy, beautiful Katy…'

Before I could even begin at my new school, a fundamental change in my life took place when my mother sold our nice, modern home in Eccleston and we moved with Grandma to a very big nineteenth century house that my Auntie Beatrice had just bought. It was in Aughton, just outside Ormskirk, eleven miles away. It was called Highfield, and it had eight bedrooms, a four-room cellar, a very large garden, a little wooded bluebell copse on the side, and, behind it, a Victorian pavilion that had been originally used as a nonconformist chapel. For me it meant there would be three lawns to mow every week in the summer, and three buses to catch every morning to get to my Catholic grammar school in St Helens; and then three buses back again.

Ormskirk was a pleasant little town with a church that had both a tower and a steeple, a market in the main street on Thursdays and Saturdays, and was surrounded by flat miles of farmers' fields in every direction. For me, one of the best things about living there was that my cousins, Pauline and Julie, lived in a grocer's shop half a mile away. Pauline was about a year older than I was, and it must have been she, or her mother, who organised a trip to the Liverpool Empire to see a matinee performance by…yes, the great Guy Mitchell, who was on a tour of the UK. Fifteen years later, I would tell John Lennon about that trip to the Empire. He was a bit disparaging. He'd been there, too, at about the same age, he said, but he'd gone to see Frankie Laine who 'was much better'. I disagreed. But that's boys. They can get very nerdy and possessive about their chosen heroes.

As for the show itself, it was my first live pop music experience, although, in those last days of variety, the other acts included jugglers, acrobats and a very young Morecambe and Wise. I was enthralled, anyway. It wasn't just that Guy Mitchell was a star and the first famous person I had ever seen. He was much more than that. He was an *American* star, and America, with its seeming abundance of everything glitzy, was, in the early Fifties, a Never-Never Land.

While waiting for my bus home from school by St Helens Town Hall, I would watch American soldiers queuing to go back to the US Air Force base at Burtonwood. In their light cotton uniforms, their trousers usually an inch too short, I thought they looked impossibly glamorous. But so did everything American. Hollywood films were more exciting and colourful than British ones, and even American chewing gum, five flat strips in a Wrigleys packet that was made in Chicago, Illinois, seemed cooler than the same British product which came in shiny white pastilles. It wouldn't be quite right to say that my generation felt cowed by Americana. It was just that they seemed to do everything bigger and better over there, a perspective that others of my generation would change dramatically when they grew up.

The talk at school was about Radio Luxembourg, and, as soon as we had a record player, I spent what little money I had on buying Guy Mitchell records. They came as ten-inch 78rpm singles, and I would regularly iron their brown paper sleeves if they got crumpled. For some reason, that seemed to amuse everyone in my family. The records were my treasures, and I would pore over their labels, memorising the numbers and the writers of the songs, noticing that Bob Merrill, who wrote 'My Truly Truly Fair', had also written 'There's A Pawnshop On A Corner in Pittsburg, Pennsylvania' and 'She Wears Red Feathers'; while Terry Gilkyson had composed not only 'Christopher Columbus' but 'The Day of Jubilo'. Wow! Years later the American first wife of Charles Wintour, who would become my editor and mentor at the London *Evening Standard,* was astonished that I'd heard of her second cousin, Terry Gilkyson. All she knew was that he'd written 'Memories Are Made of This' for Dean Martin. Clever bloke that Terry Gilkyson.

At about the same time as falling in love with records, I began going to a riding school near where we now lived. My cousin, Julie, came, too. I loved the horses, but not so much some of the other children, who were mainly Pony Club type girls, whose fathers were important people in the area, like estate agents. On my first day I went on my bike and wore my oldest trousers. The girls, however, all turned up in brand new jodhpurs and hacking jackets, riding crops in hands and hard hats on their pretty little heads. Joe hadn't stipulated that I wore jodhpurs when I sat on Daisy and he walked me around the fields. I was wearing the wrong clothes at the riding school, and, for the first time in my life, I became aware of a class distinction.

I have very little recollection of my daily trips to and from school. Sylvia, who was at the Notre Dame Convent also in St. Helens, and I always sat together and read all the way there and back. It meant leaving home at 7.30 in the morning and not getting back until getting on for six at night, so it wasn't ideal. Nor did I enjoy school. In those parts, the Catholic Grammar in St. Helens was known by its location as West Park and was famous for its rugby team. As an eight stone weakling, at best, even when I was in the sixth form, rugby was never an area in which I was likely to excel. The solitary nature of long distance running suited me better.

In those days there was always quite a bit of casual brutality around in boys' schools, usually involving a cane or a clout by some puffed up martinet of a master. But, looking back, I can see that at West Park the teaching staff were probably doing the best they could within the limits of their own experiences of life. So, I continued my school career by making myself as invisible as was possible, and by ignoring the 'K-K-Katy' jibes, which sometimes graduated into 'C-C-ConnOlly'. That was from a teacher, too.

Only on Friday mornings was I really happy, when I would buy a new weekly newspaper called the *New Musical Express* and lose myself in the pop charts. At thirteen years of age, seeing Johnnie Ray's 'Such A Night' at number one was truly exciting; even though I had no idea what he might have been doing on that special night, or that his version was a cover of an r and b hit by the Drifters. I suppose when *'SUCH A NIGHT'* was used as a newspaper headline for Roger Bannister's running of the first (under) four minutes mile that same week, thus linking the two events, it became personal for me. I was good at picking hit records and running, as well.

Memories of school days are threadbare now, but we always retain moments of dispiriting hurt, and one hangs around me even now, seventy years later. I was twelve and we'd been asked to write a short story for our English homework. Excited by the task, I spent an entire weekend planning my story and then writing eight pages in rough, before copying it in my very best handwriting into my English exercise book. I was really pleased with it, and expectant of high praise. But, a week later when our books were returned, I saw that the teacher had only made a couple of red punctuation marks on the first page and ignored the rest, simply writing at the end, 'If this is your own work it is very good'. She obviously hadn't read it.

I suppose that should have prepared me for the rejections that all writers get from editors and producers who haven't had the time, the interest or simply been bothered, to read scripts and stories sent to them with fervent hopes and prayer. Perhaps it did. I wouldn't write any fiction again until I was thirty.

When we'd first moved house, my mother had given up her job to help in the grocer's shop that my aunt had. But they must soon have realised that money was tight, so when a young gym teacher in his first job at the local grammar school knocked on our door wondering if, as we had a big house, he could stay for a few nights, he was given a room. He was Phil Downing. And when his friend, a geography teacher called Brian, also needed somewhere to live, he came, too. Brian only stayed for a couple of years, but Phil was with us until I went to university. They were the first people I knew who had degrees. And, as I grew into my teens, the *Biggles* books I was reading were cast aside for the John Steinbeck and Ernest Hemingway novels that they brought into our home. I probably read them too early, but their influence on me would be much greater than the Walter Scott that we were reading in English lessons.

By this time, I had a new and lifelong friend. He was John Rimmer and was the same age as I was. He lived around the corner in Swanpool Lane. John had also failed the scholarship, which meant, as his father was a stockbroker, that he was sent off to a boarding school in North Wales. We were then only friends in the holidays. But what holidays we had. Freed by our bikes, and in a world with few cars on the road, we pursued one craze after another, our unworried parents confident that we would come to no harm.

Armed only with torches we would go slithering on our stomachs down what was known as the 'Mousehole' into two hundred years old Crank Caverns. Then, finding a way into the dilapidated remains of the once grand, eighteenth century Lathom

Hall, we climbed up into its clock tower, where one of the clock's fingers lay abandoned. We took it home with us. John now lives in New Zealand where the clock finger hangs on his sitting room wall. That part of Lathom Hall has since been demolished, so it was lucky that we nicked the clock finger when we did. Without our thieving, it could have ended up in a landfill site.

Most exciting of all was our Roman coins adventure. A hoard of them had been discovered in the banks of stream a couple of years earlier about two miles from where we lived. Our logic said that if a hundred coins had been found, there must surely be a few that had been missed.

Wearing wellies, and equipped with huge shovels, that we borrowed from the local farm, we began the task of shovelling silt from the bottom of the stream into a riddle, before carefully carrying it to a place where the water flowed more quickly. There we washed out the mud and stared, like gypsies into tea leaves, at the remaining pebbles.

The first coin we spotted looked like a dull, grey piece of metal. But two more soon followed. The next day we hit the jackpot. From virtually the first riddle we pulled out three almost perfect coins. They were a Nerva, a Hadrian and a Trajan, all with their heads and names impressed into the silver. A not-so-good Augustus Caesar came next.

For two weeks we worked that stream, turning the whole riverbank until it looked like a scene out of the Klondike. Then in the evenings we would pore over a Roman coin reference book we got from the Ormskirk public library.

In total, we found thirty-three coins. Then I suddenly lost one on the bus to school, and with it I lost interest. John was convinced I'd given it to the bus conductor by mistake for a sixpence, because a denarius is nearly the same size, although thicker. That's unlikely. But we were now falling out over them. So, one day, I just put my share into a handkerchief, wrapped it up and gave it to him. 'You'd better keep them,' I said. The fun had been in *finding* the coins. John would be a much better bank than I was. He still has them. The Roman coins had become his hobby. It wasn't mine.

I had a new obsession.

4.

'You're too jerky...'
'It's my gimmick, sir'

John was the perfect friend, except for one thing. He wasn't into music, and, while he was away at school in the Spring term of 1956, 'Heartbreak Hotel' was released. From then on, I could talk of nothing else and think of little else. What I didn't realise, was that I was hearing, for me, a new form of music, with a new kind of dominant instrument. I know now that it was probably a Gibson 29 hollow body electric guitar, but, with the whole sound distorted by echo, it sounded as though Elvis and the guitar were at the bottom of a deep well.

Electric guitars had been invented in the Thirties, mainly for jazz musicians, but this was the first time I'd heard one used on a pop, bluesy song. Technologically it was revolutionary, because that sound would have been impossible to create just a few years earlier. Not everyone liked it, and Elvis's record company bosses didn't even want to release it. But Elvis had his ear closer to the ground than they did. He knew better and his high tenor voice did the rest. Quickly, young American bands began to play Gibsons and Rickenbackers, or, like Buddy Holly, Sunburst Fender Stratocaster, electric guitars. While in Britain Keith Richards and George Harrison would always point to the sound of 'Heartbreak Hotel' as the moment they knew what instrument they wanted to play.

There was something else, too. A Fifties' change in British hire purchase regulations which was designed to encourage sales of domestic electrical goods like fridges and cookers, also included musical instruments. That meant that budding musicians in Britain could now buy electric guitars on the never-never.

And the guitar was the main event. A development in electrical engineering had, in effect, created the perfect instrument for rock and roll. Dance halls had, for generations, waltzed, smooched and quickstepped to the sounds of big bands. But electric guitars would now make those bands redundant. Why hire a small orchestra, with horns and strings, when all you needed to dance, was an amplified four-piece rock and roll band, with a singer who could perhaps play and sing at the same time?

Until then, music on the radio had been limited to the BBC request programmes that rationed the records I wanted to hear. Radio Luxembourg was better, but the American Forces Network stations in Munich, Frankfurt and Stuttgart which served the US forces in Europe, were best. Their signal was always weak, except late at night, but it was worth staying up just to hear the bluesy riff of Jimmy Forrest's 'Night Train' at ten o'clock, as disc jockeys brought us the latest US hits. That was where I first heard 'Love Me Tender' in September 1956, with Elvis singing so quietly he could have been speaking to a girl on the back seat of his car. Until then ballad singers had been crooners. 'Love Me Tender' was intimate, not much more than a murmur, a new kind of singing completely.

What a year it was. Already Elvis had given us 'Don't Be Cruel' and 'Hound Dog' on the two sides of one record. Then came a long player. Unable to afford it, I would get off the bus one stop early on my way to school, just to stand outside a record shop and look at the album cover in the window. The lettering, just the words, *'ELVIS'* in pink down the left-hand side and *'PRESLEY'* in green along the bottom, against a black and white photo of him, aged 20, looking as if he was howling at the moon, made it the best album cover he ever had. It was the best album he ever released, too.

When I got more confident, I would go into the shop and ask that they play me something from it, maybe 'Mystery Train' or 'Lawdy Miss Clawdy', then make an excuse that it wasn't quite what I wanted, having had no money to buy it, anyway. I didn't need to. The tune, the voice, the guitars, the rhythm and the echo would be lodged on repeat in my head for the rest of the day.

I was never a Bill Haley fan, instead discovering rock music through Fats Domino's ('Yes it's Me And) I'm In Love Again', the Crickets' 'That'll Be The Day' and the Everly Brothers' 'Wake Up Little Susie'. The very idea of that song seemed so daring. What had the boy and girl been doing in the car that they were rehearsing fibs about falling asleep because 'the movie wasn't so hot, didn't have much of a plot', and worrying that their friends would say 'Ooh-la-la'? Just the idea of going to a drive-in with a girl was impossibly exciting.

I used to go the cinema with my sister. That was when I first fell in love. The girl was a cool blonde called Grace and she was in Alfred Hitchcock's film *To Catch A Thief.* I was very disappointed when she got off with, and then married, Prince Rainier and went to live in Monaco while I was still a schoolboy.

Our school was nothing like those I heard about on the American records. Romance seemed to be what mostly went on in high schools, where the key word of the time was 'teenager'. Just the word itself was thrilling. 'Why must I be a teenager in love?' sang Dion and the Belmonts on AFN Munich and Marty Wilde on Radio Luxembourg. But, once Grace had settled for someone else, I wasn't in love anymore, so I didn't understand why it was even a question, or why Frankie Lymon of The Teenagers sang 'Why Do Fools Fall In Love'? Did you really have to be a fool to fall in love? Nor was I the sort who, according to the *Daily Express,* tore up cinema seats or went around in hoodlum gangs, as the Coasters seemed to do in 'Yakety Yak'.

That said, despite my school blazer, bicycle clips, Confession when I had nothing to confess on a Saturday evening, and Mass on Sunday morning, I was, by virtue of my first shave, a teenager. Nothing could stop me now.

I'd never seen actors improvising before I saw James Dean in *East of Eden,* as he and Julie Harris overlapped their conversation as though they didn't know their lines. Maybe they didn't, but it was fascinatingly realistic. Dean had already been dead by the time the film reached Ormskirk, so, when the headlines appeared around the release of his second film, *Rebel Without A Cause*, I was keen to see it.

It was showing at a cinema in Maghull, which was a few miles towards Liverpool from where we lived. It was a school night, and I had to ask my mother for the money to get in, which she happily gave me, before announcing that she'd be coming with me.

Going with your mum to see James Dean in *Rebel Without A Cause*, infamous in the newspapers for its chicken run and a knife fight, even though the British censor had already cut that bit, was not the coolest situation for a fifteen year old to be in. As we took our seats, I glanced furtively around at the local kids. They looked more streetwise than we did in Ormskirk, tougher and more mocking, with a few Teds and their molls among them. I kept my head down, hoping that no-one would notice this rebel of a teenager…with his mum.

Only later did I realise that *Rebel Without A Cause* sold us a dishonestly glamourised version of Californian youth in which middle class kids went to school in cars, which was hardly representative of the US education system. All the same, even ordinary American high schools seemed sexy to me, and never more so than when Chuck Berry sang about lunchtime in his anthem, 'School Day'.

'Drop the coin right into the slot,' he sang, 'you gotta hear something that's really hot. With the one you love you're making romance…'

Crumbs! That you knew somewhere near your school that had a juke box you could play at lunchtime was more than cool These American kids knew how to live all right.

Until then, this kid had been an invisible schoolboy, who couldn't talk properly and who kept his head down. But the music I was now hearing was giving me a new identity. I was the one at school who knew about rock and roll. Some boys would come top of the class, be brilliant at Latin or physics, or stars on the rugby field, playing for Lancashire and England. I had an encyclopedic knowledge of rock music. It would later come in handy.

Other boys of my age, John Lennon and Paul McCartney in Liverpool, and Paul Simon and Art Garfunkel in New York, and many other fifteen-year-olds, too, were also hearing the clarion calls coming from the radio. Some of them went on to join groups and make music themselves. I didn't know anyone who was in a band. So, I ploughed my own path as a rock and roll nerd, before they were called nerds, who sang to himself and who believed in the myth of American youth that the records were telling me.

Fifteen years later, while travelling in a limousine in upstate New York to a Native American reservation with John Lennon, I was discussing Fats Domino's 'Ain't That A Shame' and singing some old rock and roll songs with him, when the recently former Beatle said: 'If you'd been in my class at school I'd have had you in the Quarry Men.'

To which I replied: 'My mother wouldn't have let me.' Which would have been true.

'I'd have forced you to join to rebel against your mother,' came back John.

At which point I went into 'Peggy Sue', which John began to sing with me. Then, noticing that Yoko was looking bored, he stopped and said: 'I'm not a fucking juke box, you know.'

Back at school, I still stammered, of course, although not when I sang. Unfortunately, my stammering reputation had gone before me. 'You're too jerky, Connolly,' the Latin master, who thought himself a bit of a tenor, said to me when it was my turn to sing 'Do-Re-Mi' as a test for the school choir.

Too jerky? I'd only sung three flipping notes. Was he imagining that I'd stammer when I sang 'Tantum ergo sacramentum' and ruin benediction for everybody? Or perhaps he thought the 'Agnus Dei' would defeat me? It's possible. He was the clown who had called me 'C-C-ConnOlly' and must have been the only person in the world who didn't know that stammerers don't stammer when they sing.

'That's my gimmick, sir,' I came back, suddenly a smart-ass now that I was a teenager. Every singer had a gimmick in those days, according to the *Daily Express*.

'Next,' he said and turned to another boy. I'd failed my audition.

Courtesy of the beneficence of the National Health Service, the school eventually sent me to see a psychiatrist about my stammer. It was worth a shot, the holy water I'd secretly sprinkled on to my lips on a school trip to Lourdes not having worked the magic. The psychiatrist didn't get very far either, so she passed me on to a speech therapist. That was better. She was in her early thirties, and I enjoyed our sessions. I would lie on a mat on the floor with my arms out and she would kneel next to me and lift one of my arms and let it drop, and then lean across me to lift up the other arm, accidentally brushing my chest with her breasts as she did. She wasn't Grace Kelly, but, you know…

I'm sure she thought she'd affected a miracle cure by the time the course finished, because the better I got to know her the more confident and fluent I became. But, when I left her office and went to catch the bus to go home, I couldn't get the words out to pay the fare.

What I didn't realise then was that I was learning to put on a performance as a boy who didn't stammer. It would take me many more years to perfect it.

In the sixth form we studied *Hamlet* and on the bus I read *The Grapes of Wrath*. By now my sister had gone off to college so I sat with my friend Jim from Scarisbrick on the way to school, secretly fancying a girl who wore a green uniform and lived on a remote farm from where the bus would pick her up at the end of her long drive like a taxi. They were journeys of gloomy adolescent introspection.

The truth was, I didn't know much, if anything, about girls. John from Swanpool Lane and I were still friends of course, and one Christmas we were invited to a party that his girl cousins were holding at a farm. There were about eight of us, and it was all very pleasant, until, with Pat Boone singing 'Love Letters In The Sand' in the background, they put the lights out and we began to play Spin The Bottle. It was, they said, 'a necking game'.

Now, I knew about kissing and I knew about snogging, but I didn't know what 'necking' meant. So, taking it literally, as one girl after another moved around the room and sat on my knee in the dark, I managed to dodge any proffered lips, and rub my neck against theirs in the manner of a young giraffe. If they had a party the following year, I wasn't invited.

By its own hormonal nature, teenage is a selfish time, so I probably wasn't paying much attention to what was going on around me. In retrospect, however, it's clear to see that the nation was getting better off. Prime Minister Harold Macmillan said before the 1957 General Election, that we'd 'never had it so good', and, although it may have been an election boast, and a line pinched from a former American president, for a lot of people it was true. The austerity of the post-war years was being replaced with a general optimism. The Festival of Britain's dream of modernity was starting to come true. The consumer society was getting into gear.

On a purely personal level, I can now see that my mother was realising it, too, when she gambled her life's savings on opening a woman's dress shop in our little market town. I'd always thought she was a timid woman, and she must have felt pretty bleak on that first day when it rained and she sold only one blouse. But, within a few weeks, as more and more stock arrived, she discovered that she had a thriving business. With her name soon over the shop window, within a couple of years there would be a commercial for her shop on the screen in the Pavilion cinema round the corner. She'd seen that there was nowhere for women to buy their dresses in Ormskirk, so she'd provided it. I, of course, being a self-obsessed teenager, never realised the risk she'd taken, or the quiet business acumen she must have had. If she'd asked my advice, I would have recommended opening a record shop or a coffee bar with a juke box. Luckily, she didn't ask. But, within a couple of years, she'd bought herself a car, a blue Hillman Minx, and at seventeen I passed my driving test. She didn't know it, but she was a small part of one of the revolutions that would shape the Sixties.

Against all my school's expectations, I did very well in my A-levels in 1959 but ended my career at the Catholic Grammar leaving hardly a ripple behind to show that I'd ever been there. They've certainly never asked me back. Not having planned what to do after school, and obviously unsuited, as a profound stammerer, to go to teachers' training college, which was what nearly all my classmates in Upper Six Arts did, I hitch-hiked around France for four weeks with my sister's medical school boyfriend. You could do that then when drivers were often glad of your company. Then, on return, I went to see the headmaster at the local co-educational Ormskirk Grammar School, and he took me in to do scholarship history and top up on some missing O-levels. It was wonderful. After seven years at an all-boys school, to be having classes with girls was like escaping from a penal colony and finding myself in a Club Med. The girls all seemed so pretty, and clean and starched. They smelled nice, too.

There was an innocence in that pre-Pill time, when all my friends, boys and girls, were, I'm sure, virgins. I don't believe we ever thought to become otherwise. Still studying, and probably young for our age, a co-educational sixth form bred pedigree celibates, unaware and consequently un-frustrated. The big city of Liverpool, with all its enticements, was only half an hour away by train, but it might as well have been 2000 miles distant for all its allegedly decadent influence had upon us.

Never interested in rugby at my boys' school, where I'd been a cross-country runner, and as lonely as the book title went, I soon found myself playing twice on Saturdays. In the morning I was in the school's second team where you would attract the girl hockey players who finished their game before us; and, in the afternoon, in the fourth team of the town rugby club, when their older sisters would support us along the touchline. I was never any good, just a winger who rarely got the ball or dirtied his knees. But the lure of possibly admiring girls, in a place where everybody knew everybody else, and relationships took on a form of non-sexual serial monogamy was a real magnet.

That was when I first got to know Plum. Calling in at my mother's shop on my way home from school one day, I was asked to take the car and deliver a skirt that had been altered to a Mrs Balmforth at the top of Ruff Lane. Everyone in Ormskirk new the name Balmforth. It was the name of a company that Plum's family used to own which sold tractors and combine harvesters to farmers in the area; and Ruff Lane was where the richest people in the town lived.

The house I was looking for was just beyond some woods, and, as I pulled up in the lane, I saw, between the Scots pines, a very large, newly built house with plate glass windows. Built way back from the road, in front of it was a sweeping drive, where three cars were parked, and alongside them a boat. At the side of the house, past a pretty, careful laid-out shrubbery and a wide lawn, was a summer house and a hard tennis court.

To me, it was like suddenly being asked to make a delivery to a home in Beverly Hills, a situation not unlike that in the film *A Place In The Sun* when Montgomery Cliff first meets Elizabeth Taylor.

It wasn't Elizabeth Taylor who answered the door. It wasn't Plum, either. It was Ruth, her pretty, older sister. I vaguely knew Plum from school because she was in the same class as my cousin, Julie. But she was nearly four years younger than I was, which was a lot then. The following day I found an excuse to talk to Plum and asked her if she could fix me up with her sister. She did, which was lovely. But, in the end, it was Plum, the go-between, I wanted, even though she didn't want me. Ruth, meanwhile, fell in love, and then married, my best friend, John from Swanpool Lane. Like I said, Ormskirk was a very small town.

These days, when we go back, we see that our old house, Highfield, has been turned into a care home for elderly people, while the town itself has grown younger. The small teacher's training college has now spread across acres of farmland and become Edge Hill University and the town now has cafes, bars and gymnasiums for the students. But there's something else, too. In our day the local dialect was flat West Lancashire. Now, with urban drift, it's become increasingly Liverpudlian posh.

I don't know whether there's a juke box in Ormskirk these days. I suspect not, as everyone now has Spotify. But the day that a friend called David Heys, who lived near me, happened to mention that his dad worked for a juke box company, and was regularly sent sample records, was up there along with my Roman coins discoveries as one of my epiphanic moments. And when he cycled round to my house the next day bringing 'Everyday' by the lately deceased Buddy Holly, Jimmy Jones's 'Handy Man' on that yellow MGM label with the lion and Neil Sedaka's 'Oh Carol!' my life was complete.

My first records had been 78s and easily cracked or broken. Now I was collecting 45s, the perfect size for hit records. So many memories are captured and stored for life in those 7-inch, three minute, slices of plastic, moments never dramatized on film better than when Harrison Ford manages to start an old car in a barn in the movie *Witness* and the radio suddenly comes on playing Sam Cooke's 'What A Wonderful World'.

'Don't know much about history, don't know much biology. Don't know what a slide rule is for...' goes the record and viewers the world over mouthed the words.

'I used to love this one,' Harrison says to Kelly McGillis.

Didn't we all.

Later, in the mid-Sixties, serious rock people would start banging on about how this album was better than that album. It was always albums they talked about. But I was a singles man when the individual song was at its most perfect. I loved it when you could stack eight 45s on a record player and wait for them to drop, one after another. I've still got all my singles, and wish I still had the juke box that I bought in 1985 when I was quite well off. I sold it because its glass and chrome dome made it look like a cartoon space-station, that its colours were bilious and didn't match the curtains and that it took up too much space in the dining room, as someone very close to me pointed out. But no hi-fi or YouTube ever played the Platters' 'Smoke Gets In Your Eyes' better than my jukebox. It was almost as good as that wonderful moment in *American Graffiti* when Ron Howard and Cindy Williams slow dance together at the high school prom and she starts to cry.

I'd never heard of the London School of Economics and Political Science until I went to Ormskirk Grammar School. It was mentioned by my new headmaster, when he realised that Oxbridge was out for someone who could never pass maths. So, I looked up the LSE on a London street map and realised that it was situated just off the Aldwych, up the road from Fleet Street. The fact that John F. Kennedy, the Democrats' boyish choice that year to be President of the United States, had studied there, gave it a vogueish air. It didn't matter to me that I'd so far shown no interest whatsoever in social anthropology, sociology, psychology, philosophy or economics, the subjects I was about to study. The LSE's location near Fleet Street was what mattered. That was where I had to be.

Most people I knew had a choice to make about what career they were going to pursue. I never had a choice. I'd already realised that writing seemed to be the only thing that I could do reasonably well, so journalism had already become the only thing I wanted to do. With my university fees paid for me and a living grant provided by my local authority, as one of the stipulations of the 1944 Education Act, the LSE would be my stepping-stone.

But there was something else that would change my life, and the lives of millions of others since. All the way through school we'd heard dire warnings that 'two years in the Army will make a man out of you, young man'. But, having seen newsreel of the army in action in Suez and Cyprus, I didn't want to be made a man in the way the army would do it. Nor had *The Goon Show*, a radio programme created by a group of young comics intent on ridiculing their own National Service years, helped the army's image. Anarchic in its silliness, *The Goon Show's* absurdist view of the world was a weekly riposte for authoritarian tinpot schoolmasters and military officers, mimicries of its characters echoing through classrooms and corridors right through the Fifties.

So, it was a day of immense relief when the Government, with a steadily diminishing empire to police, abolished National Service in 1960. Being still at school, I would, I realised, miss call-up by a matter of weeks. From then on, any fighting would be done by other young boys who would be happy for the Army to make them into men.

5.

'God, Ray, I feel randy tonight'

Like the Roaring Twenties, the Swinging Sixties has for the last sixty years become a legend that we like to tell ourselves about the way we were. But, as the Twenties didn't roar for everyone, and certainly not for some people, the Sixties didn't swing for everyone either. And, barring the music, hardly at all for lots of others. Neither did that celebrated era begin in 1960. Rather, we stepped timidly from the sedate decade of the Fifties to the next one with no idea of the cultural revolution that was quietly fermenting around us. The transition into 'the Sixties' itself didn't take place until 1963.

Living in 1960 with three other boys from various London colleges in a room in a students' hostel in Lancaster Gate (it's now a swanky hotel), I was feeling overwhelmed by the roaring self-confidence of London. In my first month at university, I agreed, for some crazy reason, to write and deliver a paper on the Nuer, a tribe in the Sudan, in my social anthropology class. For days I worked on it in the library, but, when I had to deliver it, I began stammering dreadfully. The other seven students in the class kept their eyes down while I struggled, nodding sympathetic congratulations when I finished. But, I knew, it had been bad.

So, it wasn't a complete surprise, although it was a shock, when at a one-to-one the following week my tutor said: 'I suppose you realise that we found it very difficult to tell what you were saying.'

I hadn't realised that. I don't think she meant to be cruel, just up-front honest, but I was devastated. She could probably see that, because she then suddenly said: 'We have a very good psychiatrist here at the LSE. I wonder if he might be able to help you.'

The college psychiatrist was a kind, studious man and listened intently as I told him of my stammering history. Then he asked me if there were any specific moments when my speech was really bad. In truth, it was terrible all the time at that point, but I told him that it was probably at its worst when I had to get the Tube from Lancaster Gate in the morning. If I had the exact money, it would be fine. But, when I didn't, I would get stuck on the words 'Holborn, Kingsway', very aware of the queue of people behind me.

He nodded understandingly. Then he said: 'Have you ever thought it might be a sexual problem?'

I thought I hadn't heard right. 'I'm sorry?'

'A sexual problem?' he repeated.

'No,' I said. I hadn't ever thought that.

'Well, don't you see,' he explained. 'When you go to buy your ticket and have to speak, you're projecting your voice into the hole in the glass booth.'

I still didn't get it.

Probably thinking that I must be a bit dense, and wondering what I was even doing at a university, he proceeded to make a ring with his thumb and first finger on his left hand through which he then projected the index finger on his right hand. 'Don't you see?' he said. 'A sexual problem.'

Now I got it. 'I don't think so,' I said.

'No?'

'No. It can't be a sexual problem. I've never had sex.'

And so began my three years at the London School of Economics. In those pre-motorway days, London was a very long way from Lancashire, a five-hour journey, at best, on a smoke billowing train; eight hours if you travelled overnight. And I was lonely at first. Everyone was.

Phones were expensive and the booth in the hostel was usually occupied, so students would make few calls home. Instead, everybody wrote letters, with up to three deliveries a day then in Central London. And young people, away from home for the first time, would look forward to receiving them, collect them in the hall and take them to their rooms to be read over and again. Everyone pretended not to be homesick and boasted in the letters that they wrote about the wonderful time they were having and all the exciting new friends they were making. But the writer, and probably the reader, too, knew that they were faking it. So many songs then were about letter writing, Billy Williams even getting a hit when he covered the old Fats Waller song 'I'm Gonna Sit Right Down And Write Myself a Letter (and make believe it came from you)'.

At home, I'd always had my own bedroom and never shared with anyone, so I soon left the communal squalor of Lancaster Gate and moved into the solitary squalor of my own room in Bayswater at the Camborne Hotel. The building has now, like the houses in most Victorian squares in West London, been transformed into several two and a half million pound-plus apartments. But, back then, I paid five pounds, twelve and sixpence a week for bed with breakfast and an evening meal thrown in. The only time my mother saw it, she condemned it a slum. I thought it was wonderful. Twenty years later it would make a fond fictional debut in a novel I wrote called, *Sunday Morning.*

The best part of any week would be going to a café in Queensway on Sunday evenings after mass, where I treated myself to steak and chips. I was always alone, the *Observer* propped in front of me as I ate. That was the newspaper that every student read, the one I needed to discover what my metropolitan opinions should be.

The LSE could be a very political college, but I wasn't. So, I never bothered to join any political societies, not even CND. I did go to a wine and cheese party at the LSE Catholic Society one night, though. As we were leaving the attractive daughter of a high court judge said to me: 'God, Ray, I feel randy tonight.'

I was so surprised that I said: 'I think Harry Lofthouse is having a party at his place. You might meet someone there.'

To which she replied. 'That's bloody rude.'

Which I suppose it was. But the daughter of a high court judge had never come on to me before. And she a Catholic, too.

In the end, it was through writing that I began to get to know people, after I joined *Sennet*, the University newspaper, for which I reviewed the Ingmar Bergman film *The Virgin Spring*. It was a pretentious little piece, but it was the first time I'd seen my name in print and I liked the buzz it gave me. After that a visit to the Academy Cinema in Oxford Street became a regular occurrence. They mainly showed black and white European films, which, obviously, they never did in Ormskirk, and soon I became a regular little cinephile snob, seeing François Truffaut's *Les Quatre Cents Coup* and *Jules et Jim* there, and never calling them by their English titles. By my second year, I'd even become an associate editor of a student film magazine called *Motion*, borrowing £40 from a girl I fancied to help pay the printing costs.

Of course, I didn't tell her or the other *Motion* movie freaks about Elvis and me. The Academy obviously didn't show his films, so I'd have to sneak off to an ABC where I hoped no-one knew me, to see *GI Blues* and *Blue Hawaii*. Even a besotted fan had his dignity, although, by now, ex-Army, Hollywood Elvis seemed to have lost much of his.

What I didn't realise then was that the films and the music that I liked would be part of my preparation for what became my career. Some film freaks would, years later, spot a nod to Truffaut in my screenplay for the film *That'll Be The Day*. There would be moments pinched from *East Of Eden*, too.

In those days Britain was a very white country, and, before I went to university, I'd never met a black person. There weren't any in Ormskirk, nor any Asians. But LSE students, undergraduates and postgraduates, came from everywhere and from every walk of life.

One of my first friends was an Ashanti boy from Ghana called Maxwell, who was also studying social anthropology. He was a little older than I was and would sometimes tease me by holding my hand as we walked along the street together. This threw me a bit at first, before I realised that other African boys would sometime hold hands, too. It didn't mean anything other than that you and he were pals.

Maxwell was excited to be in London and would regale me with stories of how Ghanian schoolchildren had to stand along the pavement and wave when a Rolls-Royce drove past carrying a member of the Royal Family. I think he rather liked that memory of home. If he was ever faced with race prejudice in finding a place to live, and I know other African students were, he never told me. Instead, he invited me back to his home one night for a 'good Ashanti meal of jollof'. I think it was probably rice, beans and chicken. While we were eating, he told me how he'd had an American girl stay with him for a couple of weeks.

'A girlfriend?' I presumed.

'No. Just a friend.'

As there was only one small bedroom, I asked him where she'd slept.

He laughed. 'Oh, Ray, you are so naïve,' he said.

Only one thing about the LSE disappointed me. Every Friday night there would be a bar social for drinking and dancing in the student's union building, The Three Tuns. Unfortunately, the only music being played there was trad jazz. In this apparently intellectual emporium, Kenny Ball was still king, with rock and roll considered to be a cheap music style for thickies and teddy-boys. So, I rarely went. Instead, I would hide the *New Musical Express* inside my *Manchester Guardian* (as it still was in those days) and study the Top Twenty in the British Library of Political and Economic Science.

Something else was out of kilter about those days, too, although it's almost embarrassing to admit it. Those of us who were at a university considered ourselves, solely by virtue of good luck and an ability to get decent enough marks in exams, to be something of a cut above everybody else, even old school friends who were now at teacher training colleges. Prejudice based on gender and educational attainment chopped and sliced our generation.

If we were pathetic in our snobby status consciousness, our dress sense was just as bad. There we were in our uniform of lumpy sweater and striped college scarves thinking how intellectual we must look. All that would soon change, but not yet. In the meantime, as the Shirelles sang 'Will You Still Love Me Tomorrow', a song I didn't realise was about sex, and Little Eva's 'Locomotion' became a dance song without a dance, the Berlin Wall went up and Marilyn Monroe was found dead in bed 'in the nude'. While back home in Lancashire, vacations meant delivering the Christmas post around Ormskirk and working on farms in the summer.

Memory is very choosy, retaining only snapshots of our passage through life; frozen moments that meant something to us. A girl called Solveig was one of those moments. I saw her first in a social psychology lecture. She was twenty and dazzlingly pretty, neat and serious, but she couldn't have been a regular student or I would have spotted her at the first lecture of the Lent term in 1961. She was there again the following week and the one after and so on, until one day I managed to walk out of the lecture room alongside her and somehow suggest that we have something to eat together at a little cafe in the college.

She was French, although her name was Norwegian, and she came from Nimes. Working as an au pair for a family in Essex, this was her regular day off and social psychology was the only lecture she'd been able to get into. What she really wanted to talk about over a meagre lunch, however, was the Allisons, whom she'd seen on television the night before singing a song called 'Are You Sure?' They were, she said, certain to win the Eurovision Song Contest. Not having access to a television, I hadn't seen the Allisons, but if she liked them, that was good enough for me. I was going to like them, too. She had no plans for the afternoon, so I fibbed and said I hadn't either.

It was a lovely, sunny day just before Easter, and we spent the rest of the afternoon together, climbing the spiral staircase of the hollow Doric column of the Monument that commemorates the Great Fire of London. Then, after taking the Tube back to Charing Cross Station, I ordered two Cokes in a café. Our drinks came with straws enclosed in little paper packets. Tearing off one end of her packet, she suddenly blew into the straw and giggled as the packet went floating across the café. The camera shutter in my memory clicked at that moment. It was the most daring thing I'd ever seen anyone do. I've tried to get it into a film script a couple of times since then, but it's never quite worked. Only French films have the sort of girl for that kind of scene.

We parted company at the station as she went off back to Essex. It had been the last psychology lecture of the term, and I never saw her again. But I've thought of that moment every time I've seen the Monument on a Tube map or heard the Allisons' 'Are You Sure?' As it turned out, she got that wrong. Their song didn't win the Eurovision Song Contest. It came second. It was probably too good.

I suppose she must be eighty or so now. But, in the picture in my mind, she will always be twenty. As will I. There's a kindness in memory.

Change was in the sky, if not the air, when, a year later during the summer of 1962, the communications satellite, Telstar, brought the first live images across the Atlantic via Goonhilly Down to television viewers in Britain. My sister, Sylvia, and I sat at home watching in astonishment that such a thing was even possible.

Hardly less possible were the first rumours I heard about a fabulous group called the Beatles who were just fifteen miles away from Ormskirk in Liverpool. I didn't pay such silly talk any attention. And, with money earned on a farm getting the pea harvest in, I bought my first car. It was a twelve years old, red Alvis TB14, a two-seater sports tourer and I thought I looked pretty flash driving it around. My hope was that Plum might finally fancy me. But, when she preferred the companionship of a German boy, I gave up on the summer and returned to London to edit the LSE magazine *Clare Market Review*. At least, in a journalistic sense, I might get somewhere.

Notwithstanding her German flirtation, Plum wrote to me that autumn term and told me that the Beatles had now made a record called 'Love Me Do', and that she'd been to see them at the Floral Hall in Southport. I was unimpressed, convinced that nothing good in rock music could ever come out of Liverpool, or even England. Ever the purist, to me, rock music had to be born in New Orleans or Memphis, New York or Los Angeles at a push. I was such a music snob. Besides, Plum had broken my heart in the summer. What was she doing writing to me now? She was a schoolgirl in the sixth form. There were girls in London, too. Older girls. Student girls. I didn't have a radio, and, living in my academic ivory tower, I never even heard 'Love Me Do'.

Besides, I had other things on my mind. President Kennedy had just told the Soviets to take their missiles out of Cuba, and for a few days Armageddon hung over us all. It seemed possible that we might all be vapourised in our sleep. So, when I woke up the following day and found that I was still alive, I wrote some instructions to fellow students in our Georgian hall of residence: 'Missile watching from the balconies is not allowed due to the building's architectural fragility'. It doesn't seem so silly now when we reflect on the Russian missiles that have bombed Ukraine.

The world hadn't ended during the Cuban Missile Crisis, but my world changed radically in another way on Friday January 11,1963. I was reading a newspaper in our college hall sitting room when I heard the announcer on *Housewives Choice* say something about a record that 'is being released this very day by John, Paul, George and Ringo...the Beatles'. I stopped reading the newspaper and listened.

It was 'Please Please Me' and I knew by the end of the first verse that I'd been completely wrong. The rumours that I'd heard the previous summer, Plum's enthusiasm and the excitement I'd read about in the *New Musical Express* were all justified. The Beatles were as astonishing as everyone was saying. How could I have been so blind?

The winter of 1963 was, and remains, the coldest and snowiest in Britain in living memory. Britain, it seemed, was cut off from itself. The sea froze on the beaches, villages were isolated by blizzards of snow, and drifts of frozen slush and ice lay heaped beside London's suburban roads until March.

But the Beatles had broken through. They were on everyone's lips, on the BBC radio's *Saturday Club* and on ITVs *Thank Your Lucky Stars*. Neither snow and ice nor fog could halt them as they toured the country in their van, stiff with cold, to promote their number one record, before dashing back to London to record their first LP in a day. They had to be something special to leave 'I Saw Her Standing There' as merely an album track. Fifteen months later it would be an American smash and Elvis's favourite Beatles' song…or so he told me. Now it's reckoned to be an all-time rock classic.

In Britain, 'Please Please Me' was interpreted as a simple pop song, just a boy asking his girlfriend to be nice to him. When it was first released in America, however, it was banned by some radio stations who feared its lyrics might be a request for fellatio. I never heard that mentioned once in Britain. Years later, when I worked with producer George Martin, I asked him if he'd thought there might be some *double entendre* at work when the Beatles had recorded it. He was adamant in his denial, before adding: 'But I dare say it might have crossed the boys' minds.' He would always refer to the Beatles as 'the boys'.

Like almost everybody of my age I became a Beatles convert instantly. They were so flipping good. But what was it about 'Please Please Me?' I recognised that it was structurally very similar to the Everly Brothers' 'Cathy's Clown'. But what else? Was it that harmonica opening, that, I would later read, John Lennon had borrowed from Bruce Chanel's 'Hey, Baby', having nicked the instrument itself from a shop on his way to Hamburg? Yes, partly.

Or was it the literary play on the two meanings of the word 'Please', which he also pinched, this time from a pre-war Bing Crosby hit? ('Please lend your little ear to my pleas.') That helped. Or what about both the speed and the gusto with which, at producer George Martin's suggestion, the Beatles attacked the song when they recorded it, having originally intended it as a Roy Orbison type of ballad? Absolutely. But, to top everything, was the harmony between Lennon and McCartney, with Paul, the tenor, singing, as he always would, a third higher than John, especially in the song's climatic moments. Some critics thought the early Beatles sounded raw. To me, from the very beginning, they were incredibly sophisticated. After years of playing and writing together in relative obscurity, they appeared on the national, and then the world stage, fully formed.

There was something else, too. It had forever been a rule that singers should emote while singing. Elvis had taken that a step further by emoting with his thighs in what some considered a suggestive manner. The Beatles did none of that. They just stood on the stage and sang and played; their most exciting physical manifestation being to 'shake the dandruff out of their hair' when they sang falsetto, after newspapers and comedians made fun of their haircuts. Their secret was, and would always be, in the brilliance of the Lennon and McCartney songs.

With three of them having been grammar school boys, who had also been too young for National Service, they, like me, had been born at the right time. John and Ringo were a few months older than I was, and Paul and George a little younger.

It probably didn't happen as quickly as my memory tells me, but attitudes towards rock music soon softened with the Beatles' emergence, with the trad jazz sounds at the LSE's Friday night bar social being replaced by a rock band, although unfortunately not the Rolling Stones. I didn't know Mick Jagger when we were both students there. He was a year behind me, and, of course, not yet famous. But I remember him being pointed out as 'someone who sang in a group'. My impression was that he didn't look much like a rock star.

From the Beatles on, rock and roll music would no longer be dismissed as mere entertainment for teddy boys. Soon Paul Jones would drop out of Oxford University to join Manfred Mann, Brian Ferry, after reading fine art at Newcastle University, would become part of Roxy Music and Brian May would break off from studying astrophysics at Imperial College to join Queen.

By the time the Beatles' second number one hit, 'From Me To You', was released in April, much else was happening, and 1963 was becoming a year like no other. The Beatles were exciting the young, but sex among posh people now began to mesmerize adults as a photograph of the Duchess of Argyll and a naked but 'headless man' was shown to a court at her divorce hearing. Guessing the identity of the headless man (he must have taken the photo,) became a national talking point, to be quickly rivalled in its public fascination by an even steamier story. The Conservative War Minister, Jack Profumo, had, it transpired, met an attractive, twenty-one-year-old girl called Christine Keeler when she'd gone skinny dipping, as you do, at Lord Astor's Cliveden estate one weekend. An affair had ensued, with the whole matter getting stickier when it was revealed that the lady had, at the time, also been sexually involved with a Russian naval attached called Eugene Ivanov.

And that was just the start. The headlines went on for months. In retrospect the Beatles singing 'Please, please me, oh, yeah, like I please you, oh yeah, like I please you, oh yeah…' could almost have sounded like the chorus of the times as sex became the nation's imaginary sport.

Two years earlier, the first contraceptive pill on the NHS had been introduced by Health Minister Enoch Powell. A small cyclone of disapproval had followed amid claims that it would lead young women down the primrose path to immorality. Well, sexual attitudes did inevitably change, but not that quickly.

What caused more of a ruckus in the newspapers, and what became increasingly mischievous as the decade wore on, was satire. The London stage show *Beyond The Fringe,* and the lampooning magazine *Private Eye,* had started the fashion of debunking authority and with it the previously sacred institutions of the government, the Church of England and the Royal Family. But when satire appeared on BBC television in *That Was The Week That Was* it acquired a nationwide audience. One of the few complaints the Beatles were said to have made, as they toured the country in the Spring of 1963, was that they couldn't watch *TW3,* as it became known, because they were invariably on stage at the time it was broadcast on Saturday nights.

The Beatles and satire were very different from each other, but they shared similar roots. Their leading figures, John Lennon, Paul McCartney, Peter Cook, Alan Bennett and David Frost had all grown up in a post-war Britain when the corset ties of the establishment that had held tight their parents' generation were being rapidly being loosened. They, like Timothy Birdsall, who drew the most famous *Private Eye* cartoon in which Piccadilly Circus was reduced to a bedlam of spivs, tarts and pop stars, were the advance parties for the rest of us.

6.

*'I don't think you're cut out to read
News At Ten, do you?' Geoffrey Cox,
editor of ITN*

The USA had been untouched by the tumult of excitement that was erupting in Britain, when, after my finals, in July 1963, I sold my car to buy an airline ticket to New York. From there, with my university friend, Ian Harkness from Taunton, I set off to 'look for America', as Simon and Garfunkel would later sing.

In those days there would be advertisements in *The New York Times* that sought drivers to deliver usually old cars to new owners in various parts of America. So, we took a worn-out Ford Galaxy from New York to a farmer in Iowa, and then moved on across country to Colorado. Brought up with the BBC's rationing of rock music, it was like Christmas for me as the radio record shows never stopped and Lesley Gore's 'It's My Party', The Tymes' 'So Much in Love' and the Beach Boys' (by way of Chuck Berry) 'Surfin' USA' accompanied us on those endless roads.

I was hopeless at the first job we got, which was selling magazines house to house in Denver, so I left on the second day, and took myself up into the Rocky Mountains to work on a dude ranch, which I discovered was a sort of log cabin, Western style vacation. It was terrific, mainly saddling and unsaddling horses, mowing lawns, and driving a truck to and from the Rainbow Valley dump. Then at the end of the day, I'd ride bareback with just a bridle as I helped drive all the horses down the valley to an overnight pasture.

Warner Brothers' Western series like *Cheyenne*, *Bonanza* and *Wagon Train* were a staple on Saturday night television then, and there I suddenly was, a bit part player in a movie dream. For the wranglers, who, in between rodeos, worked on the ranch during the summer, it was, of course, more than a fantasy, it was a grown-up lifestyle based on a celluloid myth. And I would watch as one of them oiled his guns and took great care of his own expensive, highly strung pony, which he rode as though it was a motorbike. He was a friendly guy, but I think he might well be a Second Amendment zealot now, so we probably wouldn't have much in common anymore.

I learned a lot about the geography of American music that summer and how it changed from place to place. On the ranch, Bobby Bare's muscular country and western 'Detroit City' was the current favourite, with its refrain 'I wanna go home, I wanna go home, Oh, how I want to go home'. But later, when Ian and I went up to Vermont to a students' summer camp, it was the humming opening sequence of Thurston Harris's r and b record 'Little Bitty Pretty One', when the entire refectory began to sing as one, that was most popular. To be followed by an intense young lady with flowing hair and a guitar as she reflected on Peter Paul and Mary's 'Five Hundred Miles'.

Back in New York in late September it was unseasonably hot, and walking down East 11th St, where I was staying, and which was then a Puerto Rican area, was like being in a pavement juke box as the sounds of different records emerged from every open window. It was the start of the Motown era and Little Stevie Wonder's 'Fingertips Part 2' along with Martha and the Vandellas' 'Heatwave' were playing constantly, as was the Ronettes' 'Be My Baby'. Then one day I heard a WINS disc jockey announce a new record by saying: 'It's a smash in England. See what you think of it?'

That was the first time I heard the Beatles' 'She Loves You'. An American student I was with was disdainful. He said it sounded quaint. I thought it was terrific. I also thought that it was time that I went home. I was missing all the excitement.

My three years' student journalism and a degree didn't get me the job in Fleet Street I'd expected. Nor did an interview at ITN go well. 'I don't think you're cut out to read *News At Ten*, do you,' Geoffrey Cox, the editor, told me, as I stammered unhappily away. Nor was the BBC interested, nor even the North Thames Gas Board's house magazine. So, with my rent being paid by the National Assistance, I was running out of options when I rang Plum.

I'd met her mother in the street in Ormskirk, shortly after I'd got back from America, and she'd given me Plum's phone number. 'She's at a secretarial college in London now. If you go back to London, I'm sure she'd like to see you.'

I wasn't at all sure that she would. But I wanted to see her. It was a couple of weeks after the assassination of President Kennedy, and we met in the Wimpy Bar in Earls Court. I got there first, and watched her pass the window before she came in. She told me later that she'd borrowed the coat she was wearing from a roommate, because she didn't want to meet me in something I would have seen before. We hadn't spoken for sixteen months, so we had a lot to catch up on, but mainly we talked about friends and music. She'd now seen the Beatles twice, 'I Want to Hold Your Hand' had been released and the Beatles had topped the bill on ITV's *Sunday Night at the London Palladium*. It was, we agreed, as though we were living in an entirely new world. As I didn't have any money, she bought me a Wimpy and chips and then I walked her back to her young ladies' hostel in South Kensington.

Plum rang me from a public phone there the following Friday night. She'd just bought the Beatles' second LP, *With The Beatles,* and wondered if I'd like to hear it. Half an hour later she was at my bedsitter in West Kensington carrying the LP in one hand and her Dansette record player in the other. The cover for *With The Beatles,* four unsmiling monochrome faces half-lit on a black background, was unlike any other album of the time. The Beatles were making new rules as they went along, their overall style screaming 'art students', although only John Lennon had been to art college.

As for Plum and me, that was, more-or-less, when we started getting together, save for a week's interlude when, the following night, she met a boy who played the harmonica in a group.

It was the Sixties. A boy in a group trumped everything.

It *was* also a new world. America was no longer the cultural mecca. In fact, most American stars suddenly looked grinningly middle-aged. Past it. Nor was there much sympathy around for the *ancien regime* of British pop stars who had modelled themselves on Elvis, terrific guys like Marty Wilde and Billy Fury, but who, with unfashionable hair and the wrong clothes, seemed old fashioned. It mattered not that John Lennon was slightly older than Cliff Richard. In their collarless suits, Chelsea boots and with a conveyor belt of terrific songs, the Beatles weren't so much ahead of the curve, they were the curve, and the curve was a tidal wave; and surfing in their slipstream came a flotilla of new groups. There were other

Liverpudlians from the Cavern, Gerry and the Pacemakers, the Searchers, the Merseybeats and Billy J. Kramer and the Dakotas. While from London came Brian Poole and the Tremeloes, Manfred Mann, and, best of all, the Rolling Stones. Soon a rivalry was being imagined in tabloid newspapers between fans of the Stones and those of the Beatles, which was silly. Lennon and McCartney had even given the Stones their first proper hit, 'I Wanna Be Your Man', a throwaway number that Lennon and McCartney had let Ringo sing because they didn't think it was strong enough to be a single for them.

Nor were the Rolling Stones and the Beatles even pitching to the same audience. The Stones, were, and have remained, an r and b band, in the tradition of John Lee Hooker's 'Hi-Heel Sneakers', which was a big hit that year. But, while 'The Last Time' and 'Satisfaction' would fit into any all-time greatest hits of the Sixties, Jagger and Richards didn't write brilliant songs outside their rock format, Lennon and McCartney wrote a bewildering array of different kinds of songs.

By 1964, the Beatles were even about to make their first film, *A Hard Day's Night*, with even more songs. Hardly ever off the TV pop shows and news programmes, they were everywhere, the entire nation seeming to have spiritually joined a nationwide Beatles' fan club. Then America fell for them, too. With 'I Want to Hold Your Hand' at the top of the American charts they flew to the US for a few days in February to appear on the Ed Sullivan Show on TV.

As we watched television news reports of the fan bedlam at their departure from Heathrow Airport, and the instant hysteria on their arrival at the recently renamed (in honour of the recently assassinated president) Kennedy Airport in New York, we were in awe. The Beatles were 'our boys'. And when they came back, emerging from the Boeing 707, we felt as though we were personally welcoming home our friends. Within a year, the Beatles had become proxy members of all our families. No-one before or since had had that kind of relationship with the public. It was something very new.

Another national change of gear occurred a few weeks later, when, on Easter Saturday, 1963, the first pirate station, Radio Caroline, began broadcasting to London from a ship anchored just outside the Thames Estuary. With financial backing from wealthy investors, it was a dodgy venture in a country where the BBC held a monopoly on radio broadcasting, but the spirit of its young Irish managing director, Ronan O'Rahilly, gave it a youthful glamour. Playing nothing but pop music day and night, other pirate stations would soon follow its lead, either on old forts outside territorial waters off the coast of Essex, or on other ships with large transmitters. Meanwhile, the original Radio Caroline sailed off around the west coast to begin broadcasting to the northwest of England, Scotland and Ireland.

Radio had never sounded so friendly and conversational as a new breed of radio personalities, all in their twenties, Kenny Everett, Tony Blackburn and John Peel, did their apprenticeships on air. It would take nearly four years before Harold Wilson's government sank the radio pirates by banning British companies from advertising through them. But, in the meantime, the ships were showing that there was a young audience eager for what they were doing. For Britain it was a radio revolution, the effects of which are still with us.

Over in America, by virtue of the erratic nature of their records' releases there, by the first week of April the Beatles occupied all the top five places in *Billboard's* best-selling singles chart, as well as seven other songs further down the Hot Hundred. No performers had ever done that before (or since), and the youth of the United Kingdom was proud of them. It was like supporting a winning national football team. Only better.

Still locked out of Fleet Street, I was, that Spring, following events from a desk in the Economic Intelligence Unit of the Westminster Bank where I would now hide the *New Musical Express* inside the *Financial Times*, while advising bank customers on the wisdom of investing their nest eggs in... caravan sites, I seem to remember, about which I knew nothing. I'd had to do something to earn a living.

Soon it was the end of Plum's secretarial course and one week in June she went for a week's holiday to Devon. With nothing better to do, I was back at the LSE one night having dinner in the refectory when a guy I knew spotted me. He was an older man, called Sean, who always wore a grey shirt and suit, and who had done his A-levels in a Belfast prison while serving seven years for

IRA terrorism activities. Presumably he was now a reformed terrorist.

'Hello, Ray. Where's your girlfriend this week?' he asked.

'She's gone to Torquay for a week with some other girls,' I told him.

'Oh really,' he said. 'And do you trust her while she's away on holiday?'

'Oh, yes. Of course.'

He looked doubtful. 'In my experience when a woman wants it, it doesn't matter if it's a man or a monkey.' And, having laid the seeds of suspicion in my mind, he went on his way.

Thirty years later I was recalling this incident to my friend Ian Harkness from Taunton and his wife Lyn, with all of us laughing at what Sean had told me, when Plum said quietly: 'Well, it wasn't a monkey.'

7.

'You know, son, God loves a try-er'

It was back in the North that I made my entry into newspapers, as a graduate trainee at the *Liverpool Daily Post,* which, at the time, was a formidable morning newspaper. It was the best training I could have wished for in that the *Post's* method was to take on a couple of young graduates every year and chuck them in the deep end. If they swam, and could do it, they kept them. If it was felt (sometimes unfairly) that they couldn't, they let them go after a couple of months.

Until then, I'd only really known Liverpool as the city from which I caught the train to London. But, working there, I began to see its grandeur and history, from the noble buildings at the Pier Head to the ferries that would paddle backwards and forwards across the River Mersey to Birkenhead and New Brighton. I would later understand the romance of Gerry Marsden's 'Ferry Across the Mersey', which was a much better song than Gerry ever got credit for. That often happens.

Both Plum and I were now back in Ormskirk and living with our parents. Then, in the October of 1964, Plum's mother died. We became even closer after that and married in April 1966. Plum was 21. I was 25. People married young in those days. Years later I would often say that if you can marry your best friend and make your hobby your job, you stand a good chance of having a happy life. At that stage, I'd achieved the first part of my ambition.

Our first home was a bright, new, expensive, rented flat north of Liverpool in a very pretty corner of Blundellsands. There, sometimes on Saturdays, we would loll in the sandhills, watching the ships going into the Mersey, while listening to the Beach Boys' 'Good Vibrations' and the Mamas and the Papas' 'California Dreamin''on Radio Caroline North. Antony Gormley's statues are on the beach there now.

My job at the *Liverpool Daily Post* was as a sub-editor. Subs are the engine room of any newspaper in that, night after night, they make the paper, checking and correcting the articles and reports for facts, spelling mistakes and libels, writing the headlines, choosing and measuring up the photographs, and, in those days, laying out the pages. I loved that part of the job. But it was a treat when I would deputise for the stone sub and work overnight with the compositors as the paper was physically put to bed. Those were still the days of hot metal, and the banter between the Liverpool FC and Everton FC supporting compositors was a nightly comedy show. In the end, I chose to support Liverpool, although, at the time, I'd never been to a football match in my life.

It was 1966 and England won the World Cup that year, and Plum and I watched the final in our flat. After the match, driving back to Ormskirk in my new car, a little red MG Midget, was like being in a national victory parade as passing cars tooted their horns in triumph, the face of every driver stretched in smiles. We were young, we were excited, and in the then fashionable sweaters and caps we'd recently bought at Jaeger in Liverpool's Bold Street, we were, in our own eyes, stars ourselves. Every young person should have a day like that.

Not everything was perfect, of course, because what I really wanted was to be a *writing* journalist. So, when my colleague Robin Oakley (who was also newly married and who would later become the BBC's political correspondent) and I were asked to look after the features part of the paper, we both took the opportunity to write articles for our pages under pseudonyms. The *Daily Post* had missed the Beatles when they'd been in Liverpool, pop music not being high on the paper's conservative agenda then. And, as they weren't very enthusiastic when I suggested using the lyrics of 'Penny Lane' to do a spread of pictures and quotes from ordinary people, such as a real 'pretty nurse selling poppies from a tray' or a real fireman and his engine, 'it's a clean machine, very clean', I began to do interviews instead.

Roger McGough was 29 then, an assistant lecturer in English at a technical college, as well as being a member of an alternative comedy trio, The Scaffold, and a poet. So, he and Thelma, his girlfriend (later his first wife), were among my first subjects, Roger having just published his *Summer With Monika* collection, with that languishingly romantic end line 'when I had summer with Monika, and Monika had summer with me'.

They lived up the hill overlooking Liverpool's vast Anglican cathedral in a flat 'with a rouge ceiling and a wall in Clayton Square yellow'. That was Roger's description. It was in one of the once grand early nineteenth century terraces in Liverpool 8, built when Liverpool had been seen as the 'second city of the British Empire'. I'd never known that this historic part of the town, with its cluttered population of students, immigrants, artists and even a Russian fencing instructor, even existed.

Forty years later, I would write a radio play and novella about what might have happened to the Beatles if producer George Martin had rejected them and set some of the action in a flat like Roger McGough's. The play was called '*Sorry, Boys, You Failed the Audition*', and I imagined that the unfamous John Lennon, having left the Beatles to become a Liverpool wit, was living there with his wife, Cynthia and their son, Julian.

Catholics always like to tell each other about their upbringings as little pillars of the church, and Roger McGough told me how he'd bribed God, or, more specifically, 'taken out a bit of insurance', which was one of the perks of being a Catholic. He'd sat the examination for the scholarship to go to a grammar school early – when he was only ten. So, when the results were due, he'd decided to make a novena, which meant getting up at 6.30 in the morning and going to mass and communion for nine consecutive days. This he did. But when on the eighth day, his teacher read out the names of all the boys who had passed the scholarship, he discovered that his name wasn't amongst them. Despondent, he went home, wondering whether it was worth going to mass the next day to complete the novena. But he'd made a promise to God. So, dragging himself out of bed the following morning off he went to mass and communion.

When he got home, he let himself in by the back door just as the postman was delivering the post at the front. Lying on the mat in the hall was a brown envelope from the Lancashire Education Department. Inside was the news that, as he was so young, he was being awarded a scholarship to take effect from the following year when he would be eleven.

Some people, ultra keen Catholics, probably, might think of that as a nod from God, because of the novena that young Roger had made. Others might deduce that Roger, aged ten, was just a clever boy who kept his promises.

The Scaffold were gaining a following through their TV appearances at the time, and, through Roger I met one of his partners in the group, Mike McCartney, who was then known professionally as Mike McGear. The younger brother of Paul McCartney, through Mike I met his father, Jim McCartney, and Jim's second wife, Angie. You couldn't meet a nicer man than Jim McCartney.

I learned a lot doing those early interviews, most interesting being that my stammer might be less of a handicap than some, and even I, had presumed. A stammer didn't show on the written page.

The London *Evening Standard* had been my goal since I'd been at the London School of Economics. It seemed younger and more keyed into the moment than any other newspaper. So, when, every day, a couple of copies of the *Standard* were sent up on the train to the *Liverpool Daily Post,* I would grab one, not least for the articles that Maureen Cleave was writing in her Disc Date column. Maureen didn't know much about rock music, but she asked brilliant, pertinent questions and was a beautiful, careful writer. From a military background, Maureen was posh, very bright and very pretty with a fashionable bob and fringe.

Born in India in 1933 (so she was already thirty, but looking much younger, when she began writing) she'd been on a passage home in 1940, when her ship had been torpedoed. She and her mother, and a man playing 'It's A Long Way to Tipperary' on a mouth organ, had floated in a lifeboat for six hours, before a passing cargo ship had rescued them. Back in Ireland it had been mainly boarding schools, and then a degree in modern history at Oxford, before she took a job as a secretary at the *Evening Standard.* That had been the usual way into Fleet Street for untrained girls in the early Sixties. Then, one day, the editor, Charles Wintour, gave her a column, and she'd begun to write the first intelligent pieces in British newspapers on rock stars. Her profile in March 1966 on John Lennon, with whom she became very close, was masterful: 'He still peers down his nose, arrogant as an eagle… He looks more like Henry VIII than ever now that his face has filled out; he is just as imperious, just as unpredictable, indolent, disorganized, childish, vague, charming and quick-witted.' That was John.

But it would be something that John told her for the same article that was to make her name; and to cause him all kinds of problems. 'Christianity will go,' he said. 'It will vanish and shrink. I needn't argue about that, I'm right and I'll be proved right. We're more popular than Jesus now. I don't know which will go first, rock and roll or Christianity. Jesus was all right, but his disciples were thick and ordinary. It's them twisting it that ruins it for me.'

You didn't read stuff like that in the *New Musical Express* or anywhere else then, and, when I first saw it, I was both amused and full of admiration for the writer. Written for a sophisticated readership, there was no outrage in Britain at the comments. John Lennon was just a guy airing his opinions, views that many others shared. But when the article was republished in an American teen magazine a few months later, fundamentalist Christians erupted by lighting bonfires of Beatles albums across the Bible Belt.

Those quotes would become Maureen's footnote in history. She left the *Evening Standard* shortly after that when her husband went to work in Peru. And that left something of a vacancy.

A few weeks before I joined the *Evening Standard,* Plum and I went house hunting. Buying our own house was an achievable ambition for young couples then, and driving down a leafy lane in Carshalton, South London, we were listening to the pirate ship Radio London, when the first airing of *Sgt Pepper's Lonely Hearts Club Band* came on the car radio. To Plum's annoyance, I insisted we stop. I then listened intently for well over an hour as Kenny Everett played the album in full. It was, Plum agreed, a major cultural moment, but had I forgotten that we had an appointment with an estate agent? I kept listening. Sometimes not even the best girl in the world can be quite as intent as her man when it comes to rock music.

As for *Sgt Pepper*? Well, I've always preferred *Rubber Soul* and *Revolver*, and I can't have been the only Beatles' fan to have lifted the pick-up off George Harrison's 'Within You Without You' and put it down again on the second track on side two, 'When I'm Sixty Four'. George Martin would later tell me that was why he put George's song as the opening track on that side – so that fans like me could skip it if we wanted. I know the album was a 'brilliant, innovative and a period defining piece of work', as all the critics in the world seemed to agree, but for me it would have been even more brilliant if they'd left off George's bit and John Lennon's 'Good Morning, Good Morning' and included the first two songs recorded at the *Pepper* sessions, 'Penny Lane' and 'Strawberry Fields Forever'. Nor did I ever see a single theme to the collection, although many others believed they could.

The year 1967 was already being called the 'Summer of Love' when, on July 3, I started work at the *Evening Standard*. Procol Harum's 'Whiter Shade of Pale' was already a justifiable sensation, a sunny song about 'San Francisco' ('be sure to wear some flowers in your hair') was becoming a hippy-dippy anthem and the Beatles' 'All You Need Is Love' was released that very week. Wearing beads, bells and kaftans was now *de rigueur* among many who had never been further east than West Ham, while, as boys' hair got ever longer, talk of psychedelia, hippies, pot, happenings, LSD and the 'Underground', peppered what was thought to be cool conversation. Soon, in a spasm of conspicuous groovyness, two Beatles would own flower-power decorated cars, John Lennon's a psychedelically illustrated Rolls-Royce, and George Harrison's, as perhaps befitting his lower status in the band, a Mini-Cooper.

At the Festival of Britain, sixteen years earlier, the totemic word had been 'modern'. Now the word was 'young', as models, artists, photographers, fashion designers, artists and rock stars became what some liked to call the 'young new aristocracy'. Others called it the new 'meritocracy', neither of which was right. Whatever it was, though, it was war babies and baby boomers making all the noise, as the cultural mutiny in music and fashion that had begun in Liverpool's Cavern and Soho's Marquee, as well as Biba and Carnaby Street and at art colleges across the country, became ever-more inflamed. In 1966 *Time* magazine had invented the term 'Swinging London', and now London was trying to live up to that soubriquet, with the Rolling Stones being arrested for possession of drugs at a weekend party at which Marianne Faithfull was rumoured, sadly, untruthfully, to have discovered a new place with an appetite for a Mars Bar.

The arrests of Mick Jagger and Keith Richards completed the trinity of sex, drugs and rock and roll. Drugs had always been a part of American jazz and blues, but while purple hearts and uppers had attracted Mods in this country, it took until the late-Sixties for cannabis to catch on in any wide sense. Even the Beatles, for whom amphetamines had been a regular diet when they'd played for hours in Hamburg, and who saw themselves as being at the forefront of everything new, hadn't smoked pot until they met Bob Dylan in America in 1964. After which they had quickly become keen advocates for both it, and in 1966, for the laboratory made hallucinogenic lysergic acid diethylamide, commonly known as LSD.

'I saw God,' Paul would tell ITN of his first LSD trip. Well, maybe he did. Or perhaps in his acid hallucination he saw a hedgehog and mistook it for God. It's easily done. It was foolish of him to tell ITN what he'd taken and what he'd seen; but, to me, even more foolish of ITN to broadcast their scoop, thus advertising it to fans who might be too young to know better than to try it themselves.

Whether Paul did or did not see God or a hedgehog, by 1967 the use of drugs had become commonplace in the rock world and was becoming so among students, too, thus engendering much newspaper space, especially when anyone famous was involved. Creating smaller headlines at the time, though vastly more important, were Acts of Parliament that legalised both homosexual acts and abortions.

So, it was a moment of all kinds of change in which to start a new job. And ten days later, I got my first front page lead when Ronan O'Rahilly from Radio Caroline, told me he was going to fight the banning of pirate radio ships by staying on air despite the strictures of the Marine and Broadcasting (Offences) Bill. He did, too. But as British advertisers were no longer allowed to buy space for their commercials on the ships, it wasn't much more than a token gesture.

Ronan was always a bit of a rascal, but he had huge energy, opening and closing night clubs at one point and managing James Bond actor George Lazenby at another. In later years it was always amusing to bump into him as he regularly played billiards at the Chelsea Arts Club. There he would be, still ranting on about how the FBI killed President Kennedy and flying a kite of a conspiracy theory about the death of John Lennon. He died in 2020, back in Ireland in the place where his family's company had originally equipped the ship that became Radio Caroline. Nothing he ever did later in his life was as influential as his launching of a pirate radio station, but he left his mark. Within two months of the Act of

Parliament which metaphorically sank the pirate radio ships, nearly a dozen young disc jockeys had been employed to front the BBCs new pop station, Radio 1. That was my second front page lead.

Because I was so late to the Beatles party, I never met Brian Epstein, so I was of no use to the *Evening Standard* when he was found dead of a suspected sleeping pill overdose in August, 1967. Instead, my new colleague, Julian Norridge, covered that story. My value only began in the September when I was instructed to chase after the psychedelically painted *Magical Mystery Tour* coach that, carrying the Beatles and a film crew, as well as wrestling dwarfs, priests playing blind man's bluff, a fat lady, a stripper, and a sinister looking eccentric who called himself Mr Blood Vessel, was making its way through the south-west of England.

I caught up with the party that night in the Royal Hotel, Teignmouth, when, going into a very large bar, I saw for the first time the close relationship that the Beatles and their coterie had with Fleet Street. In those days, national newspapers didn't have any dedicated rock journalists, the covering of pop groups being the job of seasoned, mainly older, show-biz reporters. To those guys the Beatles weren't unapproachable superstars. They were boys. In fact, the accompanying Press seemed to be sharing in the same adventure with the Beatles.

Everyone knew everybody else, it seemed, apart from me. Taking an empty chair near the door I watched the general camaraderie as if from afar, wondering how I was ever going to become part of it.

Then someone sat down next to me. It was Paul McCartney. I obviously had to say something. But what? In the end I just said: 'I know your father.'

It turned out to be the perfect line. From then on Paul made it easy for me. And for the next few days, as I got to know the Beatles' Liverpool lieutenants, Mal Evans, Neil Aspinall and their fan club secretary Freda Kelly, I followed the Magical Mystery coach by way of Widdecombe-on-the Moor, my little car, now part of a two-mile caravan of Press and fans.

I didn't then know much about making films, but I could see that, as extreme fame was locking the Beatles out of the world, it was impossible for them to film much outside the coach.

When the resulting film *Magical Mystery Tour*, was shown on Boxing Day on BBC-2 it was met with derision by TV critics. It was the first time the Beatles had failed, and, asked to write about it for the *Evening Standard,* I called Paul McCartney. His father, who had been staying with him for Christmas, answered the phone. Paul was still asleep, he said. Best if I called back in half an hour. Which I did. Twice more.

In the end he gave in. 'You know, son,' Mr McCartney said, 'God loves a tryer. I'm going to wake him up for you.' And off he went upstairs demanding that his elder son talk to me.

'I suppose if you look at it as good Boxing Day entertainment we goofed really,' Paul admitted immediately. The film had been a joint Beatle venture, but Paul had been the director.

'Of course, we could have got together a good director and editor, even some good song writers, and asked them to produce a first class show for Christmas with the Beatles in it. It would have been the easiest thing in the world. Perhaps we should have done it that way, but we wanted to do it ourselves.'

The problem for the Beatles was that everything they did was in public. Being a Beatle didn't allow for private error.

Magical Mystery Tour was certainly a setback. With the inclusion of outtakes of Greenland from the *Dr Strangelove* film, a working-class singsong on the bus, the Beatles wearing bald, egg shaped wigs and John Lennon in a walrus suit, it was certainly difficult to follow. Nor were the five new songs among the best in the Beatles' cannon, John Lennon's favourite 'I Am The Walrus' being only the flipside of Paul McCartney's 'Hello Goodbye' for a Christmas single. It wouldn't be until 2012, 45 years later, when *Magical Mystery Tour* was shown again on the BBC, that it finally found an audience. By then a new generation had been born and reared on *Monty Python's Flying Circus* and MTV, for which film students would experiment with new techniques to illustrate popular music.

Was it really as bad as the critics suggested in 1967? I thought so at the time, a view which didn't go down well when Paul asked for my honest opinion. 'You're the only person I know who says he hasn't enjoyed it,' he said.

But with no plan, no script, *Magical Mystery Tour* was *cinema verité* verging on an expensive home movie. The Beatles had wanted to see themselves in the tradition of art school students who had been given a camera and a few rolls of film with which to play. And it hadn't worked.

8.

'A fish wouldn't get caught if
he kept his mouth shut' –
Jimi Hendrix

The Sixties and Seventies were terrific times for written journalism, the last moment in history when the word would arrive before the pictures. Today we see instant images as events happen in some of the furthest places on the planet. But, when I arrived in Fleet Street, war reporters and foreign correspondents would file their articles by phone, the TV pictures only arriving the following day, or even later, after having been flown in. In 1962 Telstar had given us a glimpse of a future when satellites would link the world's populations, but television news wasn't there yet. The writing journalist still acted as the middleman, or occasionally the middle-woman, to best tell the foreign story.

But nor was it only in the telling of foreign news that the writer was paramount. The newspaper industry was still the most dominant medium in a Britain with only two, then three, TV stations. For an author, actor or musician to build a following, the main route was through newspapers and magazines, which meant that the interviewing journalist was in a prime position. If stars in any field wanted the world to get to know them, journalists, like me, were their best way of achieving it.

Today, if a well-known artist has a record, film, show or book to promote the quickest way to reach the maximum number of people is to appear on a popular TV chat show, like Graham Norton's on the BBC. Every country has similar shows, and radio programmes, too, for those artists and writers not quite famous enough the get the big TV treatment. And every name, in every field, big and not so big, has publicists aiming him or her at those programmes.

If a newspaper writer wants to interview a top star today, the odds are the journalist will be waiting in a queue at a West End hotel where a publicist will say, 'you have thirty minutes flat' because the proposed interviewee has a 'very heavy schedule'. In the Sixties the journalist was as likely as not to be invited to the star's home to ask the questions; and would often feel free to stay there for as long as the conversation took. Sometimes it took me hours.

I began doing interviews in my first few weeks at the *Evening Standard*. London had become *the* place to be for rock music, as new young stars appeared overnight, and other young people set up businesses to spot, create and maintain talent. Denny Cordell at 24 would tell me that two years earlier he'd had no idea what he would be doing but had just independently produced Procol Harum's 'A Whiter Shade of Pale'. With Matthew Fisher playing what sounded like variations on Bach's 'Air on a G String' on a Hammond organ and with teasingly enigmatic lyrics by Keith Reid, the record had just become one of the all-time greatest hits. Meanwhile Chris Blackwell, at 30, had launched his own record label, Island Records, 23-year-old Andrew Loog Oldham was managing the Rolling Stones, and Jonathan King had written and recorded 'Everyone's Gone To The Moon' while still at Cambridge. Richard Branson had only begun his career a year earlier when, at 16, he'd launched the magazine *Student, and* was about to go into selling mail order records from a phone box near his flat. Then there was Tony Elliott, all of 20, who would soon be laying out the first edition of *Time Out* on his mother's kitchen table, and Nigel Davies, who having rebranded himself as Justin de Villeneuve, had already discovered Twiggy. When Jonathan Aitken, who at first sat opposite me at the *Evening Standard,* titled his book about these go-aheads, *The Young Meteors,* he named it well.

Although rock stars were my first subjects, I quickly recognised that therein lay a problem. As articulate as many of them were, it wasn't always easy for them to express what it was they did that made them successful. No newspaper article would ever be as magical as a record or a performance. So, I chose not to pursue musical nuance with them.

Jimi Hendrix was a case in point. We didn't get into why he played his guitar with his teeth or where the skill in his fingers came from. It was a given that he was a highly talented and original musician for whom improvised electronic feedback and distortion were a major part of his music. There was no point in asking him why he did it. He just did. What was more interesting to me was that his quiet, almost meek, demeanour was the direct opposite of his provocative stage persona.

He was living with his manager, ex-Animal Chas Chandler, in a modern flat near London's Marble Arch, which was a light, functional place with G-plan Sixties furniture. Jimi's bedroom, however, was more like a Mephistophelean parlour. There were crimson curtains and blood coloured matching sheets and carpets, a giant panda, peacock feathers, a rag doll, Rip Van Winkle slippers, a cloaked Swedish Superman, and flying above the bed a vast granny shawl from which hung monstrously vivid spiders' webs attached to a candled chandelier.

Was that all publicity staging, I wondered at the time. I still don't know, but amongst it all sat Jimi in tangerine pants, telling me very quietly about his troubled childhood in Seattle, Washington. 'My mother and father used to fall out a lot,' he said, 'so I always had to be ready to go tippy-toeing off up to Canada to stay with my grandmother. My dad was very level-headed and religious. But my mother liked having a good time and going out. She used to drink a lot and didn't take care of herself. She died when I was about ten.'

At fourteen he left school because his father needed the wages: 'Dad was a gardener and things got pretty bad in the winter when there wasn't any grass to cut.' By the time he was fifteen he'd left home and hadn't been back since. 'I have a half-sister of six I haven't even seen. There may be more now. I sent my dad some money, but he sent it back.'

Somehow, while serving in the US Army he'd got a guitar and taught himself to play. Music came intuitively to him. Soon he'd been given a discharge by the army and began backing Little Richard, followed by the Isley Brothers.

Then, suddenly, he was in London and was a shy star. 'My dad was very, very strict and taught me not to speak until I was first spoken to by grown-ups. So, I've always been very quiet. A fish wouldn't get caught if he kept his mouth shut.'

Jimi was then 25, a waif and talented stray. I heard later that he could become loud and violent with drink or drugs. But he was very pleasant with me. He had just two years left to live. In 1969 he would be found dead due to inhalation of vomit following barbiturate intoxication, making him the first casualty of the '27 Club' of rock stars who died at that age.

I would spend much time with people who would become rock casualties over the next few years. I was never into drugs, and rarely drank much. Perhaps I was just too nervous, too straight, or too ambitious. But I didn't like anything that altered my perceptions. And, the more obituaries I would write, the straighter I became.

Although drugs were becoming increasingly common in music, they weren't universal. Some musicians preferred to talk about their hobbies. Chris Farlowe had an odd one. He was a Cockney ex-schoolboy boxer, who'd once sung 'Silent Night' as a boy soprano at the Royal Festival Hall. But when I talked to him, he'd recently had a hit with the Mick Jagger/Keith Richards song 'Out Of Time'. It was his side-interest, however, that took over the interview. Working from a market stall in Islington, he was a part time trader in Nazi memorabilia, and sold swastikas by the dozen. They were on dagger handles, alongside the runes and skulls on shroud black SS uniforms, and even on the Mothers' Cross for women's services to the Fatherland on the labour bed.

'It's just a business,' he said as I gazed around in astonishment at his collection of Third Reich insanity. 'I was singing in Hamburg and saw an Iron Cross in the window of a junk shop, and I just had to have it. That was it. I just started collecting. The other day there was an American lady in here. She was shocked when she saw what we had. I asked her what she was doing in the war, and she said that she'd been in New York. I said, "Well, I was here in Islington, and our house was bombed out twice. I was only four, but I can still remember the sound of the sirens".

'I've no political motives. I'm a Conservative, actually. Occasionally, we get people up here wanting to salute in front of a picture of Adolf Hitler, and asking if they can try on the helmets and uniforms. But we throw them straight out.'

I didn't know what to think as I made my way home that night. Yes, it was a hobby and a business. But a business trading in the impedimenta of evil, which at that time would still have been raw in some people's minds? Chris Farlowe seemed such a likeable bloke. I needed time to think about it. Over fifty years later, I still am.

I'd met him to talk about his follow-up record to 'Out Of Time'. It was 'Handbags and Gladrags'. Written by Mike D'Abo, it would, 34 years later, become the theme song to *The Office* TV series. Somehow, though, we'd got off the subject of pop songs.

At that time Plum and I had just bought a pretty, little, modern house in a delph surrounded by trees in Bromley, Kent. It seemed a good Sixties place to start a family, which we did four months after we moved to London. Louise was our first born. Everyone congratulates the husband when he becomes a father, and all my colleagues did, but that seemed to me to miss the point. To Plum and me, and I think for most other people, becoming parents, and sons Dominic and Kieron would later join Louise, meant that we were creating our lifelong best friends.

I never really got on with Mick Jagger. He was polite enough, but, though I met and talked to him several times during those early years, he was always somehow aloof. I felt that he was slightly grand, too, in a way I didn't find with the only other two Stones I met, Charlie Watts and Keith Richards.

At the time, the newspapers were gleefully full of Mick. He was a gift to the tabloids. When he and the Rolling Stones had first emerged, the joke had been whether any mother would want her daughter to marry him. After that he became Mick the Dandy and Mick the Toff and then Mick the Martyr when Judge Block sent him to prison for three months for a drugs offence. When the Lord Chief Justice released him the following day, he became Mick the Championed to be soon followed by Mick the Spokesman for his Generation after Granada TV hired a helicopter to fly him from prison to a 'summit discussion' with Malcolm Muggeridge, the Bishop of Woolwich and William Rees-Mogg, the editor of *The Times*. Always, of course, he remained Mick the Sexy and Mick the Provocative, but mostly, and perhaps surprisingly, because he never had a great voice, Mick the terrific front man for the Rolling Stones.

I first met him at his large flat near Regent's Park. He was then 24, and his dyed hair hung on to his shoulders making him look like a camped-up Robespierre. We sat, uncomfortably, on an island each of violently coloured Dunlopillo cushions, Mick, cross-legged and shoeless in puce pants with a clown's cravat to match, and a cosmic cotton shirt with stars and moons and other celestial objects printed on it. Around his waist was a sequined, tasseled belt that he'd bought on the Kings Road. His socks, he said, were from Marks and Spencer.

There was absolutely no sign then that he was thinking of marrying anybody's daughter, believing that marriage was becoming outdated, and that, in Western society, it was going into gradual decline. He turned out to be right about that.

'It's just one form of social behaviour,' he said. 'We're all animals, really. And marriage is just a primitive institution that we still have. Personally, I like the idea of two people living together. It's better than ten people living together,

'I can understand women wanting to get married, because they know their man can always run off with another woman. And as they are dependent on him, they have to make it that bit harder for him to get out of his obligations. But I don't really see why men want to get married at all, although I can see that I would if I ever met anyone I really loved and who wanted to marry me.'

Not his girlfriend, Marianne Faithfull?

'Well, she doesn't want to get married, and, anyway, she's already married to someone else, so she doesn't come into it.'

Over half a century on, and after eight children with five different women, it would seem he still doesn't see why men want to get married, although, it must he said, he's always fulfilled his paternal obligations.

Looking back on his life, it's interesting to reflect on how his social climbing and confection of contradictions has produced a self-creation. After growing up with a middle-class PT instructor for a father, he then consorted for years with a band of druggie outlaws, and while remaining a keep-fit, cricket fanatic as well as a free-spirited Lothario, he was drawn to aristocratic friends. On top of that he was a harmonica playing natural mimic who copied American blues singers while speaking in a faux Cockney dialect. A casually decadent drop-out from university, he would later manage his and the Rolling Stones' careers with a steely financial realism. He was clever, too.

From the beginning his stage performances were deliberately burlesque, the lyrics to some of the Stones' early hits being cheekily sexy. 'Let's Spend The Night Together,' he sang on TV, to a blizzard of protest from angry parents. The Beatles had veiled sexual desire in metaphor, but the Stones got straight to the point. John

Lennon once told me, 'Mick Jagger wears a codpiece on stage'. Whether that was true or not, I have no idea, and for sure that wasn't Mick Jagger's bulge and zip-fly in a pair of jeans on the front of the Stones' Andy Warhol designed album *Sticky Fingers*. But that was the image Mick liked to put out about himself.

He might not have fancied the idea of marriage when we spoke in 1967, but a couple of years later I was among a group of journalists who laid siege to his wedding in St Tropez to Bianca Perez Morena de Macias, known forever after as Bianca Jagger. We were all there, with the groom's parents, Roger Vadim, other Rolling Stones, photographer Patrick Litchfield, Ringo, Natalie Delon, fashionable friends and Press, all staying in the Hotel Byblos and waiting around the pool for two days while Mick negotiated a pre-nuptial agreement with his bride-to-be. A pre-nup? They always said he was canny with money. 'I grew up in the war,' he would explain.

Every journalist who covered the Rolling Stones has a favourite Mick Jagger story. I've got two. As a boy, he would help his father make television films promoting rock climbing and canoeing, of which he would later say: 'I was thinking I was a star already. Never mind the bloody canoe, how does my hair look?'

The other concerned the Montreux Music Festival where the Rolling Stones appeared in 1964 as fledgling stars. 'Did you know that in those days Montreux was reckoned to be the gay capital of Europe,' my friend Christopher Matthew asked the singer years later when they met at a cricket match.

To which, Jagger replied: 'Not on my watch, it wasn't.'

One of the perks of my job was that every day the record companies sent me their new singles, fifty or so a week. Ten years earlier I would have thought I was in heaven, but the thrill soon became a chore when I had to sort through the records to find half a dozen to review. I was surprised to realise how few had any commercial potential and would wonder what it was that made a long-lasting hit. Was it the tune, the arrangement, the rhythm, the lyrics or the singer? Obviously all five were involved, but I suspect that I often overlooked the potency of a good lyric.

Bobbie Gentry's 'Ode to Billy Joe', however, grabbed me immediately. It was a dark, short story, its events being told in casual conversation by a rural Mississippi family sitting around a table having dinner. Even without the doom-heavy cellos that underscore the song's shape, the bleakness of the piece was haunting. The storyteller, Bobbie herself, obviously knows she's had a part to play in why Billie Joe McAllister jumped of the Tallahatchie Bridge, but she isn't saying, and she didn't tell me either, after I asked her when she came to London for TV appearances. She didn't need to. The song was about a mystery. A relationship had broken up and a young man had killed himself, and now this local family were nonchalantly saying, 'Papa said to Mama, as he passed around the black-eyed peas, "Well, Billy Joe never had a lick of sense; pass the biscuits, please".'

For me, 'Ode to Billy Joe' from 1967 has one of the best lyrics of any popular song, in that it depicts time, place, sadness, the rural struggle, unspoken guilt and casual cruelty in matter-of-fact conversation. Bobbie Gentry could have been a novelist.

I didn't know much about mods and nothing about auto-destructiveness in music when I met Pete Townshend, once of Ealing Art College, and since then of The Who. They'd become famous as the West London group who decorated their umbilici and bosoms with bullseyes, and who appeared at gigs wearing what looked like only half a shirt each. Apparently, their managers, Kit Lambert and Chris Stamp, had invented the term 'Pop art music' for them to link their mod followers with art school fashion. So, as Keith Moon hammered his drums into submission, and Roger Daltrey sang 'Pictures of Lily', which is about masturbation, Pete Townshend, their main writer, was coming up with ultra sharp lyrics such as 'I was born with a plastic spoon in my mouth' for their song 'Substitute', while whirling his arms like a windmill as he played lead guitar. I wanted to know why he did that.

'It's all because of me hooter,' he explained one afternoon in the Soho office of Track Records. 'When I was a kid, I had this enormous great hooter and I was always being baited about it. So, I used to think, "I'll bloody well show 'em. I'll push me huge hooter out at them from every newspaper in England, and then they won't laugh at me".

'I used to go up on stage and forget I was Pete Townshend, who wasn't a success with the ladies. Then, all of a sudden, I'd become aware that there were little girls giggling and pointing at me nose. And I'd think, "Sod 'em. They're not going to laugh at me". And I'd get angrier still.

'My whole absurdly demonstrative stage act was worked out to turn myself into a body instead of a face. Most pop singers are pretty, but I wanted people to look at my body, and not have to bother looking at my head if they didn't like the look of it.'

From this came his routine of smashing his guitar on stage every night. 'The Who are a pantomime. But not one you'd take your children to. Showmanship is what the smashing up of instruments and equipment is all about. It's traumatic, melodramatic, theatrical, pure basic emotion. We couldn't get the crescendo any other way. We don't like to smash all the gear up. It costs money. But there isn't really any other way.' What he didn't tell me was that after every performance he would glue his guitars back together…if that was possible.

'It's like an auto-destructive ballet, as though every performance we do will be our last, and every audience thinks they've seen the last. We're good circus entertainment.

'Our song "My Generation" in which Roger stutters "why don't you all f-f-fade away" was originally about anger and communication, but by the time we got it on record it came out as a pilled-up kid, who, for the first time in his life, becomes aware of things. But, unfortunately, the taking of purple hearts has incapacitated him and he can hardly speak.

'He wants to say things, but he can't. It's like having a big nose. You can't communicate because of it. That's what the stutter in "My Generation" means.'

Which was interesting to me because my stammer (and I always used the English word for it, not the American 'stutter') was at last beginning to sort itself out. It could still be very, very bad on occasions, which sometimes made me wonder (and no doubt others) why Charles Wintour, the *Evening Standard* editor, had ever employed me as an interviewer. But he had, and my years there were among the happiest of my working life.

The paper didn't have a huge circulation, probably no more than 450,000 a night, which was about half what the rival London paper the *Evening News* sold. But the *Standard's* writers mirrored its readers. That is, they were mainly younger, educated, and metropolitan in outlook and ambition. It didn't matter how many people read you: it did matter *who* read you. I wouldn't have had the success I had on any other newspaper.

From the outside, the *Evening Standard* office wasn't the most prepossessing of places. Built in the nineteenth century, it was on the corner of a side street which ran down to Farringdon Street, under which was the sewer channeling the River Fleet into the Thames at Blackfriars. The inside of the building was Dickensian, the entire second floor being given over to journalists: sport in one section, news reporters in another, crime somewhere else, and, in the middle, the engine of the newspaper, the news sub-editors. There was also space for the Londoner's Diary people, a place for fashion, another for photographers to hang around, and a couple of long desks for the specialists and the feature writers. Occasionally there would be a whirring sound as a mechanical contraption sent a photograph racing along a wire from the picture desk to the processors, like one of those things they used to have in a department store. And, all the time, there would be little border wars as one writer, such as this one, exceeded the boundaries of his specialist field and invaded the area of another.

The editor would be in an office in a corner, only to spend most of his afternoons sitting on the backbench alongside his deputy, Roy Wright, overseeing the main pages of a newspaper that changed its main news pages five times a day as the news dictated, and fighting a duel with the *Evening News*, edition by edition. From where the editor sat, his back to the window, every journalist on the floor could see him; and know that he could see them.

In those days before the invention of computers, the tools of the journalist were modest. All he or she needed was a hook on which to hang a coat, a phone, a place at a long wooden desk, a chair, a typewriter, a long spike for unused pieces, and a stack of paper which came in wads of five, with carbon in between the sheets, so that copies were available for the editor, the lawyers, and the sub editors.

In many ways, a newspaper was a microcosm of a small society in one building. On a floor below the journalists, the compositors turned our stories into sandwiches of metal, while underneath them the printers tended their roaring machines and gigantic rolls of paper. Meanwhile, outside the building, vans waited, like carrier ants, to rush the latest editions to the street sellers and shops throughout the city; and, above everyone, on the top floor, the advertising department sold space and the management plotted the way forward.

As a specialist writer, I was mainly in the middle of the room, along with the arts editor Sydney Edwards, film critic Alexander Walker, writer Valerie Grove and Sally Baker, the features' department secretary and a close friend ever since. Behind us sat a guy who seemed to be the paper's main link to the constables of the Metropolitan Police. Respectable newspapers always deny that they pay for information, but once a month the *Evening Standard's* police reporter would have a stack of fresh banknotes on his desk together with a pile of envelopes. Then, going through a little book he kept for this purpose, he would bung a 'thank you' into each envelope, address it and send it to the home of PC 49, or whoever had provided the tip off about the car crash and ensuing gridlock on Westminster Bridge, or the 'gruesome murder victim' in Whitechapel. How else would newspapers have got their news stories? It must still go on, although now in a more sophisticated way.

9.

'It was beautiful and quiet, with baboons eating your breakfast...'
- John Lennon

It is impossible to exaggerate the fascination the Beatles had on the general public in 1968, and, with this in mind, I went to Paul's McCartney's house in St John's Wood. It was about half a mile from the EMI's Abbey Road recording studio, a large, square 1830 brick-built mansion behind a front garden wall, the kind of dignified home that a captain of industry or a foreign ambassador might have had. I was there to catch up with Beatle events before all four, plus wives (or partner in the case of Paul's girlfriend, Jane Asher), embarked on a trip to the Himalayas to relax and meditate with the Maharishi Mahesh Yogi. The Yogi was an odd little man, with a high-pitched giggle, who had become a figure of some ridicule since the Beatles had plucked him from obscurity the previous summer.

What Paul wanted to talk about, however, was Apple, the management company that the Beatles had set up since the death of Brian Epstein. 'When we first started,' he said in his living room as he watched while his cats clawed at his green velvet three-piece suite, 'we were eighteen and wanted to get rich. And, if there was a possibility of getting rich by singing we were willing to forget everything. Well, let's face it, that's what swinging London is really about, isn't it?

'But now we don't have to do things just for ourselves so much anymore. So, instead of trying to amass money for the sake of it, we're setting up a business concern called Apple, which will be rather like a Western Communism. We want to make it a complete business organisation on the lines of ICI, not just for us, but for the general good. Apple could be a social and cultural environment, as well as a business environment. The concept will spread. It will be fantastic.

'We've got all the money we need. I've got the house and the cars and all the things that money can buy. So now we want to start directing this money into a business. Not as a charity. No one likes charity, it makes them wince. Too sickly. We want to get something going where the underwriters and the staff will get a decent share of the profits, not two pounds a week, while we make a million.

'We've had to do it for ourselves. When Brian Epstein died, we had to take a look at what we consisted of, and who owned bits of us. Now we're really looking for someone like Brian, not in the managerial sense, but someone we could respect and who we'd listen to and take advice from. We meet lots of people who are good at business, but they're not necessarily nice people. Every big company has the sort of person we want. The trouble is that they all have good jobs already.'

So, that was what Apple was intended to be. Hippy idealism. Two years later the Beatles would have broken themselves up and an American conman called Allen Klein would be running a rump of the company, albeit without Paul McCartney. The concept hadn't spread. It had disintegrated from within. John Lennon would tell me later that he realised that the Beatles 'were fucked when Brian died. I knew then we'd had it'. In retrospect, the Apple plan and the vacuum where a manager should have been, was the beginning of the end for the group. But other factors were soon to arrive, one of them in a series of letters by post to India.

Before I left that day, Paul took me upstairs to his music room to play the Beatles' latest record. 'Norwegian wood,' he said indicating the little studio's wood panelling. Then, fiddling with some knobs, he found some music that at the time sounded to me like a waltz in a Calcutta discotheque. 'George wrote this,' he told me. 'It's beautiful, isn't it. It's translated from Chinese.'

It was 'The Inner Life', and by playing it to me before his own song, he was, I assume, showing an awareness of George Harrison's growing unhappiness at the guitarist's lower status in the Beatles. It was the first time that one of George's songs had been on a single.

Another song, with Paul playing a barrelhouse piano, followed. It was 'Lady Madonna'. When it finished, he waited for my verdict. 'Do you like it?' he asked.

Clearly, he liked it very much, but I recognised its roots. 'Humphrey Lyttleton's Bad Penny Blues', I told him.

He smiled sheepishly. 'You're not supposed to say that.'

A few days later, the Beatles were off to learn about transcendental meditation at the feet of their yogi in an ashram in

Rishikesh. It was a two-hour taxi drive from New Delhi, in the foothills of the Indian Himalayas. The plan had been for a three month break for all of them, and that Lennon and McCartney, free from outside distractions, would come home with over two dozen new songs. But, for Ringo and his wife, Maureen, who had taken tins of baked beans and powdered milk with them, 'just in case', it was a brief holiday. Ten days later they were back.

'It was just like Butlins,' was Ringo's verdict, when I called him. He knew a lot about Butlins, having played there with Rory Storm and the Hurricanes before joining the Beatles. 'In India we all lived in chalets, went down to the canteen for breakfast, then perhaps walked about a bit and meditated. Maureen and me are funny about our food, and we don't like spicy things... But I think the biggest thing was that we missed the children. We just wanted to come home.'

He was pretty sure that Paul would be the next to leave. He was right. John Lennon, however, was going through a crisis. Yoko Ono had arrived in London with her husband and daughter, a year earlier, looking for financial support for her *avant garde* art. She'd managed to get to Paul first, but he'd shown no interest, while Ringo would say he hadn't understood what she was talking about when she approached him. John, however, had been more receptive, and he'd even considered bringing her along with Cynthia to India, before deciding he hadn't known how to broach the subject with his wife.

Cynthia, who I liked, had no idea of what was going on behind her back. She'd been hoping the break would get John away from drugs and alcohol, and that they could refresh their marriage. It wasn't to be. On arrival, she and John had been given a bungalow with a large double bed, but John rarely spoke to her, deciding, after a week or two, that he wanted to move to a separate room. 'Our love life had definitely disappeared by then, and been replaced by a brother-sister relationship,' Cynthia would later tell me. 'He was having problems, whether because of being so high on drugs or whatever. He found it quite difficult with me, although obviously not with someone else. There are many ways of stimulating someone, but I didn't know the tricks.'

John's memories of Rishikesh were different. Secretly, he would get letters every day through the ashram post office. 'Yoko wrote me these crazy postcards…like, "Look into the sky. I'm a cloud". And I'd be looking up trying to see her, and then rushing down to the post office the next morning to get another message. It was driving me mad.' Yes, Rishikesh was 'beautiful and quiet, with baboons eating your breakfast…but I was writing the most miserable songs on earth. When I wrote "I'm lonely, want to die" in "Yer Blues", I wasn't kidding. That's how I felt, up there, trying to reach God, and feeling suicidal.' That was John, off on one of his exaggerations. But, for sure, Yoko had been getting inside his head.

The Sixties was a time when many young couples who had been brought up in towns were scraping together enough money to put down a deposit on a house and moving to the suburbs. Three of the Beatles, guided by their accountants, did exactly that, albeit on a grander scale than anybody else. George went to live with his wife, Patti, in Esher, Surrey, while John and Ringo chose houses not far away in what was known as the stockbroker belt of St George's Hill estate, near Weybridge. While the other Beatles were still away and Ringo was at a loose end, I went there to see him in March 1968. He was one of the most open and unassuming people I ever interviewed, but slightly sad in his little rich boy indolence. Wanting to show me his new home, he took me up to his playroom when I arrived. It was the top floor of an annexe built on to the living room of his home, a place of flashing lights, panda rugs, a fruit machine, a table for snooker and table tennis, and miles and miles of taped pop music. The last word in Sixties youth clubs, I thought. Outside was a terraced garden, with a Wendy house in a tree. Beyond that was a golf course. 'We get quite a few foxes around here,' he said, nursing one of his Siamese cats. 'The first time I heard them I thought some girl was getting assaulted down at the end of the road.'

He and Maureen had moved there shortly after Zak, their first son, had been born. 'We were afraid some fan would pinch him and take him home to put in her scrapbook,' he joked. Zak was then a toddler; their second child, Jason, was eight months old. They had a nanny who lived in, a chauffeur, a gardener and a lady who did the housework. While they'd been in India, Maureen's mother had come to stay and was still with them. 'Maureen's Dad's at sea. He wouldn't give it up for anything.'

After lighting some joss sticks, Ringo chatted as we played pool. 'John lives just up the road. Sometimes I go up there to play with his toys, and sometimes he comes down here to play with mine.'

They rarely went out in the evenings and watched a great deal of television, he said. There were six sets scattered throughout the house. He liked situation comedy, or a good play and the Cilla Black show. Their neighbours, who were mostly hidden by the wooded hills, were still mainly strangers.

'Maureen is friendly with some of the girls who work at the hairdressers she goes to, and they come back for tea some days, and I've got a friend in Liverpool called Roy. He's a joiner, and he's only got about thirty records, but he gets so much pleasure from them. Yet, I've got a cupboard here with about five hundred LPs, and, when I want to play one, I have to close the cupboard again, because I don't know which one to put on anymore.'

He had, he said, a passion for hobbies and consumed new ones at an enormous rate. His current one was developing his own photographs. A few weeks earlier it had been using a movie camera ('We used some in *Magical Mystery Tour* so that gave me an extra push'), and before that it was photography, snooker, making light machines with coloured slides, and painting eight-foot-tall sunflowers on the garden walls. The rain had washed most of them off. 'Next week it might be fixing up my new fountain by the fish pond, or sorting out my favourite records

'I've always had crazes, but now if I want to do something I go out and buy all the equipment. Then sometimes, if there's a lot of setting up involved, I go off whatever it is. I don't stay with one hobby for much more than a couple of weeks. Sometimes I'll have a week and I'll just play records; then I might spend a day just playing with my tape recordings. Sometimes I put the video tape machine on and film myself playing snooker.

'I suppose I get bored like anyone else, but instead of having three hours a night, I have all day to get bored in. Even this house was a toy. In Liverpool I'd always lived in a four-roomed house and the height of my ambition was a semi in Aigburth', which is a middle-class Liverpool suburb. 'Sometimes I feel I'd like to stop being famous and get back to where I was in Liverpool. There don't seem to be so many worries in that sort of life, although I thought there were at the time. But I had to come here to realise that they counted for very little.

'Still, the happiest times of my life have been as a Beatle. What I regret most is never being able to see a Beatles' stage show from the audience. I would have loved that. It isn't the same when you see it on film later.'

Going back into the cathedral that he called his living room, television replaced the constant records. Despite his five headlined years (or perhaps because of them) he was still remarkably touchy about newspaper reports, and surprised that his movements should attract the attention they do.

'It's amazing,' he said several times. 'They must be barmy. Why everybody had to be so set against our doing meditation, I don't know. What would have happened if we'd suddenly turned Catholic instead? I suppose, if we'd been sitting with the Pope every day we'd have been "good old Beatles". Reflecting on the newspapers, he suddenly said for no apparent reason: 'You know, I went through a stage of thinking seriously about having plastic surgery on my nose, because that was all the papers seemed to write about. I never noticed "my feature" until the Press pointed it out. It didn't hurt me, but I got fed up with reading about it.'

He had no real ambition, he insisted, but rather fancied the idea of seeing himself in comic film roles, because his face made people laugh. He was, it seemed to me, the supreme fatalist. Nothing ever seemed to get on top of him. He had problems, he said, but he could cope. 'I've never really done anything to create what has happened,' he admitted. 'It created itself. I'm here because it happened. But I didn't do anything to make it happen apart from saying "Yes".'

Neither did he know the cost of anything: 'I haven't had any real money worries since I was eighteen, although I probably only had £10 in the bank then. I could now afford never to work again, I suppose. But I'd have to be careful, and probably have to sell this house in about ten years. 'I'm rich by working-class standards, but not immensely rich, and not by the standards of those who really do have money. I spend money like water, you see. A lot of it went on this house.'

As a Sixties home, it was as colourful as a butterfly, and chock-a-block with knick-knacks, ornaments and souvenirs. There were pictures of John and dozens of psychedelic posters. When he first moved down to Weybridge he had a bar built because he couldn't go out to pubs. He smoked between twenty and forty American cigarettes a day, he said, and the house was littered with ash trays and squashed filter tips.

He looked very small and vulnerable wandering around his mansion in his purple pants and flowery yellow shirt, and he was so open and guileless it was disarming. 'Do you remember when everyone began analysing Beatle songs? I don't think I ever understood what some of them were supposed to be about,' he said in one minute, and then in another: 'As a drummer I'm fair, that's all, and I don't care about being good anymore'; then straight after that another admission. 'I'm not very good at singing because I haven't got a great range. So, they write songs for me that are pretty low and not too hard.' And finally: 'I didn't feel that I was really involved with the Beatles for the first couple of years.'

At that moment Maureen's Mum called us for our tea and we moved from one television to another.

10.

'I'm a romantic and a lecher and a lover of women' - Leonard Cohen

It didn't take me a year at the *Evening Standard* to realise that I had the best job for me in the world, my life being consumed by covering anything and everything connected with popular music, and anything remotely allied, as well as writing a page interview for Saturday's paper. The freedom I was given was extraordinary. The editor, Charles Wintour, was a shy man, but he encouraged me all the time. I used to joke that when he took me out to lunch we didn't say much, because he never did, and I couldn't. But he had a talent for spotting young journalists and giving them their heads, and, with the paper's promotion, it made their names. It wasn't a national newspaper. It was better than that. It was a local newspaper that was read by all the nationals, and everyone else of influence in London. Sitting at the desks around me at that time were some very bright writers, several of whom would go on to be Fleet Street editors themselves within a few years – Max Hastings, Simon Jenkins, Suzy Menkes, Trevor Grove and Magnus Linklater, while Liz Forgan went on to run BBC Network Radio among much else. We, and many others, cut our teeth at the *Evening Standard*. It was a nursery for journalistic talent.

To have my own page to fill every week was every young journalist's dream, but it was an endless worry finding good enough interviewees for it. Failure wasn't acceptable. Every Monday I would have a list of the people I wanted to interview and, usually, I would get one. But, sometimes, a big name would fall through at the last minute, or do a big interview for a rival newspaper, which would rule him or her out. Popular music was a cottage industry and publicists would ring all the time offering the artists they were employed to promote; so, I would often find myself fibbing and pretending that senior people on the paper had rejected their suggestions. Actually, that didn't happen. It was always my decision whom I chose to talk to, and which publicist best convinced me. That was how I came across Leonard Cohen.

I'd never heard of him when a friend at a record company begged me to listen to Cohen's first album. I needed some persuading. The guy was almost 35, virtually middle-aged. It seemed to me that he was probably just another ageing folkie who wrote poetry and novels that no-one bought. He was Canadian, too. This was pre-Joni Mitchell and Neil Young, and, at that time, Canada wasn't known for producing superstars. All the same I agreed to play the record. That was when I first heard 'Suzanne' and 'So Long, Marianne'. I met Leonard Cohen the following day.

He was staying, at his record company's expense (though actually the amount would be deducted from any royalties he was owed), in the plush Mayfair Hotel, having arrived in London with his belongings in just a scuffed old leather bag. He was a small, dark-haired man with that deep voice that everyone now knows. But he surprised me. You might not guess it from his songs, but he was a mischievous, funny man. He was also a ladies' man. That *was* obvious from his songs. We talked first about his career as a poet.

'I must have looked extremely absurd, because I wrote all my poems to ladies thinking that was the way to approach them,' he explained. 'So, I put them all together in a book and was suddenly taken seriously as a poet, when all I was really, was a kind of stud. And not a very successful one either. Because the successful ones didn't have to write poems to make girls...'

Summing himself up, he was, he said, 'a romantic and a lecher and a lover of women. Women are indeed in control. It isn't necessary to declare a matriarchy, but it exists. Everything that a man does is laid at a lady's feet, whether it is a battle or a song or an amalgamation between two great companies. At some time in the day the man comes home to his woman and says, "Look what I've done".

'I remember one day I was in a very excited state, and I saw a bunch of cows in a field, and I noticed how beautiful they were. They were so beautiful that I got down on my knees to worship them. And, you know, the cows were so happy. And the more I worshipped them the happier they became. And, to make a metaphor out of it, it's the same with ladies...' And he left the thought hanging, as I wondered what he'd been smoking that day.

Cohen's lady at the time was a Norwegian called Marianne, as in the song, who lived with him on the Greek island of Hydra. 'I met her one day when I was sitting outside a store, and I thought she was the most beautiful woman I'd ever seen. She had a three-month-old child, and her husband had just fallen in love with an American girl. So, I went to him and said that if he went off with the other girl I would like to go and live with Marianne. We had a lot of drinks together and talked about it and everything worked out all right.''

Marianne, he continued, had now learned to accept his need for other women. 'She knows that is what my nature is. I say to her, "What are your appetites?" She knows what I mean, because she is attracted to other men. And I know she's had that feeling.'

So much for Marianne. I wanted to know about Suzanne and those oranges that 'come all the way from China'.

'Ah. Suzanne... She's great, but she's half crazy. The other week I was in New York or Los Angeles or somewhere and a guy comes up to me and said he liked my song and that he'd lived with Suzanne for a while. And I asked him if he was still with her. And he said, "no", he couldn't stand it anymore. "She's half crazy".'

After that day, it came as no surprise to me that in 1984 Leonard Cohen would write one of the great lyrical songs of the last half of the twentieth century, 'Hallelujah'.

Or that women, particularly, loved him. As we know, he loved them.

Having left the pirate ships for the BBC's new station, Radio One, disc jockeys were now quickly becoming as famous as, and often more famous than, the artists whose records they were playing. In the case of sunny Tony Blackburn, who was always easy to talk to, he'd gone from being a buccaneer to becoming a housewives' choice. John Peel, on the other hand, took himself and the music he played seriously. Very seriously. Just old enough to have been called up for National Service, during which, he told me, he'd played at being a 'toy soldier' for two years, his programmes were of studied eccentricity. With a column in the underground newspaper, the *International Times*, he was a sort of agitprop, provocative DJ who was said to have inflamed listeners by playing a Vietnamese lullaby on his late-night show at the height of the Vietnam War. Why listeners were upset I don't know. Lullabies and babies hardly took sides.

British radio was quickly changing. And movies were, too. Since the introduction of talkies, composers had been engaged to score music to accompany the action on the screen. That led to

Elmer Bernstein's music for *The Big Country* and Anton Karas's zither on the soundtrack of *The Third Man* created audible mental pictures for those films. You heard the *Harry Lime Theme* and immediately your brain showed you Orson Welles.

Then, in the Sixties, for the first time, pop records, that had nothing to do with the story, began to be added to movie soundtracks. At first, they were just played over title sequences, especially on James Bond films, where Matt Monro sang 'From Russia With Love', and Shirley Bassey did 'Goldfinger'. The next step took the symbiosis of film and song further when, in *The Graduate*, which starred Dustin Hoffman and Anne Bancroft, three tracks by Simon and Garfunkel accompanied the action. The film was a huge hit and became a trailblazer, ensuring that the appeal of Simon and Garfunkel justifiably mushroomed. Without those songs, *The Graduate* would still have been a very good film. But with Paul Simon's compositions and Art Garfunkel's peerless voice, their harmonies matched the mood on the screen, making a perfect union of two art forms. Within a few months Burt Bacharach and Hal David had added 'Raindrops Keep Falling On My Head' to *Butch Cassidy and the Sundance Kid*. Others would quickly follow, including *American Graffiti* and *That'll Be The Day*, for which, by the way, I would write the screenplay. Then, just over a decade later, MTV, would demonstrate how music would in future be sold through three minute promotional films when it launched its online channel with 'Video Killed the Radio Star' by the Buggles.

Music, radio, TV and films weren't the only things changing. Two years after England had won the World Cup in 1966, Saturday night's *Match of the Day* was turning everyday footballers into big stars. The game was transmuting from sport into entertainment, where it remains. This struck Plum and me forcefully when we went to an afternoon party in the garden of friends who had a swimming pool and watched in astonishment as three muscular Chelsea FC players used a hair dryer after going for a swim. Today a footballer's hair is his crowning glory, changing with the fashions and the football seasons, but until that day it had never occurred to me that sportsmen were vain.

George Best must obviously have been vain, too, but, looking the way he did, that was understandable. With that hair and those eyes, he was football's first pop star, even though he didn't sing. What he did was dribble, and no matter how often big defenders knocked him down, he just got straight back up again and carried on dribbling. It was something to see. In 1968 he was the Footballer of the Year, so I went to Manchester to meet him.

It was bedlam at the boutique that he now co-owned. A little boy of about five with a Union Jack stuck in the handlebars of his tricycle was wanting to know 'is Georgie Best cummin' before bedtime', girls with backcombed hair were taking peeps into the changing room and leaving love letters and photos of themselves, and knowledgeable lads surveyed an S-type Jaguar as it arrived.

And then there was George in a tangerine sweater, the dark, pretty, slight lad from Belfast who'd joined Manchester United at 15, and who, at 22, was the most famous footballer in the country, telling them all to clear off because people couldn't get into his shop to buy things. 'People used to think that footballers were big blokes with short haircuts, but I'm just an ordinary young bloke who happens to play football,' he said. Actually, he wasn't ordinary at all. He had, it seemed, all the gifts. Well, all but one.

In a family of six children, he could have been working in the Belfast shipyards, nine to five-thirty, like his father, for whom he'd just bought a fish and chip shop, but he had a talent. 'You can't make a footballer. It's either born in you or it isn't. I've been kicking a ball around for as long as I can remember. I went to a grammar school when I was eleven, but I left because they played rugby and not football. United spotted me when I was playing with a youth club and brought me here and put me in digs with a widow and her family.'

He was still there. 'I'd like a flat, but they won't let me. I suppose they think I wouldn't be able to look after myself, and it wouldn't do for me to come home screaming in the middle of the night and bringing people back and all that. You need lots of sleep if you're going to play football. Matt Busby [the manager] still gives me a talking to, but not too often. And I haven't smashed up my present car yet.'

And the gift that he didn't have? You could tell from what he said that day that he already knew what it was. Certainly, Matt Busby and Manchester United knew. George couldn't say 'no'. He couldn't look after himself.

Five years later he laughingly told a story about himself on the BBC's *Parkinson* show, on which I was briefly involved. Manchester United had by now given up on him, and, going out with a lady who had become a Miss World, he had one night won a lot of money that had been paid in cash. Driving his Jaguar to a hotel, he and Miss World took a room and then rang down to reception for a bottle of champagne to be brought up.

A few minutes later an elderly porter delivered the champagne. Seeing Miss World already in bed and the money that George has just won spread out on the sheet in front of her, he shook his head sadly, and said: 'Tell me, George, where did it all go wrong?'

The story got a hoot of laughter from the studio audience that night, but it really wasn't funny. George, the most talented and loved footballer of his generation, was already well on his way to becoming an alcoholic as his football degenerated into a cycle of failure. The beautiful girls didn't stay around forever, his good looks became raddled and the money got thinner. After years of struggling with alcoholism, he died at the age 59 in 2005 from a kidney infection.

It was the *Evening Standard's* readers who rang in and tipped me off about the great Apple give-away. As the first part of their plan for self-management, the Beatles had opened their own shop in London's Baker Street and hired a couple of Dutch dress-designers to come up with the clothes. They wanted it to be 'a beautiful place that sold beautiful clothes', Paul McCartney would say. But it wasn't and it didn't. The main problem was that too many of the beautiful people who shopped there didn't believe in paying for what they wanted, and quickly developed a beautiful kind of shoplifting. None of the Beatles had any experience of running a shop, so one weekend they simply decided to close it down. When the staff arrived the next morning, they were told that every single item was to be given away free to customers. 'We weren't getting rid of the clothes fast enough, so we went out into Baker Street and stopped passers-by,' said an assistant. Their shop had gone from being a Beatles Take-Away to a Beatles Give-Away. What no-one admitted was that the clothes were fancy dress absurd, anyway, and not well-made.

It really didn't matter that the Beatles lost money on the venture. They could afford it. But it was another signal to them that they were musicians, not businessmen. It was another warning, but they didn't see it, simply going on to form other companies under the umbrella of a central one called Apple Corps.

When, in 1919, Charlie Chaplin, Mary Pickford, D.W. Griffith and Douglas Fairbanks had set up their own Hollywood studio and called it United Artists, the fabled joke in the film industry was that the inmates were taking over the asylum. That may have been a jaundiced reaction, but it was to be replicated to the very smirk when the Beatles created Apple Corps. Placing an advertisement in the Underground bugle of the day, the *International Times*, they invited readers to send in their film scripts, songs, poems, tapes, fashion designs, inventions, plays, electronics, novels and recordings for possible financial backing.

Big mistake. Within days a trickle of hippy hopes had turned into an avalanche of useless dreams being delivered to the Beatles' newly renovated Regency house in London's Savile Row. Staffed by many of the group's old friends from Liverpool, Apple Corps soon became a financial whirlpool as money was sucked away to places unknown. One rumour was that a Mercedes car had somehow vanished into thin air.

But it wasn't all naïve failure. Apple, as a small, short-lived record company, wasn't without its successes. Who knew that both Paul McCartney and George Harrison played on the original recording of James Taylor's 'Carolina On My Mind', that Apple released a Modern Jazz Quartet album, and that it was at Ringo Starr's insistence that John Taverner's 'The Whale' was recorded for the label?

There was something magnificently crackers about Apple's open house policy where friends could drop in for a chat with whoever happened to be about, while outside on the pavement the teenage girls, whom George Harrison christened Apple Scruffs, stood sentinel. On one day you might meet the young, then long-haired, James Taylor, whose first album was being produced by Peter Asher (brother of Jane Asher), with the rumour that Taylor had spent time in a mental hospital marking him as someone especially exotic. And, on another, there would be Sweet William and Frisco Pete, a couple of Hell's Angels from San Francisco, who said that they were stopping over in the UK on their 'way to straighten out Czechoslovakia'. Eventually one of them tried to straighten out the Apple office Christmas party, going eyeball-to-eyeball with a Santa John Lennon, who was wearing a red robe with a stuck-on white cotton wool beard, after which they disappeared back to California with their Harleys between their legs.

Meanwhile, at one end of the many tentacled Apple spectrum, was well-scrubbed seventeen-year-old schoolgirl Mary Hopkin from Swansea, whom Paul decided should sing 'Those Were The Days', a Russian folk song he'd heard in a club; and, at the other end, a girl who wanted backing to make some nude sculptures of herself out of patent leather. History doesn't record whether she got the money, but there were always a lot of pretty girls around. If the Beatles, at their peak, couldn't attract pretty girls, who could?

It seemed that every day young, long haired, denim clad Americans were beating a path from London Airport to the Beatles' front door. Once there, they could rarely get past the lovely, but unbending, Debbie in reception, a place described at the time as closely resembling 'the waiting room of a Haight Ashbury VD clinic'.

What the visitors really wanted was to bump into a Beatle on the stairs, and, in the early days at least, that could often happen. There would be George talking earnestly, and usually to blank faces, about Krishna, John ordering acorns to be planted at Coventry Cathedral in the cause of peace, and busy-busy Paul interfering all over the place as he saw his Apple dream going wrong. Ringo was, the drummer liked to say, 'just the office boy'.

What is astonishing, however, is the amount of music that was still being generated in and around the general bedlam. George Harrison was playing on sessions for Jackie Lomax, Billy Preston and Doris Troy along with his pals Eric Clapton and Keith Richards; while Paul McCartney was writing top ten hits for Badfinger and Mary Hopkin, and Cilla Black, too, for whom he composed 'Step Inside, Love'. It was going to be called 'Come Inside, Love' until someone pointed out that such an invitation might be misinterpreted.

Meanwhile John Lennon's affair with Yoko Ono was a constant river of a story. I learned later, mainly from Cynthia Lennon, that the affair had started properly when she'd gone to Italy for a holiday, and, in her absence, John had invited Yoko down to their house one night. When Cynthia returned the following day Yoko had, in effect, moved in. 'John was sitting in his dressing gown. Yoko was facing him wearing my dressing gown,' Cynthia said. 'It was a betrayal of such considered callousness that it still shocks. You had to be in the situation to realise the horror of it. It was vicious. I'd phoned to say I was on my way. He knew I'd be coming.' After going out with John since they met at art college in 1959, they'd been married for six years at that point.

Yoko was an enigmatic, mystery lady in black, who had suddenly appeared seemingly from nowhere, and who hid more than half of her face behind two curtains of long black hair. That she'd made a film showing the bottoms of famous people, was all anyone seemed to know about her, which, not unexpectedly, provoked ridicule in the tabloid Press. And which then turned to phoney indignation when John and Yoko released an album of various sounds, with photographs on the front and the back showing the couple naked. The album was called *Two Virgins*.

Who was this woman who'd come over here and broken up the marriage of one of our Beatles, ran the ribaldry of some popular newspapers? The Beatles were 'national treasures' and she was a foreign interloper. Not only that. She was a zany, *avant-garde* Japanese interloper, a nationality that some papers abbreviated by saying that she was a 'Jap', a term not often heard since World War II. Its reference opened a wound that John Lennon would never forget or forgive.

I didn't know much about John Lennon's private life, but, intrigued, I arranged to meet Yoko at Abbey Road Studios. It was the first time Yoko had been interviewed, and her notoriety didn't prepare me for the very small, smiling, charming and slightly nervous woman in white tennis shoes.

'The idea for our *Two Virgins* album came from John,' she explained as George Martin and John Lennon were mixing 'Cry Baby Cry' in the background. 'I know some people may think "ah, that bottoms-girl Yoko has persuaded John into this" but that wasn't how it was. I don't think my bottoms film inspired him. I know some may think that I have a bottoms fetish, but when we made that film, I was so embarrassed that I was never in the same room as the filming. I'm very shy. I just set up the camera and allowed the technicians to do it and my friends went before the camera as though they were being x-rayed.

'John is very shy, too. I don't think he's seen the bottoms film. He heard one of the tapes of my voice pieces and said this should be an LP record, and that if it were made it should have a picture of me naked on the cover. I don't know why he said that. I suppose he just thought it would be effective. He didn't even know me that well at the time. Anyway, he sent me a drawing of me naked, and I was terribly embarrassed. But, when we decided to make a record, we decided that we should both be naked on the cover. He took the photograph with an automatic camera. We wouldn't have had anyone there to photograph us. The picture isn't lewd or anything like that. Basically, we're very shy and square people. We'd be the first to be embarrassed if anyone was to invite us to a nude party.'

She was thirty-five at the time, twice married, and had been brought up in Tokyo and America. Her family were rich (her father was a governor of a bank, and she had an uncle who represented Japan at the United Nations), and her childhood had, she told me, been authoritarian and dedicated to education.

When she was eighteen her family had gone to live in New York, and she had enrolled to read philosophy at Sarah Lawrence, which was, she said, 'a school for girls who thought of nothing but marrying Harvard graduates.' Gradually, while she was there, she'd become interested in instructional art.

Her biggest problem was that there wasn't anyone who would produce or accept her ideas. So, she rented a loft, converted it into a studio, and held happenings every other week. 'I remember I bought a baby-grand piano and at the first concert I played it with my body, by rolling along the open string part. It snowed that day. Another buzz I got was when we boiled a still of water and listened until it evaporated.'

This was all unlike anything else being said in the rock world at the time, and I began to see what John Lennon had meant when he said, 'I've finally found someone as barmy as I am'. Yoko was a conceptualist. She thought of an idea and others performed it. When she asked people to cut off her clothes, as she had at a New York happening, it was their reaction which made the event.'

She'd first been married eleven years earlier to a Japanese composer. ('He used to write Stravinsky-type material, but now he's the foremost *avant-garde* composer in Japan'). After six years, and some affairs and resulting abortions, she left him, and returned to Japan where her family had her institutionalised. Her second husband was an American artist and documentary maker producer, Tony Cox. They had one daughter, aged five, Kyoko.

'Both of my marriages were elopements,' she told me that night. 'Basically, I'm a romantic and believe in long-lasting relationships, but somehow I've failed up to now.' Her later marriage to John didn't fail, although it went through a very rocky patch. But something else she said to me that night lingered in my mind. 'Because John is so creative, we can collaborate together,' she told me.

Which is exactly what they did. Whether he realised it or not, from then on John lost interest in the Beatles, pouring his energies into John and Yoko, his new craze. Yoko was self-obsessed. She wanted to be recognised as a famous artist, and that is what John came to want, too. He certainly made her world famous. Whether she will be remembered as a great artist, we'll have to wait and see.

That night was one of my first visits to Abbey Road, and, after our interview, Paul McCartney turned up. Suggesting I join him in a music room, where there was a grand piano, he then gave me a solo performance of a few old rock and roll favourites, before suddenly going into a churchy gospel fragment that included the line 'Mother Mary comes to me.' The lyrics and tune were unfinished. I wouldn't hear it again for a further sixteen months when it would be released as 'Let It Be'.

All my interviews were now being taped on a little Sony cassette machine. It went everywhere with me and would see me through hundreds of conversations. Unfortunately, I was only being paid thirty-five pounds a week, and, if my memory serves me well, at that time a two-hour cassette cost about four pounds. I couldn't afford to keep buying them.

So, what did I do? I simply taped over some earlier interviews, thus wiping John Lennon, Paul McCartney, Muhammad Ali, Mick Jagger, Tom Stoppard, Leonard Cohen, James Baldwin and dozens more. I was meeting these people all the time. It didn't seem such a big deal then.

I still have some of them, of course, but a complete set would have been quite a selection. At least, I kept the printed newspaper versions of the interviews.

11.

'Hey, d'you want a tooth with the
Stars and Stripes on it?' –
Ken Kesey

When we think of the Sixties, we often imagine pretty girls. In the Sixties myth they were everywhere, a new, shining army of free, post-Pill spirits. 'Dolly girls' was the name the tabloids gave them. Never before had a generation of young women seemed so healthily beautiful with their eyes, bigger and rounder and their lashes thicker and longer. Their skirts went up and up and later down and down as fashion dictated, while a buoyant patina of self-love shone from them as, in their Courreges boots, they strode so confidently through magazines and newspapers. They were the flipside of the male rock groups. It seemed every girl wanted to be one. And although they didn't all look like Julie Christie in *Darling,* that was the template at which to aim, the new, proud, self-aware and self-possessed woman of the Sixties.

It's often said that behind every successful man is a better woman. In the Sixties it was sometimes a case of in front of every beautiful woman was a guy with a camera. And thinking of the model and the photographer as a pair it brings to mind the line in the song 'Love and Marriage…go together like a horse and carriage'. Which was the horse though and which the carriage when it came to model and photographer? Who was pulling whom? Would David Bailey have had such an early and meteoric career if he hadn't met the beautiful Jean Shrimpton? He was a Cockney guy with all the chat. She was Home Counties, a bit further up market, who liked horse riding. Together they became a formidable pair. But, in the very nature of things, photographers were always going to have longer careers than their models. Beauty inevitably fades. Cameras just keep getting better and better.

I always thought Jean Shrimpton was the most beautiful woman I'd ever seen. Actually, she was better than that. She was nice, too. I met her a couple of years after she and Bailey had broken up. She was 26, living mainly in New York, but renting a little house near Harrods. When I interviewed someone, the *Evening Standard's* picture desk would usually send Roy Jones, who photographed for the arts pages, or a young Irishman called John Minihan. Unknown to me, on this day, neither was available, so they sent the only person who was. He'd got there first, taken his picture and left before I arrived.

Jean Shrimpton was both bemused and amused when she opened the door to me, and asked me if I knew the photographer. I didn't. So, she described him for me. He was elderly and wore a pork pie hat, she said. And, apparently, he'd seemed to have no idea who she was or that she was one of the most expensive models in the world. But he'd been very nice, quick and efficient and had said: 'Show us a bit of leg, girl.'

'What did you do?' I asked.

'I showed him a bit of leg and pulled up my skirt a little.'

He'd then snapped a couple of times, and left, happy with his picture. At a time in her career when photographers would have given anything to photograph Jean Shrimpton, she simply thought it was funny.

I learned later that the main job of that photographer, who was near to retirement, was to cover the greyhound racing. He never did portraits of famous people. But he had on this day. And his picture was so good he was given a big by-line in the paper, very probably the biggest in his career, while his photograph of Shrimpton has been used hundreds of times since. It was a lovely picture.

Part of my job was reviewing the stars' appearances on stage. And, as the West End's supper venues, The Talk of the Town and the Savoy, were the only place in London where singers played for more than one night, I would be a regular at one or the other about once a month for some 'grown up' entertainment. It absolutely wasn't my thing, but then it wasn't really the thing for some of the artists either, who were simply doing their best to copy the sounds on their records.

Judy Garland's appearance at the Talk of the Town at the end of December in 1968, was special, as she summoned memories of past youth and glories. At the time, I wrote: 'She is still Dorothy on the way to Oz; still the little girl from Kansas finding her way to "Somewhere Over The Rainbow". A compound of pathos, self-mockery, guts and comedy, she bawls, she totters, she does a mocking little tap dance…as she sings "The Man That Got Away", "Rock-a-Bye-My-Baby" and "You Made Me Love You".' After a career of drink, drugs, divorces and financial problems, it was like watching someone on the edge of a precipice, fearful that, at any moment she would lose her balance and tumble into the orchestra pit.

The custom at The Talk of the Town then was for critics to go around to the star's dressing room after the show, something I hated doing. (In the theatre, too.) But, on this occasion, I was glad I was able to thank this little bird of a woman. She looked genuinely grateful. Eighteen months later, she was found dead in her hotel room by her newest and fifth husband. She was 47. Fifty years later, Renee Zellweger's performance as her in the film *Judy* would justifiably win an Academy Award for the actress. Although, I didn't care much for the film.

I covered dozens of cabaret acts: Matt Monro, the great Roy Orbison, who wasn't quite so great in that setting, Tom Jones, the beautiful Sandie Shaw, Cliff Richard, Dusty Springfield, and Frank Sinatra, who, though past his best, was still the best. And then there was Sammy Davis Jr. who, without explanation, was introduced by Richard Burton wearing what looked like a mini-dress over his trousers and who said: 'I'm wearing Elizabeth's frock because she can't get into it anymore'. After which Sammy Davis gave a two-and-a-half-hour performance as the cameras filmed him, presumably for a TV show. On and on he went. He wasn't just a singer, or an impressionist or a comedian. He was everything and more. I never liked all that Ratpack stuff that he did with Frank Sinatra and Dean Martin. To me they just looked like a gang of middle-aged drunks showing off. But, without his drinking pals, he was brilliant.

For me, the rock concerts at the Albert Hall were much better. The setting alone gave the artists who appeared there an element of gravitas. It could be a bit hippy, and the drums and guitar solos of Cream went on a bit, but Crosby, Stills, Nash and Young were special. So was Janis Joplin. I'd met her the previous day. I think she'd probably been drinking on the plane from Los Angeles, and she was coming on, pretending to grope me in the lobby of the Dorchester Hotel where she was staying. Perhaps she was showing off for a girlfriend who was with her, trying to live up to the wild girl image that had preceded her. It was embarrassing. She was talented. She didn't need to do that.

She probably didn't need to sing at the very top of her register either, so loud it sounded as though she was hitting several notes at the same time, I thought, when I saw her on stage the following night. 'Piece Of My Heart' was classic intensity, but that technique didn't suit every song. When she wasn't trying to sound like an electric saw, she had a sweet natural voice. She had a sad life, a plain, acned scarred young woman in a spotlight that demanded a beauty she didn't possess. At high school she'd been mocked by boys for her looks. As a star nobody ever described her as a dolly girl. She died a couple of years later in 1970 from a heroin overdose. She was 27.

After every show, it was my habit to drive to the empty *Evening Standard* office and sit alone in the midnight gloom as I typed out my reviews. I could easily have gone home, written them there and phoned my copy through the following morning for that day's paper. But my stammer still made me avoid having to read out my own copy, whenever possible. Very gradually, however, I was beginning to devise ways of coping with my speech, becoming increasingly deft at avoidance techniques when I got stuck, which usually meant substituting a word I couldn't say for one that I could. I even began to make the odd appearance on BBC World Service programmes, where I was pretty sure that no one I knew would ever hear me. It was a little peak for me. Until I did it, radio had seemed to be an impossible mountain for me to climb.

When I'd gone for my interview at the *Evening Standard* in 1967, I'd bumped into a couple of young blokes who'd written a song for the paper's 'Girl Of The Year' competition. I'd never met songwriters before, and we chatted as we waited to be called in to see the editor. We met again on the way out. They'd sold their song, and I'd got a job.

They were, I discovered later, Tim Rice and Andrew Lloyd Webber, and one night, eighteen months later, I went to St Paul's Cathedral to review the first public performance of what would become *Joseph And The Amazing Technicolor Dreamcoat*. Using a schoolboy choir to sing the chorus, was for me a new way of doing a musical, and I loved it. I liked it even more when they used my St Paul's review as an advertisement for the album on the London Underground.

For news people, some years simply astonish from beginning to end. 1969 was such a year. A man walked on the moon for the first time, Concorde made its maiden flight, the Kray twins went to jail for murder for the rest of their lives, acolytes of the Charles Manson 'Family' murdered the pregnant actress Sharon Tate and her neighbour, half a million rock fans laid waste a place called Woodstock in New York state and *Monty Python's Flying Circus* made its debut on television. It was also the year when the Beatles made their last public appearance… well, semi-public.

Once again it was the *Evening Standard's* readers who were first with the news, phoning in to tell us that something extraordinary was happening in the West End. As all the world now knows, it was the Beatles performing on the roof of their Apple headquarters. Fearing that the police would stop them, they hadn't told anyone, and, on hearing the amplified music, shoppers and office workers quickly began gathering in the surrounding streets, gazing in bewilderment up into the air.

The performance was, we would discover, intended as the final part of a TV documentary that the Beatles were making, which showed them writing and recording a new album, *Let It Be*. It's probably better known now as *Get Back*, following the restoration of over fifty hours of film half a century later by *Lord of the Rings* director, Peter Jackson. But, most importantly, although we didn't know that at the time, it has become known as the first part of the Beatles' long goodbye.

A few weeks later, Paul McCartney married his American girl friend Linda Eastman at Marylebone Town Hall. To be followed almost immediately when John Lennon married Yoko Ono in 'Gibraltar near Spain', as he sang in 'The Ballad of John and Yoko'. Getting those stories first were two big scoops for me, although, like everyone, I didn't yet realise that, as comedian Max Bygraves used to sing, 'Those wedding bells are breaking up that old gang of mine'. Perhaps I should have paid more attention when an Apple employee, when asked the reason for the rows that were developing between the Beatles, had simply replied, 'Cherchez la femme'. But as, by then, the Beatles had become such a central part of the British cultural establishment, the notion that one day soon they might not exist was about as unlikely as the entire Royal Family abdicating. It was unthinkable. So, we didn't think it. Not even when John and Yoko had their honeymoon in bed for a week in an Amsterdam hotel as a peace protest, did we foresee the coming repercussions. That was just John, off on another craze, I thought. It'll be something else next week.

Whether John and Yoko were stoned when they were in bed that week, I've no idea. I didn't go and see them. But it seems likely. It was a druggy time. So, when I discovered that Ken Kesey, who was known in America as the Pied Piper of the psychedelic era, and the author of the novel *One Flew Over The Cuckoo's Nest*, was living in London, I went to spend an afternoon with this exhibitionist who wore a cowboy hat and drove an old Cadillac.

Brought up on a farm in Oregon, he was then in his mid-thirties, and, as he opened his front door wearing just his trousers, he looked as big as a bear, his chest coated with blond curls, his hair almost gone on the top of his head but as thick as a rug around his ears. Welcoming me inside, he put on a T-shirt and hung a Native American token around his neck. 'I shot this elk with a bow and arrow myself,' he boasted. 'And then I had Mountain Girl make it up into a leather jacket for me.'

Then, as I wondered who Mountain Girl might be, he smiled, and I saw Stars and Stripes painted in enamel on a false tooth, an upper right incisor that said a pepper-minted 'God Bless America' in red, white and blue.

'I was running from the FBI on a marijuana possession charge,' he explained, 'when I crashed into my lawyer and wrecked my car. Somehow, I caught my head, so that my tooth was hanging out by the nerves. But I had to keep hiding. So, I waited in a laundromat for a while. It's funny how you can just sit in a laundromat and no one ever thinks of looking for you there. The pain, however, was terrible. So, I finally made it over to a dentist I know.

'But he also happened to be an acidhead. And, while he was fixing me, he said, "Hey, d'you want a tooth with the Stars and Stripes on it?" And I said, "Yeah, that'd be nice". So here it is. You never think these things can really happen.' And he unplugged his plate to show me.

He'd come to London to make some spoken word recordings, but the financing had fallen through, so he was at something of a loose end. With him was his wife Faye, a childhood sweetheart.

For some reason, after college, he'd sold his body for seventy-five dollars to a clinic for their experiments into lysergic acid diethylamide, LSD. And under the surveillance of the clinic staff, he'd become, as he said, 'the world's first acid-head guinea pig'. After which he joined a hipster community, wrote *One Flew Over The Cuckoo's Nest* and became a hippy celebrity, believing that he had invented the word 'trip', which he used to describe the sensation he got when he took the drug.

Soon, he told me, he'd been turning-on everyone in his community, and when the bulldozers had arrived to remove them, they'd clubbed together to buy a 1939 International Harvester yellow school bus, wired it for the thousands of watts needed to play rock music and aerosolled it in Day-Glo mandalas. Then, calling themselves the Merry Pranksters, they'd taken themselves off on a cross-continent acid trek of the United States. Journalist Tom Wolfe had written a book about them, and with it brought Kesey national fame. The Beatles' *Magical Mystery Tour* had been a more sedate and old-fashioned imitation.

What about now, I wanted to know?

He shook his head. 'I haven't taken acid in quite some time. We're into other things. There's not a great deal of energy in dope.'

And he laughed. He laughed a lot. I could see why he called his gang the 'merry pranksters'.

Then off we went in his old Cadillac, around the edges of Hampstead Heath, down the lanes and under the blossom. Since he'd come to Britain he'd become quite an anglophile, England being the 'holiest' place he's ever visited, and Stonehenge the 'heaviest'.

'We're going down there for the summer solstice, to see the sun come up between those great pillars that are as big as two Buicks. And then we'll get my bus over here and go off to the cathedral at Chartres and then the Wailing Wall and the Great Pyramids. I haven't seen those places, but I figure that any place that took so much in human endeavour to build must be a very heavy place to be.'

Whether he ever got to any of those places, I doubt. Certainly not in a 1939 psychedelic school bus. What I do know is that he fell out with Hollywood when Milos Forman filmed *One Flew Over The Cuckoo's Nest* with Jack Nicolson in the role of the provocateur, and based, we assume, Kesey himself. Not liking the script, Kesey sued the film's makers, claiming never to have seen the film. Well, maybe. As a highly literate counter-culture bohemian, he told a lot of good stories, always being endlessly provocative, before he eventually retired back to running the family farm in Oregon, having a seat on a school board and coaching children wrestling. None of his later novels was successful and he died in 2001. That said, Jack Nicolson's performance, in the movie version of Kesey's famous novel, has taken on a celluloid life of its own.

There was a sort of *Planet of the Apes* parallel in London's Hyde Park on July 5 that year. The film was a big hit in 1969 and had one of the best 'reveals' in the history of cinema when Charlton Heston, playing an astronaut, discovers the Statue of Liberty sticking out of the sand on an 'unknown planet'. During their space voyage the astronauts had, it seemed, raced forward in time and the unknown planet they'd landed on was Earth in a nuclear wrecked future.

It seemed to me that day, that London had raced forward in time, too, and that, if an astronaut had taken off from Hyde Park in 1962 and landed again that afternoon in 1969, the scene before him would have been equally unrecognisable.

In 1962, when the Rolling Stones had played a mile away in the Marquee Club in Soho, they'd been lucky to draw a hundred fans to hear their music, which came through tinny, little speakers. Seven years later the biggest multitude ever seen at a rock concert in Britain, of 400,000 denim clad fans, was sitting waiting for them on the Hyde Park grass, their hair, boys and girls, generally a good foot longer than that of those in that little crowd in 1962. While, on the stage, a battery of amplifiers and huge high-powered speakers waited, too. None of that technology would have existed when the Stones had been at the Marquee.

That the fans were *sitting* on the grass seemed remarkable. Seven years earlier they would have preferred to stand rather than besmirch their clothes with the soot that coated everything from the millions of coal fires that were still then burning across the city. The

Clean Air Act of 1956 was taking a while to become effective, and in 1962 there had been another terrible smog. By1969, however, the grass looked and felt like new.

For the Rolling Stones to hold this free concert at all was a coup, so uncertain were the times for them. Two days earlier, guitarist Brian Jones had been found dead in his swimming pool, probably a casualty of drugs, alcohol and asthma, after having been sacked by the band a month earlier. Would the concert even take place, fans wondered, as the hot afternoon wore on under the careless eyes of fifty or so local Hells Angels hired to police them?

Then, suddenly, there was Mick Jagger on stage, wearing what looked like a little white dress over his jeans, sharply ordering 'Quiet', and then reading 'a poem for Brian by Percy Bysshe Shelley'. It had been chosen for the occasion by the singer's ex-girlfriend, Marianne Faithfull, while his new girlfriend, Marsha Hunt, dazzling in a white suit, her Afro hair a halo around her head, watched from high on a scaffolding at the side of the stage. There was a lot to look at that day.

But, while Mick sang 'Sympathy For The Devil' and the Stones' replacement guitarist, Mick Taylor, probably wondered what the fans were making of him, a sad little minor drama was also taking place. It happened at most Stones' gigs and concerned the band's former member, Ian Stewart. Stewart was better known as Stu, and on this, the biggest day the Stones had ever had, he slipped quietly, and unannounced, on and off stage, to play keyboards now and again, or perhaps to adjust an amplifier.

He looked like an interloper or a roadie, but in fact he was both a servant and a fellow musician. More important than that, he was a rarely acknowledged sixth Rolling Stone.

Stu, a quiet chap with thick, dark hair who wore an old polo shirt, baggy kahki trousers and Hush Puppies, was a victim of fame. He'd been with the Stones from the beginning, and he was, according to Keith Richards, the man more responsible than anyone for forming the band.

'He basically hand-picked all of us,' said Richards in his autobiography, remembering his own audition and how Stu had later been insistent that the Stones should have Charlie Watts on drums. Stu had been the man who used his phone at ICI, where he worked as a shipping clerk, to get the group some of their first bookings.

And he was the man who, through a friend, arranged their first recording session.

But he was also the man who had suddenly found himself demoted by their first manager, Andrew Loog Oldham. Overnight Stu went from life as a Rolling Stone, with a golden future beckoning, to a job as their van driver. Having seen the Stones play an early gig in Richmond, Surrey, in 1963, the eighteen-year-old, self-opinionated Oldham laid the law down. 'I can only see five Rolling Stones,' he is said to have told Mick Jagger and Brian Jones. 'Not six.'

Stu, the pianist with his Desperate Dan jaw, and tough square build, was too ugly to be a pop star, he insisted. He was four years older than Mick Jagger and he spoiled the look of the band, which, in those days, was thin and androgynous. Stu could play his Chicago blues style on the records and do radio with them, Oldham said, but he couldn't appear on TV or in any photographs.

It wasn't Oldham's place to sack Stu. That was the decision the Stones themselves had to take. They didn't like doing it, but no-one confronted Oldham.

And why? Because they were young. None of them imagined the lifelong ramifications of their actions. They suddenly saw a slight chink of a possibility and they went for it. But for Stu it meant being permanently cast into the shadows of rock and roll.

Would it have been different if he'd combed his hair another way, he must have wondered. Having suffered unhappy teenage years, during which an abnormal growth of his chinbone led eventually to corrective surgery, after which his teeth had been wired up for months as the bone reset, he couldn't not be conscious of his looks.

When the Stones rejected him, he could have walked away from them, bitter that the band he'd helped mould had deserted him. But he didn't. Stoically, he accepted the situation.

Working quietly in the background, he stayed loyal and proud of the Rolling Stones, at first driving them around the country in his pink Volkswagen van, later helping establish them on the world stage.

'He always chose which songs he wanted to play on,' Richards remembered. And although his photograph was not on the front of the albums, it was Stu who played his favourite boogie-woogie piano on 'Satisfaction', 'Honky Tonk Women', 'Brown

Sugar' and dozens more. If he didn't like a song, he would just walk away from the piano, saying, 'I'm not playing this. It's got Chinese chords'.

The most enigmatic of men, he was more influential than he appeared. When Brian Jones became a liability, he had a large say in who replaced him. And, although he was an employee, while the other original Rolling Stones were partners, and unknown, while the others were stars, he could be the calm at the centre of the storm, keeping confidences, with more than a share in the decisions and the music. Unpretentious, he hated it when Truman Capote, Princess Lee Radziwill and other New York socialites lionised the group, loathed the Stones' psychedelic period, and was the only one of them who never took drugs.

But when Keith Richards was busted for heroin in Toronto, it was Stu who stayed with him when the guitarist was not allowed to leave the city, and Stu who coaxed him into a recording studio there.

Some of the Stones' girl friends were always puzzled by his position in the band. 'I just couldn't understand why he wasn't one of the Rolling Stones,' Jerry Hall would say. 'I felt sorry for him that he didn't get everything on a silver platter like his mates. But he didn't resent it, which was even more admirable.'

Then, one day in 1985, Stu died of a heart attack while at a doctor's surgery in London's Harley Street. He was 47. Keith Richards had been waiting for him in a hotel, wondering why he was late, when a phone call came from Charlie Watts. 'That guy,' Richards would say, 'had the biggest heart that I've ever known…a guy that puts a band together and then gets kicked out of it, and then says, "I'll drive the van…"

'I don't think it was ever obvious, but he was the daddy of us all. He made the band.' A few years after his death Stu was inducted posthumously into the Rock and Roll Hall of Fame in America, as 'Ian Stewart: The Rolling Stone'.

So, if you were at that concert in Hyde Park in 1969, or indeed at almost any other Stones' concert until 1985, and wondered who the guy was, who, almost unnoticed, came on stage and played keyboards with them, now you know. He wasn't just a roadie.

When Charlie Watts died in 2021, I was reminded of an afternoon we spent together at an antiques sale in Lewes, Sussex, a couple of weeks after the Hyde Park concert. A very private person, it was the first time he'd agreed to be interviewed in years and would be the last for the next couple of decades when he didn't like the headline on my article. It was: 'Wealth is a pound of peaches'. The full quote being: 'What I like about money is that if I want to buy some peaches, I don't have to buy half a pound, I can have the pound. And that's nice, isn't it?'

'I know I said it,' he told me years later. 'But I didn't like it as a headline.' Which, I suppose, tells us quite a bit about the shy, slightly lugubrious, expressionless Charlie, the collector of antiques and first edition books, who, on the side, had a little band of his own playing jazz, with Stu on piano. Only after his death did he get the credit he deserved as the bedrock of the Rolling Stones. He never liked touring, and, former art student that he was, he drew his bed in every hotel room he ever slept in. Nor did he take drugs, that is, until, late in his career, when he tried heroin and was instantly hooked. It took Keith Richards, who knew a bit about heroin, to get him unhooked. 'Keith did me a favour there,' he told me.

A thoroughly likeable man, he would tell me he found Mick Jagger endlessly interesting. 'I like to go to bed after a gig, but sometimes Mick will drag me out, and wherever we are in the world he will know of somewhere interesting. That's Mick'. That was also the Mick whom he once clouted for having introduced him to someone as 'my' drummer. 'I'm not your fucking drummer!!' Charlie roared. Quiet though Charlie might have been, he knew his value to the Rolling Stones.

One of the many most wonderful things about having children is that early memories of their childhoods ghost with their parents for the rest of their parents' lives. The first beach holiday that Plum and I had, since we'd been married, was when Louise was about eighteen months old, and we took her to Portugal. Plum had bought me a camera as a wedding present, and, as film was expensive then, every shot had to be carefully framed and focused. In those days before camera phones and selfies, Zoom and video, those pictures froze forever the little moments of our lives, some in colour, but mainly in shades of grey.

The Algarve was empty then. Salazar was still president, donkeys carried the farmers' produce to market every day, and

Portimao hadn't yet succumbed to the tourism which would shortly arrive to enrich and disfigure it. But nothing can disfigure my photographs of Plum and Louise on that shining, rippled beach after the Atlantic tide had gone out. Louise was in her little blue sundress and pink hat, and Plum in her bathing suit, all of 24, and already the centre of our little family. I must have taken tens of thousands of photographs of her and the children and then our grandchildren since then, many stored these last twenty years on various computers, discs and USBs. But nothing can match the anticipation of collecting those first snaps from Boots after they'd been developed, then opening the envelope and reliving the holiday.

We still have them, some stuck by Plum in albums to which she added the date, the place and Louise's age. They now look like curious artefacts from history, from a time when people wore funny clothes, and had strange haircuts.

We decided to move house a couple of months after that holiday. All my work was in the centre of London and that was where I wanted to be. Looking through the *Sunday Times* one morning, we saw an advertisement for a four-storey house in Kensington. It was out of our price range, and the lease was only for 29 years. But Plum had some money left by her mother, I was doing well in my job, and 29 years seemed as near as damn it to eternity for a couple in their twenties. So, we put in an offer.

12.

**_'I wouldn't be being honest with you if I
said I wasn't ashamed of some of
the movies I've made' - Elvis Presley_**

Someone who never knew his worth, not his cultural value, anyway, was Elvis Presley, whom I finally met in the summer of 1969. It was my first visit to Las Vegas and I really didn't like the place. It was worse than godforsaken; a place of pushers and plastic hotel palaces, there were pimps, charlatans, weekend hookers flying in from Los Angeles for some quick bucks, mirrors over the beds (to get a different view, I imagine) and legions of shining, one-armed-bandits. Outside was suffocating dry desert heat and dazzling sunlight, while inside was air-conditioned chills and permanent night. It seemed to me to be a quicksand of everything that was cheap and phony about Americana. But to get to Elvis, that was the place to go.

After thirty mainly forgettable films since he'd left the Army in 1960, some of which had been truly terrible, there was nowhere left for Elvis to earn the kind of money that he and his manager, the phony 'Colonel' Tom Parker, needed. The Colonel (a Dutch illegal alien whose real name was Andreas Cornelis Kuijk) lived to gamble, while Elvis seemed to live to provide for his own wild extravagance and the retinue of old friends and hangers-on who went everywhere with him. The previous winter he'd appeared in a very successful television special, and, after an eight years' absence from live appearances, the stage pointed the way forward. Vegas paid the most for stars to draw the suckers to the gambling tables, so Elvis was the guy to get. Twice a night for four weeks, he was the carrot. The fans were the donkeys.

His image met me at Las Vegas airport in the shape of an Elvis plastic cut-out reading, 'Live at the International Hotel'. His voice was in the taxi, too, by way of a radio commercial, there was a giant reminder of him on the front of the International Hotel, and all kinds of other little reminders in my suite, in the bars and in the restaurants.

My entrée to the Elvis world had been arranged by a friend called Chris Hutchins who was a publicist for Tom Jones. So, Chris was there, too, along with photographer Terry O'Neill and another English journalist, Don Short, from the *Daily Mirror*. I joined them at their table for the show.

I don't know how nervous Elvis, then aged 34, was as he walked out from the wings that night in what looked like a black karate suit, his face and body thinner than we'd seen it in years, those famous sideboards dyed into black slashes down the sides of his face. But I certainly was. This, I remember thinking, is the man who gave us 'Heartbreak Hotel' and changed everything. I hope he doesn't let us down. Let *me* down.

He didn't. As Phil Spector said at the time: 'There's no substitute for talent.' But, all the same, the setting just didn't seem right. Guests had just finished dinner and waiters were still scurrying their plates away when Elvis came on stage. And the main showroom at the hotel was just like the Talk of the Town in London, only on a grander scale.

It wasn't only that. I'd expected Elvis to be accompanied by a rock and roll band of guitars and drums, with a pianist at the back and maybe the Jordanaires singing back-up vocals. Three new guys were doing that, along with a girl soul group, the Sweet Inspirations. That was fine. But sitting behind them all was an orchestra, which ended many of the songs with an old-fashioned closing vamp, horns blowing out over the guitars. They didn't do a lot, but to me it was a sacrilege to end 'Blue Suede Shoes' with a few notes by a brass band. I wanted to hear the hits exactly as Elvis had recorded them, as I'd first heard them when I was fifteen. And soon I began to realise that, good as he was, Elvis wasn't an Elvis fan in the way that I had been. He didn't know how perfect those early records had been, so perfect that they had changed the universe that was popular music.

For the slower songs, 'Can't Help Falling In Love With You' and 'Love Me Tender', he kept faithful to my memories, apart from the added strings, while his new song, 'Suspicious Minds', was a seven minute show-stopper. But virtually everything that was upbeat was too hurried, and intercut with silly karate chops, as he raced through a truncated 'Don't Be Cruel' into 'All Shook Up'. It was as though he couldn't wait to get rid of those boyish toys he'd played with when he was twenty-one. Over the next eight years he must have sung those songs hundreds of times, but I doubt there was ever one occasion when he sang them as well as he'd done on the original recordings. The trouble was that he didn't respect his own music.

He was good, of course. He hadn't become Elvis Presley by not being good at what he did, all of which I admired in the review that I wrote that night in my hotel bedroom and phoned over to the *Evening Standard* in London. But what I couldn't quite admit to myself, or to the *Evening Standard* readers, was that, thrilled as I was to have finally seen him, his show had also felt like a small betrayal.

At the time, I didn't want to blame him. The vast canteen that was the auditorium dining room was stuffed at every table with uncritical fans, women dressed to flirt or to pull, in love more with the way he looked than the music he made. Certainly, they didn't seem the kind of people who'd spent their schooldays studying the matrix numbers and dates of his early Sun recording sessions. I was, I realised, probably the only Elvis anorak there.

No, I didn't want to blame him, but it was his fault. A good musical director would have insisted he treated his old records with more respect. His little band was terrific, and the backing girl singers, including Whitney Houston's aunt, Cissy Houston, added a touch of gospel. But that orchestra? Elvis must have wanted it there on stage with him. It was all down to him. He gave Las Vegas what he thought Las Vegas wanted.

It wasn't just the opportunity of seeing Elvis on stage that had drawn me to Vegas, it was the promise of an interview, too. So, for the next three days our little English group hung around the hotel waiting for a call from the phony 'Colonel' Parker, and me going back repeatedly to see the show. Then suddenly, between performances, we got the summons: 'Elvis will see you now.' There was no time to go back to my room for my tape recorder, or for Terry O'Neill to fetch his camera.

When we got up to his back-stage suite. Elvis was sitting drinking from a bottle of 7-Up, surrounded by four or five of his gang, the Memphis Mafia, in a small sitting room. Wearing his stage suit, he had diamond clustered rings on his fingers, while a silver bracelet bearing his name dangled from his wrist. It struck me as funny that one of the most famous people on earth needed a bracelet to remind him of who he was.

Quickly polite, possibly nervous, he leapt from his Spanish sofa to greet us. His retinue got to their feet more lethargically. The Colonel stood behind us all watching and listening carefully, like a genial, if suspicious, warder overseeing a prison visit. To be honest, what I got that night was more an audience than an interview.

At first the general conversation was jokey and congratulatory as Elvis showed us the good luck telegram that he'd received from the Beatles. It had, actually, been sent by their road manager, Mal Evans, whom I'd tipped off about the opening, and, pathetically, I asked Elvis if he had any favourite Beatles songs. His hands went up to play an imaginary guitar. 'I like that one "she was just seventeen, you know what I mean,"' he said, beginning to sing.

Well, at least it broke the ice, and being the only Elvis expert there, I sat alongside him and ventured to enquire why he'd made all those terrible films, although I hope I put it more diplomatically at the time. For just a second, Elvis glanced up at the Colonel before answering. 'Well, I wouldn't be being honest with you if I said I wasn't ashamed of some of the movies I've made and some of the songs I've had to sing in them,' he began, surprised, I think, by the question. Did he realise that I was a journalist, I wondered, because prior to this he'd never done newspaper interviews? But he was still talking.

'I'd like to say that they were good, but I can't. I've been extremely unhappy with that side of my career for some time. But how can you find twelve good songs for every film when you're making three movies a year? I knew a lot of them were bad songs and they used to bother the heck out of me. But I had to do them. They fitted the situation. How can you enjoy it when you have to sing songs to the guy you've just punched up?'

That brought an overloud laugh for the Memphis Mafia chorus. They were good at laughing at his jokes. That was partly what they were paid to do. What his joke didn't do was explain why he'd been so weak that he'd accepted a situation in which he appeared in rotten films and sang mediocre songs.

'I was in a rut,' he tried to explain, 'I signed a lot of contracts when I was in the Army. But we've now completed all the deals I made then. From now on I'm going to play more serious parts and make fewer films.'

But why Las Vegas?

'Well, we didn't decide to come here for the money, I can tell you that,' he laughed, although he clearly had. 'I've been wanting to perform on stage again for the last nine years. It's been building up inside of me until the strain became intolerable. I got all het up about it, and I don't think I could have left it much longer. The time is just right. The money… I have no idea about all that. I just don't want to know. You can stuff it.'

At this point, Parker intervened, probably suspecting that his client was blaming him. 'The Colonel has nothing to do with Mr Presley's finances. That's all done by his father, Mr Vernon Presley, and his accountant. He can flush all his money away if he wants to. I won't care.'

I remember at the time being surprised by the sharpness of Parker's tone. It made the meeting slightly uncomfortable, but I thought little of it. What I didn't know then was that Elvis and the Colonel were locked together in a desperate need for money, Elvis to spend on his legion of hangers-on, and the Colonel to fund a gambling habit.

Elvis, meanwhile, began talking about his plans. He wanted to make a new rhythm and blues album, and would not make another film, or record another song, that he didn't believe in. And when his Las Vegas season ended, he was also thinking of doing a world tour. 'I know I've been saying for years that I will visit Britain. And I will, I promise. But, at the moment, there are personal reasons why I can't go.'

At that moment, Parker abruptly ended our conversation, although I suspect Elvis would happily have gone on chatting. As an interview it hadn't been what I'd hoped for, but it was Elvis and he'd been, for him, extraordinarily open.

The following morning the Colonel joined me for breakfast in the hotel coffee shop. 'I won't pick up your breakfast tab because I don't want you being beholden to me,' he said, and then explained why an overseas Elvis tour wasn't likely any time soon. Mrs Parker was, apparently, not well enough to travel and he couldn't leave her to go abroad with Elvis.

He was lying to me, I would discover later. As an illegal immigrant he was afraid to leave the US in case he wasn't allowed back in. And he certainly wouldn't have let Elvis go alone. He was too controlling for that.

I left Las Vegas the next day and flew to New York. Bob Dylan, who'd been recovering upstate in Woodstock after a motor-cycle accident a couple of years earlier, was soon to appear in Britain at the Isle of Wight pop festival, and, on a whim, I called his manager, Al Grossman. I'd been hoping to arrange an interview for when Dylan came to London, but to my surprise I was immediately invited down to Grossman's office, and even more surprised when he suggested that I interview 'Bobby' on the phone there and then.

Within a couple of minutes, the great recluse was on the line. Normally, my interviews were planned to some extent, but with this one sprung on me, I hardly had a question in my head. So, at first, I mentioned that I'd just been to see Elvis.

'Really! I read the review of the show in *The New York Times*. Was he good? Really good? Who was in the band? Were the Jordanaires with him? And Scotty Moore on guitar? What did he sing? Did he do "That's All Right, Mama", "Mystery Train" and the Sun Records stuff?' The questions poured out. Dylan was interviewing me.

His legend for being difficult and aloof with journalists was well known, but that day, perhaps because he was selling tickets for the Isle of Wight Festival, he could hardly have been more friendly, even chatting about his children.

Reminded of the barracking he'd received from British folk purists when he'd 'gone electric' in 1965, he explained: 'The reason I started off with just that acoustic sound was an economic one. Between about 1958 and 1963 it wasn't possible for a big rock band to make a living so they went out of fashion. But, when the Beatles came along, they opened it all up. It became economic, too.'

As for his permanent moody look?

'The reason I look so miserable in all the pictures is because when I ask the photographers how to look, they always say "Don't smile". So, I don't.'

And what about the people who say his lyrics are poetry?

'I'd sure like to be a poet. But, when I do songs, I usually fit the words around the music. It's the music that determines the words. I like to be considered a poet, but I think it's more flattering than truthful.' Nearly half a century later, in 2017, he would be awarded the Nobel Prize for Literature.

A couple of days later I was back in London and was on the phone to John Lennon when I told him, too, that I'd just seen Elvis.

'Elvis! *Yes?* Was he good?' The question was immediate. 'What did he sing? Was Scotty Moore with him? Were the Jordanaires there? Did he do his early songs? "That's All Right", "Don't Be Cruel", "Hound Dog"?' Almost word for word, Lennon asked the same questions that Dylan had wanted answering.

I came to realise something after those two conversations. No matter how famous and successful a star might become, he is always a fan of someone who went before him.

By the time Dylan reached the Isle of Wight at the end of August his bonhomie towards the Press had faded. 'I wanted to see Alfred Lord Tennyson's home,' was his reason for coming, he told reporters at a Press conference. His poker face was still there for his concert a few nights later, too, when, wearing a white suit with a lime green shirt, he came on stage at 11pm. With an air of detached cool towards the audience, rock aristocracy among them, he ran through a dozen of his biggest hits: 'Mr Tambourine Man', 'Like A Rolling Stone', 'Lay Lady Lay', etc. Then he left the stage, leaving the 150,000 fans to figure out how they were going to get off the Isle of Wight and back to the mainland, the ferries that had brought them having by then finished operating for the night.

Luckily, I knew someone, who knew someone, who knew Robert Stigwood who had provided a boat for Eric Clapton and friends. So, I hitched a ride back across the Solent to Portsmouth where I'd left my car.

I went to the Isle of Wight Pop Festival again the following year, but, although I regularly found myself charmed by the happy, easy-going multitudes on these occasions, I was always quite glad to get away. Germaine Greer seemed to get it about right when she described the festival to me as a 'psychedelic concentration camp'.

13.

'I just wanted to tell you that I've left the Beatles' - John Lennon

Sometimes in journalism misunderstandings screw things up, and sometimes accidents can be unintentionally prophetic. This happened to me in the autumn of 1969 when I wrote a piece about the rumours of disharmony among the Beatles. John Lennon had joked about 'being down to me last ten thousand', saying that someone needed to be brought into Apple soon to stop the profligacy, and Allen Klein, a tough little New Yorker, whom I found hard to like, had been employed to do just that. Consequently, there had been sackings and tears and rows, which I reported in my piece. What I didn't do was predict anything. So, I was surprised when the article appeared in the Evening Standard under the headline *'THE DAY THE BEATLES DIED'*. In newspapers the writer never writes the headline above his or her piece, and I hadn't written that the Beatles had ended. This was just plain wrong.

So, that afternoon I was half expecting a call from an Apple lawyer when instead a white rose in a cellophane box arrived at my desk with the message: 'To Ray with love from John and Yoko'. I hadn't been blessed with second sight, but, from that moment, I had my own source right at the heart of the Beatles. John Lennon himself. In the vernacular of the time, I now had my own Deep Throat.

A couple of weeks later John Lennon rang me at the *Evening Standard* to tell me he'd sent his MBE back to the Queen 'in protest at the war in Biafra and because "Cold Turkey" is slipping down the charts'. I told him that I wasn't sure it was a good idea to link the two, but John didn't care. 'No? Well, it's too late now. It's in the car and already on its way to the Palace'. Step by step John Lennon was now beginning to dismantle the Beatles' halo.

His solo anthem 'Give Peace A Chance' was at the time being sung by protestors all around the world and one Sunday night while I was on the phone to him, he said: 'We're going to Toronto to see Pierre Trudeau for our peace campaign. We'll be staying at

Ronnie Hawkins' house. Do you remember him? He used to waggle his arse when he sang. You can come if you want?'

I went. He paid. It was the first time I'd flown first class, and the first time I'd tasted mulligatawny soup, too. You didn't get that at the back of the bus.

Ronnie Hawkins was an old rock and roller from Arkansas whose biggest claim to fame was that the group he'd put together had become The Band, who now backed Bob Dylan. Ronnie was a big, likeable man who told tall, funny stories about holding parties 'that Nero would be ashamed to attend', and playing in a bar in Dallas that was owned by Jack Ruby, the man who shot the man who shot President Kennedy. 'I swear to God that one of the strippers there didn't have but one arm,' he would laugh.

He'd become involved with the Lennons through a middleman over a proposed peace festival. And he and his wife, Wanda, had been planning to celebrate Christmas at their smallholding outside Toronto when a call had come from the middleman: 'Yes. John and Yoko would be delighted to accept your hospitality during their stay in Canada,' he'd been told. And within a couple of hours a man from Capitol Records had appeared at his door with a huge, white, synthetic, gingham draped Christmas tree, together with a gilded cage, bearing two, white, live, but uncooing, doves.

The telephone company had come next and installed half a dozen new lines, then a macrobiotic cook had been hired together with his Zen recipe book, while a girl with good teeth was chauffeured out to the house to do the washing up.

Then there they were, John and Yoko; and, a day later, me. I'd hardly been in the house more than a few minutes before John beckoned me upstairs to the Hawkins' bedroom, which he and Yoko were using during their stay. Whenever John wanted to talk privately it was always in a bedroom.

'I just wanted to tell you,'he said, after I closed the bedroom door, 'that I've left the Beatles.' Alongside him, Yoko nodded, apparently pleased. He giggled.

I was stunned. John had just given me the biggest story of my entire journalistic career.

'We had a board meeting at Apple and Paul was talking about us going back on the road and playing little gigs,' he continued. 'He was going on and on. And I suddenly found myself saying, "I want a divorce like I got divorced from Cynthia".'

Yoko nodded again.

'Divorced' was the perfect choice of word for John to use to destroy the band, because to the outside world the Beatles did seem very much like a family. John was the mercurial father-figure, funny and savage in equal measure; Paul the hard-working, respectable mother who kept the family together; George could be seen as the truculent teenager (and he had much to be truculent about); while Ringo was the happy-go-lucky younger son who just went along with whatever the parents decided.

In the Hawkins' bedroom I was already envisaging world headlines, then John said. 'Don't tell anyone yet. I'll let you know when you can put it out. Allen Klein doesn't want me to make it public until after *Let It Be* comes out in Spring next year.'

So, having given me the story of a lifetime, he was now asking me to sit on it. I didn't know what to think. As a journalist my duty was to the newspaper that paid my wages. But…
as a fan, I suppose I was relieved to have time to think about it. I didn't want the Beatles to break up. Besides, how did I know that John wouldn't change his mind. So, apart from Plum, I didn't tell anyone.

I was also wondering if I'd become too close to my sources.

That was my introduction to Canada. An art publisher had sent 500 large erotic lithographs, recently drawn by John, and now the artist wanted the world to see them. Accordingly, the following day, a little human conveyor belt was assembled in the Hawkins' sitting room to feed the lithographs to the Beatle for signature. The images all involved a naked John and Yoko, several of which involved oral sex.

'Why do you draw so much cunnilingus?' I eventually asked.

'Because I like it,' John grinned merrily.

Whether the drawings were good or not, he had no idea. Nor did he care. 'They won't be taken seriously, anyway,' he said.

Yoko had no doubts. 'Better than Picasso,' she judged.

Nobody commented. John looked embarrassed, and, continuing to sign, changed the subject. 'You know, during Beatlemania, Mal and Neil (the Beatles' two road managers) used to sign our autographs for us. It was Neil who signed the photographs that were sent to Prince Charles.'

John was in his element that week. Away from the down-to-earth retorts of the other Beatles and the merrily cynical British Press, he was basking in a reverence that he didn't now get in his own country. On one day a New York art dealer, who had his eye on the marketing of the lithographs, was telling us that John should be nominated for the Nobel Peace Prize. To which Yoko nodded her determined agreement; while on the next day, a local Toronto rabbi was declaring John and Yoko to be the 'finest people I've ever met'. It was easy to see how that sort of fawning could go to a fellow's head.

John Lennon may have been on a peace campaign, but, in many ways, 1969 could be seen as the dying light of the Hippy Generation, when, on Christmas Eve, the Charles Manson Family was charged in Los Angeles with the murders of Sharon Tate and six other people. At one time Manson had been peripherally involved with the Beach Boys, and had called his movement 'Helter Skelter', after the Beatles' song. So, by association, the entire hippy movement now found its love and peace message soaked in blood and drugs. Nor was that all. In December a riot at a Rolling Stones performance at Altamont in Northern California had led to the stabbing to death by Hell's Angels of a fan.

'The violence in front of the stage was incredible,' Keith Richards told me later. 'We got the Hell's Angels at the suggestion of the Grateful Dead who'd organised these shows before. The majority did what they were supposed to do, like they did in Hyde Park. But about ten or twenty were completely out of their minds, trying to ride their motorcycles through the middle of the crowds. It was crazy.'

Like I say, the end of the hippy dream.

14.

'What a bummer it **must** be to have a life that is so public' - Joni Mitchell

On my shelves there must be over a thousand long playing records in their twelve inch square covers. Some look as pristine as the day I got them. But others reflect the battering of time and wear, after years of play. Joni Mitchell's first two albums fall into this group. On *Clouds,* from 1969, there was 'Chelsea Morning', as well as 'The Gallery', the sad story of a left-behind lover; while on *Ladies of the Canyon* from a year later came 'Big Yellow Taxi' and 'For Free'. The autobiographical message of 'For Free', is how a rich and feted singer (Joni herself) sings when she is paid to perform; but the music that moves her most comes from a guy on the street who is busking with his clarinet, and playing for the love of music. It's a short story in itself, a collision of two cultures.

So, when Joni Mitchell, the woman who had also written 'Both Sides Now', came to London, I was keen to meet her.

It didn't go well, her manager, Elliot Roberts, insisting upon sitting in on the interview and interrupting whenever I asked her anything that he considered 'personal'. Since everything Joni Mitchell had written was obviously highly personal, I didn't understand what was annoying him. I always enjoyed hearing accounts of childhood, and Joni, who was then, 26, was happy to tell me about her time with polio in an Alberta hospital when she was nine years old. Polio in the Fifties, and before the Salk vaccine, could be a crippling disease, and it took her six months to recover, during which she passed her time singing to a little boy of six across the hospital ward.

She was revealing, too, when she explained how the lyrics of 'Big Yellow Taxi' had been inspired when she had visited Hawaii. 'I arrived at the hotel at night and went straight to bed,' she said. 'When I woke up the next day I looked out of the window and it was beautiful. Everything was so green and there were white birds flying around. And then I looked down, and there was a great big parking lot. That's what Americans do. They take the most beautiful parts of the continent and build hotels and put posters up to ruin it completely.'

The Seventies was a time when care of the planet was just beginning to gather momentum, and 'Big Yellow Taxi', what Joni Mitchell called her 'ecology rock and roll', quickly became a classic for the ecology movement. What she didn't address that day was the final verse of the song about how a big yellow taxi takes away her boyfriend, presumably after a row, when she hears the 'screen door slam'.

'Don't it always seem to go that you don't know what you've got till it's gone', she choruses in regret at the end of song, as the lyrics go from the general to the personal. It was such a clever piece.

By this time in our interview, she had suggested that perhaps her manager leave us, but our conversation was still strained. I wanted to know more about looking 'at life from both sides now' and 'it's love's illusions that I recall, I really don't know love at all'. But we never got there.

On a question about the street entertainer in 'For Free' she merely said. 'The money you get as a singer is out of all proportion. They pay you to sing, but they don't pay the birds to sing in the trees. It really is ridiculous.' She'd put it better in her song: 'And I play if you have the money, or if you're a friend to me. But the one-man band by the quick lunch stand, he was playing real good for free'. I've never passed a street entertainer since and not thought of that song. That was how powerful it was.

'I don't like talking about my personal life,' Joni explained. 'I hardly ever do interviews. I don't care if I need them for my career. I remember going to a prom when I was about fourteen and while I was having my hair dried at the hairdressers' they gave me a movie magazine to read. It was all about the marriage of Sandra Dee and Bobby Darin breaking up. And I remember thinking, "What a bummer it must be to have a life that is so public, and to have so many people know so many things about you".'

Over 25 years later I began to understand the mystery of why her manager had thought I was asking too many 'personal' questions. Joni had had a baby in 1966, before she'd become famous, and had given the child up for adoption. Only in 1993 did the baby and adoption become public. Joni and her now grown-up daughter were reconciled in 1997, but it had been a sad secret at the beginning of her career. Had her manager thought I was an inquisitive British tabloid journalist who'd heard a rumour and was trying to wheedle a story out of her? Was he just trying to protect his client? I think that's likely. But he was wrong. I hadn't heard any rumour. I was just a fan of her songs.

There would be a hidden clue, that no one saw at the time, in Joni's album *Blue*, which came out the following year in 1971. 'Child with child pretending, weary of lies you're sending home,' she sang in her song 'Little Green'. 'So, you sign all the papers in the family name. You're sad and you're sorry, but you're not ashamed. Little green, have a happy ending.'

Joni Mitchell wasn't the only brilliant songwriter in the early Seventies, the Woodstock generation seeming to have opened the way for a more thoughtful, literate, educated time in lyric writing. Paul Simon led, of course, with the opening line of 'The Boxer', 'I am just a poor boy though my story's seldom told...' instantly capturing the attention. If there is any other popular song that uses the world 'seldom', I don't know it. Then, in the same song, comes his wry comment, 'a man hears what he wants to hear and disregards the rest'. Carly Simon's 'You're So Vain' took scorn and fascination to a new level with her song about her composite old boyfriend (a bit of Mick Jagger, some more of Warren Beatty and others) who 'walked into the party like you were walking on to a yacht', and who 'had one eye in the mirror as you watched yourself gavotte'. When did anyone ever 'gavotte' before, or after, in the Top Ten? It was the perfect word.

We remember the songs of the Thirties and Forties as some kind of peak of lyric writing. But the writers of the Seventies, inside a changed musical structure, told universal truths, too, with Janis Ian's 'At Seventeen' recounting how it feels to be a teenage girl and to be one of 'those of us with ravaged faces, lacking in the social graces'. The romantic, adolescent love she read about, and other people sang about, was indeed 'meant for beauty queens'. Then there was the Elton John and Bernie Taupin partnership that produced 'Your Song' ('I know it's not much, but it's the best I can do, my gift is my song, and this one's for you'), and David Gates' 'Everything I Own' with his group Bread, with lines originally written about the death of his father, but which more generally sound as though he is grieving a broken romance.

Newspapers have ferocious appetites so I was now filling as many pages as I could. It was good to talk to Tom Jones, Stevie Wonder and B.B. King, but I was now being encouraged by my editor to see my remit as covering more than musicians and singers. So, I began to branch out. Some of British society's traditional ways of doing things were, by 1970, just hanging on and I wanted to get to know about one of them before it was gone for ever, which in the case of the debutante season would be very soon. With this in mind, I went to interview a deb.

      The original point of the 'season', which ran every year from June until December, had been seen as an opportunity for the daughters of the gentry to be launched into society, where they would be presented to the monarch at court, and, in the ensuing bashes, to meet the children of other toffs. It kept all involved separate from the rest of us, and, aware that it had become an anachronism in the modern world, the Queen had abolished it in 1958. The grandest bit of it, the presenting at court, may have been gone, but the remnants were still hanging on when a very pretty 16 year old called Caroline Delevingne was, by virtue of the society columns, acclaimed 'Deb of the Year'.

      Over tea at her parents' house near Notting Hill Gate, she explained to me the etiquette and manoeuvrings of the deb ritual. 'At the beginning of the year you go to lots of parties and meet lots of other girls. And they all promise to put you on their list and invite you to their dances and cocktail parties. Your mother does all the arrangements and she writes to *Queen* and *Tatler,* and invites people to your party. No-one asks you to take part. I was in two minds whether to do it or not, but I think it was expected of me. When my mother did it, she was presented to the King. I think it's a shame they don't do that anymore.

      'Princess Anne is often at the parties, but Prince Charles isn't, although he's invited. I'd like to go out with him, although he's not obviously fanciable. I think I like the sound of his character. But you can't tell, can you...?'

      As she talked, I counted the invitations on the mantelpiece. There were parties in smart areas of south-west London and dances in Sussex and Gloucestershire. Being a deb clearly involved quite a bit of travelling. 'I'm up nearly all night, so I sleep nearly all day,' Caroline continued. 'And then I have to go out and buy clothes for the next night. It's very hard, and you never get the weekend off to relax because you have to go off to someone's party in the country.'

Her wish was that the boys at the parties, debs' delights, in the parlance of the time, were older. 'Men are so much better at 29 than they are at 20. And if you go to a dance and get paired off with someone, you get stuck with him for the night. Some of the boys have been doing it for three or four years. They just go for the girls and the free drink. Some of them are going to inherit vast amounts of money, but half of them go because they aren't very rich and haven't got any money.

'I just wish there was someone there like Mick Jagger. They aren't exactly chinless wonders: they're more like chinless wonders with hair. The trouble is that after you've spent an evening with someone, he's not likely to just let you go home and say "bye-bye" if you don't fancy him... I don't drink, but everyone else seems to get sloshed.'

The expense of doing the season, must, she believed, cost about £3000, which, my calculator says would be getting on for £50,000 in today's money. She had six long dresses, but she bought lots of clothes 'quite cheaply at the Antiques Market. I'm supposed to pay for all my clothes out of my allowance from my father, but I don't. The trouble is you can't appreciate all the dances because there are so many of them. It's incredible what people do. They have marquees and bands and discotheques. I don't know how it's possible for people to be so rich these days. I'm sure there must be a fiddle somewhere. But if anybody is rich, you can be sure you'll meet them during the season.'

Which, I suppose, was, the point of the whole thing. She was an open and friendly well-off young girl, who later did some modelling before marrying a couple of times and having four children. Her brother's three daughters also went into fashion. They are Chloe, Poppy and Clara Delevingne. Good looks ran in the family.

While Caroline Delevingne was doing the season that year, Germaine Greer was publishing her famous book, *The Femail*

Eunuch, the working title of which, or so she told me, was *The Clitoris Strikes Back*. Whether that was ever true I've no idea, but it was funny. Germaine was always funny. I interviewed her twice, once after a fictitious article she'd written about being a groupie when her conversation was so graphic that I didn't write it, knowing that the *Evening Standard* wouldn't have published it. And, a few months later, when she was anxiously awaiting the publication of the book that she already knew would cause an almighty stir.

We were sitting on the grass by the Serpentine in Hyde Park one Sunday morning when she explained the theme of her book to me. But, being Germaine, her conversation drifted through half a dozen different thoughts and moods as we talked, from 'the smell of death' having been strong in the air at the Isle of Wight Pop Festival, to a girl in the park who seemed to be wearing a pair of transparent trousers.

With a Ph.D. from Cambridge on 'The Ethic of Love and Marriage in Shakespeare's Early Comedies', she was a lecturer at Warwick University in the weeks during term time, while becoming a provocative, mischievous columnist at the weekends. On the brink of international fame, she was articulate, contrarian and a skilled and charming self-publicist. It was exactly the right time for her. She caught the tide of the moment, and feminism was the boat that carried her.

Pronouncements spurted from her that day: 'Female liberation wasn't even big when I began to write my book. They were thinking about it in the States, but it hadn't got here. And it seems to me the terms of their discourse are quite inappropriate...all these companies wanting to put women on their boards, like obligatory negroes.'

Then there was marriage, her own having lasted for just about three weeks. 'Marriage is so wrong. It's so immoral. I'm sure the sum of two people when joined together in marriage is less than the two individuals they were to start with.'

This was Germaine on merry ranting form, but I remember, too, that first unwritten interview when, probably in a mickey-taking exercise, she talked non-stop about sex, and I finally asked her, as a joke, if she ever thought of anything else. 'My dear Ray,' she said grandly, as though already savouring the coming put-down. 'Since I've been talking to you, I haven't thought of it once.'

The house that Plum and I had bought just off Kensington High Street was perfect for us. The previous owners had rented it out as separate bed sitters, and I doubt that it had been redecorated in decades. It was, therefore, a blank sheet that we could colour any way we wanted. There were no carpets or curtains, and the bathroom and kitchen were primitive, while the basement was a self-contained flat that we didn't incorporate into the rest of the house for several months. What the house did have, however, was sunshine from a west facing back garden and masses of space in big Victorian rooms. For the first time I had my own study to write in, and, armed with several large tins of Wedgwood blue paint in one hand and packets of Polyfilla in the other, I set about smartening things up, while Plum made the curtains. It would take us the best part of ten years to get the house the way we wanted it.

We hadn't been there very long when Plum went into hospital for the birth of our son, Dominic. One evening when I was going to visit her, I needed a babysitter for Louise, and was expecting Nora Wintour, the schoolgirl daughter of my *Evening Standard* editor, to come round for a couple of hours. Apparently, however, Nora had too much homework that night, so her elder sister, Anna, who was then 20 and working at the Way In boutique at Harrods, came instead. Not everyone can say that they once employed Anna Wintour as a babysitter, although I don't think she ever got paid.

When Plum brought Dominic home from the hospital, we needed help in the house at first, so we gave a home to a Yugoslav young woman whom Louise, who was just learning to talk, called Nadie, being unable to master the girl's unpronounceable Serbian name. Nadie was a terrific little worker who would entertain us with ballet and her yoga exercises in the evenings. She left us to go and work in a Wimpy Bar when Plum got stronger, only to turn up some months later asking if she could borrow a dress. She was getting married the following day and had nothing to wear, she said. We didn't even know that she was courting.

Looking through her wardrobe, Plum found a white dress for Nadie to wear for the occasion. Then, as her father was in Belgrade, Nadie asked if I would go to the registry office to give her away. I was flattered to be the stand-in father of the bride. Plum would have come, too, but she was feeding the new baby.

When I arrived for the ceremony at Fulham Town Hall the next day, and Nadie, pretty in her borrowed dress, introduced me to the groom, Antonio, a six-foot-tall Italian dishwasher, I realised that there were no other guests. We were also a witness short.

Without two witnesses the couple couldn't be married, so I nipped outside and stopped the first respectable looking chap I saw. He was in his fifties and had just popped out to do some shopping. He was thrilled to be included, and twenty minutes later the happy couple plighted their troth, and he and I signed as witnesses.

On the steps of the Town Hall I took some photographs, then, as I didn't have any confetti, I bought Nadie a bunch of flowers, and suggested we go to a pub to celebrate.

'Sorry Tee-total,' said the Instant Witness,' and hurried off home to tell his wife about his adventure.

In the pub Antonio, who I now realised spoke very little English, said he wanted a beer, so Nadie and I celebrated with a half-bottle of champagne and two bags of crisps. As Antonio tried to talk to me about football, Nadie talked to me about babies. They didn't talk much to each other. I don't think they could. In the end I drove them home to the bedsitter that Nadie now had in West Kensington. And there I left them to enjoy their honeymoon, before Nadie had to go back to work at the Wimpy Bar on Monday morning.

That was the last we saw of Nadie, until, one day, about three years later, I arrived home to find Nadie and a little boy having tea with Plum and our children.

'So, how are you getting on back in Yugoslavia?' I asked. 'Everything all right? How's Antonio?'

Nadie frowned. 'He fuck my sister.'

15.

'It simply became very difficult for me to write with Yoko sitting there' – Paul McCartney

To no-one's surprise, the opening of an exhibition of John Lennon's erotic lithographs at the London Art Gallery in Bond Street attracted massive publicity, before, on its second day, it was closed by order of the Metropolitan Police. Drawings of Yoko masturbating were considered by the Met to be obscene, although the charges against the gallery were later dropped. On sale at £41 each, anyone who bought one and hung on to it until today would have made an astonishing profit, sales per lithograph now going at anything between £3,000 and £10,000.

John and Yoko kept quiet as the public huffing and puffing over the lithographs came and went, mainly because they were in Denmark for much of the time. When they got back, John's first musical act of the year was to write and record 'Instant Karma'. I joined him, Yoko and producer Phil Spector in a Soho studio as they recorded the flip side, a song of Yoko's called 'Who Has Seen The Wind', with me, for a short time, playing the triangle.

A few weeks later when Yoko was pregnant and in a private hospital, with John sleeping at her bedside (she later lost the baby), I went to visit them. John offered me a job that day. I said I'd think about it, but purposely I didn't mention it again. Their life wasn't for me.

While we were talking, a man who called himself Michael X (full names Michael Abdul Malik or Michael de Freitas) turned up with a friend and carrying a large plastic bag of marijuana inside a suitcase. Even John was surprised by the quantity. I hadn't liked Michael X since, some weeks earlier, I'd watched him give John and Yoko a pair of blood-stained shorts, supposedly worn by Muhammad Ali in his fight with Joe Frazier. Well, maybe, I thought. In return, the couple had given him some of their hair which had been cut short while they were in Denmark. The exchange of gifts was supposed to be some kind of symbolic ceremony to mark the launching of Michael X's Black House, a community project in

North London. To be honest, I thought the guy was just another conman, who was hitting on John Lennon for money. But he proved to be far worse than that.

For the first three months of 1970, the other three Beatles stayed out of public notice. I asked John a couple of times if it was time yet for me to write about him leaving the Beatles; but it never was. Paul, meanwhile, was working on his first solo album, *McCartney*. Then on April 9, I was sent an embargoed preview of a questions and answers statement that Paul would be putting out to the Press the following day. It seemed to be mainly a document to promote his solo album, but, when asked if he had any plans to record with the Beatles, Paul replied that he hadn't, and didn't know whether the break would be temporary or permanent. My reading of the document was that he was still waiting for John, hoping his old friend might change his mind and cancel his 'divorce' from the Beatles.

I was woken at 7am the following morning with a call from the news desk at the *Evening Standard* saying that the front page of the *Daily Mirror* had broken the embargo and was splashing on 'Paul Quits Beatles'. It was a huge, worldwide story, and was filling all the papers, the TV and radio broadcasts. By obeying the strictures of the embargo, I'd missed it.

Or had I? I re-read the statement again. Nowhere did it say that Paul had left the Beatles. Had it been implied? Had Paul just been his usual cautious self, couching his words carefully, not quite saying what he meant? I tried to call him, but, not surprisingly, couldn't get through. At around lunchtime, when I knew John Lennon would be awake, I called him.

He was furious. It seemed to him that, as he'd started the Beatles when they'd been the Quarry Men, he believed it was it was up to him to announce publicly when they would be finished. Paul had now stolen a lead on him in that respect. Since Paul was already being blamed and hated for wrecking the world's most favourite entertainment it seemed a perverse argument to me, but that was how John saw it.

'Why didn't you write it when we were in Canada and I told you that I'd left the Beatles?' he snapped down the phone.

'You asked me not to,' I said.

His reply was withering. 'You're the journalist, Connolly, not me.'

Had Paul McCartney been a king who had abdicated, the convulsions of anger and despair that he'd broken up the Beatles, couldn't have been more acute. The world's favourite Beatle had become the most hated.

Then, two weeks later, he phoned me and suggested I should interview him so that he could put his side of the story. We met for lunch in a very busy seafood restaurant in London's Soho. Linda was at his side.

'It was all a misunderstanding,' he told me. 'I just thought "Christ, what have I done? Now we're in for it". And my stomach started churning up. I never intended the statement to mean "Paul McCartney quits Beatles".' Nor, he said, was it intended as a publicity stunt, which is something that had been widely suggested. Then he went through a short history of the fraught Beatles' relationships.

His first point concerned the reputed struggle between his father-in-law, Lee Eastman, and the Beatles' new manager, Allen Klein. 'Klein keeps saying that I don't like him because I want Eastman to manage the Beatles,' he said. 'Well, I thought, and still think, that Linda's father would have been good for us all. I decided I wanted him. But all the others wanted Klein. Well, all right, they can have Klein, but I don't see that I have to agree with them.

'The real break-up in the Beatles was months ago. First Ringo left when we were doing the *White Album*, because he said he didn't think it was any fun playing with us anymore. But, after two days of us telling him he was the greatest drummer in the world for the Beatles, he came back. Then George left when we were making *Abbey Road* because he didn't think he had enough say in our records, which was fair enough. After a couple of days, he came back, too.

'And then I began to feel that the only way we could ever get back to the stage of playing good music again was to start behaving as a band again. But I didn't want to go out and face two hundred thousand fans, because I would get nothing from it. So, I thought up this idea of playing surprise one-night stands in unlikely places…just letting a hundred or so people into the village hall, so to speak. It would have been a great scene for those who saw us, and for us, too.

'Then, one day when we had a meeting, I told the others about my idea, and asked them what they thought of it. John said, "I think you're daft." I said, "What do you mean?" I mean, he is John Lennon, and I'm a bit scared of all that rapier wit we hear about. And he just said again, "I think you're daft. I'm leaving the Beatles. I want a divorce."

'Well, none of us knew what to do, but we decided to wait until about March or April until our film, Let It Be, came out. But I was bored. I like to work. I'm an active person. Sit me down with a guitar and let me go. That's my job. Anyway, I hung on for all these months wondering whether the Beatles would ever come back together again… hoping that John might come around and say, "All right lads, I'm ready to go back to work". But in the meantime, I began to look for something to do. And the album, McCartney, turned out to be the answer in my case.

'At first, it wasn't going to be anything serious, but it turned out to be a great time. When we had to go to the studios, Linda would make the booking, and we'd take some sandwiches, and a bottle of grape juice and put the baby on the floor, and it was like a holiday. So, as a natural turn of events, from looking for something to do, I found that I was enjoying working alone as much as I'd enjoyed the early days of the Beatles. I haven't really enjoyed the Beatles in the last two years.'

So, did he think the Beatles had broken up?

'More than anything, I would love the Beatles to be on top of their form and for them to be as productive as they were. But things have changed. Even on Abbey Road we didn't do harmonies like we used to. I'd have liked to have sung harmony with John, and I think he would have liked me to. But I was too embarrassed to ask him.

'I must admit, I don't want to be the one to come out and say the Beatles are finished. I agree that they were an institution, and I don't want to go and break them up, but now I'm beginning to suffer because of all this. I suppose, really, I do believe now that we have finished performing together and recording together. I may not be right, but I must say I'm really enjoying what I'm doing at the moment.

'I didn't leave the Beatles. The Beatles have left the Beatles, but no one wants to be the one to say the party's over. Last year John said he wanted a divorce. All right, so do I. I want to give him that divorce. I hate this trial separation because it's just not working. John's in love with Yoko, and he's no longer in love with the other three of us. And let's face it, we were in love with the Beatles as much as anyone. We're still like brothers and we have enormous emotional ties because we were the only four that it all happened to…who went right through those ten years.

'I don't mind being bound to them as a friend. I like that idea. I don't mind being bound to them musically, because I like the others as musical partners. I like being in their band. But for my own sanity we must change the business arrangements. Only by being completely free of each other financially will we ever have any chance of coming back together as friends. Because it's business that has caused a lot of the split.'

His main worry was over a contract signed in July 1967, which tied all four Beatles together financially until 1977. Thus, the profits from all their activities (excepting song writing) were paid into Apple, the company that the four of them owned and still do. Under their agreement none of the four was able to earn separately, thus John's records, and his solo album, were treated in exactly the same way financially as their Beatle material.

In the same way, the Lennon-McCartney agreement with Northern Songs disregarded the fact that John wrote 'Instant Karma' by himself, and that all the songs on Paul's album were written by him alone. They both shared the royalties for all their songs.

'I think we should all have our independent incomes and let us work out for ourselves the accompanying problems. After all the years of work, all I've got to show is money locked up in a big company.

'Strictly speaking, we all have to ask each other's permission before any of us does anything without the other three. My own record nearly didn't come out because Klein and some of the others thought it would be too near to the date of the next Beatles' album. I had to get George, who's a director of Apple, to authorise its release for me.

'Give us our freedom which we so richly deserve. We're beginning now to only call each other when we have bad news. The other day Ringo came around to see me with a letter from the others, and I called him everything under the sun. But it's all business. I don't want to fall out with Ringo. I like Ringo. I think he's great. We're all talking about peace and love, but, really, we're not feeling peaceful at all.'

Although for the previous three or four years most of the Lennon-McCartney songs had been individual efforts, the final break in their partnership had been about eighteen months earlier.

'It simply became very difficult for me to write with Yoko sitting there,' he told me. 'If I had to think of a line, I started getting very nervous. I might want to say something like "I love you, girl", but with Yoko watching I always felt that I had to come out with something clever and *avant-garde*. She would probably have loved the simple stuff, but I was scared. I'm not blaming her, I'm blaming me. John and I tried writing together a few more times, but I think we both decided it would be easier to work separately. I told John on the phone the other day that at the beginning of last year I was annoyed with him. I was jealous because of Yoko, and afraid about the break-up of a great musical partnership.'

Looking back, he must now reflect on how right he was. But, on the day we met, he was particularly upset about a new arrangement, 'with harps, horns, an orchestra and a women's choir', that had been added by Phil Spector to 'The Long and Winding Road'.

'No one had asked me what I thought. I couldn't believe it. I would *never* have female voices on a Beatles' record. It just goes to show, it's no good me sitting here and thinking I'm in control, because, obviously, I'm not.'

After this interview was published, it was suggested that it had been Paul's way of communicating with the other Beatles, so bad had relations become. That seemed likely. John, for his part, was incredulous when he read that Paul had been upset over 'The Long and Winding Road'.

'Is that what this is all about?' he asked me when he read the interview. 'Paul ought to have thanked Spector for all the work he's done on the album, making it possible for it to be released. None of the Beatles wanted anything more to do with it. Even the biggest Beatle fan couldn't have sat through the six weeks of misery that making that film was. It was the most miserable session on earth, with the most miserable music going on and on and on, and everyone was expected to have a big smile going.' Half a century later, director Peter Jackson would beg to differ when he recut the fifty hours of the *Let It Be* sessions to make the TV series *The Beatles Get Back*.

What I find astonishing is that even today, Paul, who had always been the biggest Beatles fan of all four, is still being blamed for having broken up the band. That *Daily Mirror* headline from 1970 stuck. His explanation had come too late.

Around that time, I came home to our house in Kensington to find half a tree blocking the steps to the front door. Climbing over it, I went inside, and asked what had happened.

'A man with one arm rang the bell and asked if he could cut a branch off the tree,' said Plum, who was sitting nursing the new baby. 'I gave him five pounds.'

'Five pounds! You were done,' I said. Five pounds was a lot of money in those days.

'I know,' said Plum. 'But it's very difficult sawing a branch off a tree when you only have one arm.'

Which was undeniable.

16.

'Girls run after me a lot… I know that I'm as capable of being swayed by a girl as by a boy' - Dusty Springfield

Fifty odd years ago, it wasn't done to enquire about a person's sexuality, and especially not if that person was a famous singer who was much loved by the British public as the zany girl- next-door. Yet that was what Dusty Springfield mischievously goaded me into asking during an interview with her one afternoon in 1970.

It was our one and only meeting and we were at the Philips Records office at London's Marble Arch to talk about her new record, 'How Can I Be Sure?'. She didn't have great hopes for it. 'That comes from a backlog of doubts in myself because the last few records have gone wrong,' she admitted. 'I'm always a bit surprised to sell records, anyway. It would be a souring experience if I weren't to have any more hits, but I would survive. It would be a test of character for me. If it did happen, I'd probably get out unless I could find some other direction to go in. I don't particularly want to be a cabaret type of entertainer. Whether or not I could be defeated into accepting that type of existence, I don't know.'

To hear someone talking about possible failure was rare when self-confidence was the key spirit of the Sixties entertainment generation. But from there, as two lapsed Catholics, we began talking about guilt, mortal sin and going to confession as children, which led on to a discussion on sex and promiscuity. When Dusty suddenly said: 'There's something else you should ask me now.'

I hesitated, not knowing what she meant.

She was insistent. 'Go on, ask me. I know you've heard the rumours.'

I knew then. I'd heard the gossip that said that she preferred girls to boys. So, still hesitant, I half put the question. And off she went.

'I'm promiscuous. Not often, but when I am, I really am. I'm not a nymphomaniac. In fact, I could do with a lot more action, really. I think my laziness even spreads that far. It's an effort to be promiscuous. I don't mean that I leap into bed with someone special every night, but my affections are easily swayed and I can be very unfaithful. It's fun while it's happening, but it's not fun afterwards because I'm filled with self-recrimination. The truth is I'm just very easily flattered by people's attentions, and after a couple of vodkas I'm even more flattered.'

She was giggling by then. 'I suppose to say that I'm promiscuous is a bit of bravado on my part. I think it's more in thought than in action. I've been that way ever since I discovered the meaning of the word. I used to go to confession and tell all my impure thoughts.'

At which point she became serious again, spacing her words carefully. 'There's one thing that has always annoyed me. I'm going to get into something nasty here, but I've got to say it, because so many people say I'm bent, and I've heard it so many times that I've almost learned to accept it. I don't go leaping around to all the gay clubs, but I can be very flattered. Girls run after me a lot and it doesn't upset me. It upsets me when people insinuate things that aren't true. I couldn't stand to be thought of as a big butch lady. But I know that I'm as perfectly capable of being swayed by a girl as by a boy. More and more people feel that way and I don't see why I shouldn't. There was someone on television the other night who admitted that he swings either way. I suppose he could afford to say it, but I, being a pop singer, shouldn't even admit that I might think that way. But if the occasion arose, I don't see why I shouldn't.

'And yet, I get such a charge out of walking down a street and having a guy who's digging the road give me a whistle. This business makes me feel very unwomanly sometimes, and I love to be admired just for being a woman. I don't feel masculine. If I did, I'd have more drive. But being a woman is very precious to me, and that's probably why I could never get mixed up in a gay scene because it would be bound to undermine my sense of being a woman. I've had this reputation for years, but I don't know how I got it. I'm always hearing that I've been to this gay club and that gay club. But I haven't. I sometimes wonder if it would be nice to live up to my reputation.

'I got raided the other day by the police. But they didn't find any drugs. I've hardly ever smoked. As it happens, I think I know who tipped them off, and it relates to what I've been saying. There was a rather hysterical lady who was upset because I didn't fancy her. I think it was her.'

As we lived quite close to one another, I drove Dusty home after the interview. 'Do you realise,' she laughed, as I dropped her off, 'what I've just told you could put the final seal to my doom? I don't know, though, I might attract a whole new audience.' And, with that, she got out of my car and went inside to join the American artist, girlfriend, Norma Tanega, with whom she was then sharing her house.

Today the sexuality of stars isn't an issue. We regularly see photographs of actresses and girl singers kissing, and we know of many who are openly in gay relationships without it affecting either their popularity or their careers. Back then, however, an admission of homosexuality, whether male or female, could, it was believed, kill a career in show business. Quite why Dusty chose to come out at that moment, I've never discovered. Nor do I know why she selected me to make public her situation. I can only assume that she simply felt it was time to stop hiding.

Unwittingly, however, she'd presented me with a dilemma. I was a huge Dusty fan and we'd got on very well, but I knew that professionally she was playing with fire. Did I want to be responsible for ruining her career? No, I didn't. At the same time, she was obviously keen to clear the air. So, after consulting my features editor at the *Evening Standard,* we decided to bury the sex discussion in the middle of the article. You had to read the piece to find the candid admissions. Our headline simply read: *'DUSTY AT THIRTY'*.

Although I later learned that her manager had a fit when he saw the interview, Dusty had no regrets, phoning the day the article was published, and leaving a message to say that she was quite happy with the way I'd reported our conversation.

It had been a brave step to confront the prejudices of the era, but that was Dusty. She was a real one off. A gifted woman, she was, in many ways, years ahead of her time. But she was also contradictory and sometimes self-destructive, with, despite that voice, a profound lack of self-confidence in a life of depressions.

When most of us first encountered Dusty on television at the beginning of the Sixties, singing with her brother Tom in the Springfields pop-folk trio, she seemed not to have a care in the world. An ex-convent schoolgirl from Ealing, with an almost genteel accent, something quite rare in pop circles at the time, she personified a happy-go-lucky wholesomeness.

But she had ambition, too. Unhappy with the style of songs her brother was writing for the Springfields, she dropped him at the peak of their fame, and became an immediate solo success with the hits 'I Only Want To Be With You' and the Burt Bacharach-Hal David song 'I Just Don't Know What To Do With Myself'. By the mid-Sixties she was 'the golden girl of British song', loved for her charm and giggles, and the way she lit up television's *Ready Steady Go* with her blonde beehive, panda eyes and seemingly effervescent love for life and music.

Then, out of nowhere, she found herself at the centre of an international row. Going on a short tour of South Africa in 1964, under the impression that she would be allowed to perform to mixed black and white audiences, she refused to sing to *anyone* when told black fans wouldn't be allowed into her concerts. Despite days of cajoling by the South African authorities, she wouldn't give in. As a result, her visa was revoked, and she was escorted to the airport and put on a plane back to London.

To take on the South African Government on a matter of principle was a brave stand for a 25-year-old, and not one that drew universal admiration from other, mainly older, British acts, who had adhered to apartheid rules. They felt she'd spoiled it for them.

To many of her own generation, however, Dusty had been heroic, as was her championing of the black Motown stars of the day. She just loved black r and b music. So, when in 1968 she was invited to record in Memphis, in the studios where Aretha Franklin, Wilson Pickett and Otis Redding worked, she was exultant.

Things in Memphis didn't go well, however. Producer Jerry Wexler would later tell me that she drove him to distraction by her perfectionism in only wanting 'to record one line of a song at a time'. Eventually, the album, *Dusty In Memphis*, had to be finished in New York. It's now considered a classic, especially its hit song 'Son Of A Preacher Man', but at the time it wasn't commercially successful.

For the first time, Dusty's career had seen a real setback, and simultaneously the cracks in her psychological make-up were beginning to widen. By the time I met her, although I didn't know it, she was beginning secretly to self-harm, taking a razor blade to her arms. Behind the sunny mask, problems were emerging.

She'd been in love with the idea of America since the days her mother had taken her to see Hollywood musicals when she was a little girl, and, a few months after my interview with her, she abandoned London and went to live in Los Angeles. She wanted to make a new start on a bigger stage and was under the impression that she could become very big in America. She had the voice for it, but it didn't work out. Having left behind in Britain the team who had helped her rise to the top, she was unable to find the songs that would give her new hits.

Before long she began, like many a fading star in Hollywood, to slip into alcoholism, turning up unrecognised at an Alcoholic Anonymous meeting in the suburbs of Los Angeles without the disguise of beehive hair and black eyes and under her real name of Mary O'Brien.

The self-harming grew worse, too. Soon her girlfriend at that time would be calling for ambulances on a regular basis as Dusty began to gabble about seeing demons who were telling her to do bad things, after which the blood would always flow. At one point she had to be put in a straitjacket. On another occasion she tried to commit suicide. Whatever the reasons, as her consumption of alcohol and cocaine spiralled, her beautiful voice was damaged. One night, with her savings spent on companions who were leeching off her, her house sold and her voice damaged, she mimed for ready cash to a record of one of her old hits in a Los Angeles gay bar.

She would later joke that she'd never quite been on skid row, but she wasn't far from it, when she began her fight back, banishing alcohol and drugs from her life. And, back in Britain in the late Eighties, she found herself at the top of the charts again when her collaboration with Pet Shop Boys' 'What Have I Done To Deserve This?'

At around this time she gave an interview to another journalist explaining simply that she'd had sex with both men and women and enjoyed both, but, as middle age wore on, she was increasingly happy to live the single life. 'No drugs, no alcohol and no sex,' she said. An avid reader, she was content to read and look after her cats in her large, rented house near Henley-on-Thames, quietly amused that she had become the gay icon she'd jokingly prophesied at our interview all those years earlier.

Then in 1995, while making a new album, she discovered that she had breast cancer. Increasingly confined to her home, she was cared for by one of her former backing singers, Simon Bell. One night in 1999 they watched together a special video that the BBC had sent her of programmes she'd made for them in her prime in the late Sixties. 'She enjoyed it,' Simon Bell told me. 'When it finished, she fell asleep and died the following day having never woken up again.'

Had she made a mistake by coming out to me in 1970? I don't think so. It was time. It's difficult now to understand the anguish she must have gone through having to hide her sexuality from fans, some of whom might not have understood. What we do know is that she was a brave, independent and gifted woman with a uniquely beautiful voice. And if you can't remember just how good she was, give her version of the Carole King/Gerry Goffin song 'Goin' Back' another listen.

Some years ago, I wrote a screenplay about Dusty called *Some Of Your Lovin'*, based on a biography by Sharon Davies, and, for the one and only time, I wasn't paid by a con-man who said he was a producer. Having borrowed money to hire me and another writer to script something else, he lived well for a while, renting offices at Twickenham Studio. Then, when the money ran out, he ignored my contract, and did a runner to Dubai, leaving other debts. I'd assumed that the screenplay would be snapped up by a television company as a series, or by BBC Radio 4, because it's a great story about a woman ahead of her time, and Dusty's voice was, of course, wonderful. But, so far, it hasn't been.

'Our timing couldn't have been better,' Tim Rice said to me in December 1971. That was no exaggeration. Four and a half years after I first met him and Andrew Lloyd Webber when they were two budding songwriters earning £25 a week each, their rock opera *Jesus Christ Superstar* was a hit on Broadway. The rest of the world and a film would shortly follow.

It was all down to Jesus, of course. Their businessman manager had convinced MCA Records to allow them £14,000 (over £190,00 in today's money) to make a concept album based on the last seven days of Jesus's life. It seemed a risky venture. And, when the record was released, it hadn't caused much more than a ripple of interest in the UK.

Put to one side by the BBC because it followed the story partly through the eyes of Judas Iscariot and the prostitute Mary Magdalene, it was believed that some listeners might consider it sacrilegious. America, however, reacted very differently, the arrival of *Jesus Christ Superstar* there coinciding with a revival in religious interest and the new cult of Jesus freaks.

None of that had been foreseen by its writers. Twenty-three-year-old Andrew Lloyd Webber's only thoughts had been how to approach the subject musically, with inspiration for the theme tune coming to him when he was in a local record shop where he'd gone to buy an old Ricky Nelson album.

'I was so excited I came out of the shop with the tune running in my head and rushed to the nearest restaurant and asked for some paper so that I could write it down. Then I phoned Tim to tell him that I'd thought of the most fantastic tune.' For which Tim Rice then wrote the lyrics: 'Jesus Christ, Superstar. Who are you, what have you sacrificed?'

'We now have this absurd situation where people are merchandising Jesus Christ Superstar T-shirts and watches,' Tim Rice went on. 'There are Superstar rubber stamps, Superstar patches for your jeans, stick-on things for your cars and sunglasses... There's even a record "Richard Nixon Superstar"', and a pastiche of Christ up in heaven singing "Me-ee-ee, Me-ee-ee", to the opening refrain. And what's worse is that people think we started the whole thing, when we really wish we were able to stop it.'

I did hundreds of interviews in those years. Donovan, Twiggy, Frank Zappa, Christine Perfect (before she became Christine McVie and part of Fleetwood Mac), John Fogerty of Creedence Clearwater Revival, Allen Klein, Jane Asher, England goalkeeper Gordon Banks, Kenny Everett, Johnny Cash, Carl Perkins, Rufus Thomas, Peter Cook, Thor Hyerdahl and Ken Russell, while Jane Birkin breathed an orgasm to a tune by Serge Gainsbourg. Then there was

David Frost, who recommended I wear a suit for doing interviews, and I wondered if he was embarrassed that I was in my Levis at his smart New York hotel; and Paul Raymond who remembered that the first naked lady he'd ever seen was when, as a boy, he'd peeped through the keyhole to watch his aunt taking a bath. Some interviewees became friends for life, others I knew would have forgotten my existence the moment I left the room.

My interest in songs, however, never left me, and the Everly Brothers, to whom so many groups owed so much, had clear memories. 'Bye Bye Love' had been their first hit in 1957. 'At the time we would have recorded anything just for the studio fee,' Phil Everly told me while I was making a video with the two brothers. 'Wake Up Little Susie' had come next. 'There was a lot of tension because we knew that the follow-up record had to be a hit. We must have listened to two hundred songs before the songwriters, Felice and Boudleaux Bryant, came up with that one.

'The first time I heard "All I Have To Do Is Dream" was on an acetate with Boudleaux singing. They could have put it out just like that. We knew it was an instant hit.'

Both brothers liked 'Devoted To You', which Phil described as being like an English madrigal. 'It's a very well-structured piece, and it feels good to sing.' (I only recently realised that it also borrows heavily from 'Twinkle, Twinkle Little Star'.)

Don Everly wrote 'Till I Kissed You' on a plane back to the US from Australia. 'I'd fallen in love with a French girl called Lilian and I was afraid that I would never see her again. In those days Australia seemed like the end of the world.'

Both Everlys had a hand in 'Cathy's Clown', which was their biggest hit. 'Musically the inspiration came from "The Grand Canyon Suite",' Don remembered. 'There's a little marching section that I was really taken with that was used in a Philip Morris radio commercial. For his part, Phil wrote 'When Will I Be Loved'. 'I was upset over some girl, and I remember sitting in my car at a root beer stand near to where I lived and writing the last verse.'

The Everly Brothers wrote their last big hit, 'The Price Of Love', together. 'It reminds me of touring,' Phil remembered. 'While Donald plays to the band, I like to look around the audience and maybe pick up a pretty face, a girl I'll never see again. "You talk too much, you laugh too loud, you see her face in every crowd."'

Classic hit records are usually no more than three minutes of song. But they come with their writers' and their performers' thoughts. Then they sit in our heads, and become embossed with our own thoughts, too. That's why they become hits. They open a pathway to our memories.

17.

'There's a porn shop on the corner…'
- Ann Summers

I got on with most people I interviewed, but some who angrily bollocked minor employees in front of me for little mistakes, and then, two-faced, turned back to me, all smiles, were awful. Tony Curtis did that, as did Michael Winner. While James Baldwin, of whose books I was a huge admirer, polarised everything I said into a historical and racial context. 'You talk as though I was never on a Virginia plantation, working for you, picking your cotton, building your railroads and your cities and letting you sell my sons,' he said. It was a difficult conversation.

Stevie Wonder, surrounded by an army of devotees, told me that being blind was 'like owning a TV with a tube that didn't work'; Britt Ekland said she'd been 'hideous' when she was a teenager, which was hard to believe, while Diana Rigg, who half the men in the country fancied as Emma Peel in *The Avengers*, didn't want to be interviewed at all.

Ann Summers did, however. She was 29 and she had won the 'Evening Standard Woman of the Year Award' in 1971, having caused a stir when her shop, that sold vibrators and other sex aids, opened at London's Marble Arch. A high street sex shop, or, as Ann Summers joked, 'the porn shop on the corner', was something brand new in Britain then. Only the Germans and Swedes, had such emporia, and everyone knew about the Germans and their nudity and Swedish au pairs. Now crowds were gathering on the pavement outside Ann Summers shop to view her wares. She'd captured the moment, so she had to be someone to talk to.

On meeting her, my immediate guess was that she was a brilliant front for the business, but she insisted that the wholesome sounding 'Ann Summers' was her real name. Not quite, I discovered. Annice Summer would have been more accurate. All the same, her plump, blonde, peachy, middle-class English looks, public-school accent, and an ability to blush on cue, were as disarming as the punnet of strawberries which lay on the back seat of her Hillman Imp, alongside the basket of eggs and a small jar labelled Love Balm.

But, while she was eager to tell me, 'Our best-selling line is the clitoral stimulants, trade dropped slightly when we ran out of them,' discovering who was backing her was impossible.

A few months later, a fellow called Michael Caborn-Waterfield, better known as Dandy Kim, a good-looking conman in his day, was identified as the man pulling the strings. Ann Summers had been his secretary and girlfriend. But soon, after a row over money, she was out of the picture, and, dissociating herself from the shops in her name, she left Britain to live a private life in Italy, where she died of cancer in 2012.

Acquired by sex magazine publisher, David Gold, there are now over 150 Ann Summers shops. Gold's daughter, Jacqueline, (who died in 2023) became the chief executive, with a personal fortune reckoned at one time to be around £450 million. It was, however, the original Ann Summers, Dandy Kim and his backers who had seen the future. And it was clitoral.

Some of the nicest people didn't always have much to say, and I would worry about how I was going to fill my page. Michael Caine, however, wasn't stuck for words. When we met, he'd spent the day with Elizabeth Taylor shooting a scene in the film *X, Y and Zee* (which had been written by Edna O'Brien), and, as we were being driven back to London from Shepperton Studios in his silver blue Rolls-Royce, he, unprompted, suddenly said: 'A lot of people probably don't know that I can speak French. I'm good at German, too.' Practically no one knew that either, he said, but he was quite proud of it. 'It's an accomplishment of which no-one considers me capable.

'Sometimes when I'm in a restaurant and speak to the waiter in French, the people I'm with will just gape in stunned astonishment, because they just *know* that I ought not to be intelligent enough to have learned a foreign language.'

At this point, I began to wonder if Elizabeth Taylor had said something to upset him earlier that day; or whether Richard Burton had turned up on the set and come on all poetic.

But Michael Caine was still talking. 'And you know, sometimes I have to go off to the Gents and have a good look at myself in the mirror to see if I really do look like the dumdum that seems to be my image. I mean, it makes you wonder about yourself. Somehow, I seem to have got the image of the world's luckiest half-wit. But in my view, I'm not half-witted and I've never had an ounce of luck in my life. I've never been given any credit as a craftsman. My whole Press image has been frivolous. And, of course, there's always the crumpet thing about me.

'Everyone always assumes that the parts I've played have been those where I haven't had to think about creating a character. God! It annoys me to death to be written about as though I'm a village idiot, a real lazy, stupid, good-for-nothing, like one of those actors in the old days when it was said the studio electrician used to put the sparkle in his eyes. I suppose the Press wanted a Cinderella story and I was it. But Cinderella *was* lucky!'

Michael Caine was lucky, too. But he was also good. The part of Alfie, the London boy on the make with the ladies, had been turned down by both Anthony Newley and Terence Stamp, before Caine got it. Being a South London boy himself, born Maurice Joseph Micklewhite, the son of a Billingsgate fish market porter and charlady, he looked good and sounded right. It was perfect casting. After ten years as an actor in TV and repertory, his chatty Cockney performance and voice-over narration personified the newly fashionable working-class anti-heroes of the Sixties, people like photographers David Bailey and Terry O'Neil, and rock star Rod Stewart. What bothered him when we talked was that he'd been so good at playing Alfie, that fictitious character was superimposed upon him by everyone he met.

At that time, a new Michael Caine film was being readied for release. It was called *Get Carter* and was about a gangster, a 'real repellent character', he said, the flip side of the personality coin from *Alfie*. He had, he said, modelled his performance on someone he used to know. 'I once saw him put someone in the hospital for eighteen months. Those guys are like that. If you're born into a working-class milieu, like I was and as virtually every violent criminal is, then you're sure to want something different. And, if the world treats you violently enough, then you will act in a violent way to alter your circumstances. Or you can go another way. I became an actor which was considered a cissy thing, but it does allow you to act out your fantasies. It wasn't a case of there but for the grace of God goes me; it was there but for the grace of *me* goes me.'

As the Rolls-Royce took us back into London along the Cromwell Road in Kensington, it stopped at a traffic light, and we watched as a very pretty, leggy girl crossed the road in front of us. Then the light turned to green, and we moved on. 'You know,' said Michael Caine, or was it Alfie, I wasn't sure, 'blokes come over here and talk about the permissive society, but I think it's all a bit of a myth. They're just balling the same couple of hundred girls that everybody else has been having. I'm sure the whole thing is kept going by a couple of hundred ravers.'

The habit of actors seeming to sometimes continue playing a character off screen that they've enjoyed playing, and finding fame with, on screen, is as old as the theatrical profession. The one time I met Edward Fox at dinner, he'd just played the Duke of Windsor in television's *Edward and Mrs Simpson,* and, throughout the evening, I had the humbling feeling that I was dining with royalty. While Peter Fonda came across as a little Captain America, like his character as at tough, hippy biker in *Easy Rider,* advising me never to go upstairs in front of an FBI agent. 'If the guy is behind you, he could cut your kidney out before you know it.'
Which was, of course, something I've since borne in mind whenever climbing stairs ahead of an FBI agent.

That was the way Fonda talked, all macho, violent and hip. He was 30 and *Easy Rider*, in which he'd starred with Dennis Hopper and Jack Nicholson, had been a very big late Sixties hit, for which he'd won a co-writer's Oscar. But when his follow up, *The Last Movie,* was given a poster on Sunset Boulevard that he didn't like, he said he went back into his *Easy Rider* character and charged into Universal Pictures.

'Believe me,' he told me as though repeating lines from another script, 'I really looked like a madman… a maniac, knife in my hand. And then I see Denis Hopper, and see he's got his knife. And he goes, "Let's go cut 'em up". And the secretaries are looking terrified because we both have this reputation for being totally insane… We really figured to freak them out and they never got me out of that place so fast.' This may have been Peter Fonda, son of

Henry, sister of Jane talking; but it sounded more like things he wished he'd said.

Nor had he finished. 'When Nixon became President, I tore up my draft card and sent it to him with instructions for him to shove it up his ass.'

But he was still drafted?

'Oh, yes. I arrived for my physical one morning and they had us there naked. And we were all told to bend over and spread our cheeks. And I told the doctor there that if he touched me I'd shove my heel down his throat. He sent me to the psychiatrist who began saying some derogatory things about my mother and family.' His mother had committed suicide when he was ten.

'Which meant, I suppose, that he was trying to plumb the depths of my neurosis. So, I stood up, still naked, and walked out and across the parking lot to get my car. A little marine comes up to me and puts a coat around me. And I said, "Don't touch me, or I'll kill you. I'm a civilian". I was classified 1-Y, which means that they should re-examine me every year, but they never did.'

It sounded to me that either he'd invented the incident to fit his view of himself as a fictitious celluloid character, or he'd pulled off a very successful draft dodge to get out of being sent to Vietnam.

As an actor, and therefore part of a profession that makes fiction seem real, Peter Fonda may have had a silly, vague excuse for wild exaggeration. Donald Trump, however, made a political career out of such nonsense, and when caught telling lies, simply had a spokeswoman step forward and talk about 'alternative facts'. So, I suppose, 'alternative facts' were what rock star Marc Bolan was doing when he told me that he could both fly and could make himself invisible.

Bolan was one of those stars who bubbled up in the vacuum left after the Beatles' dissolution, and, with his group, Tyrannosaurus Rex, later modified to just T Rex, he had a run of hits. Pretty, in an elfin sort of way, he stuck glitter on his forehead and sequins like tear drops below his eyes, and, when I went to see him in his shabby flat in Maida Vale, he was the teenybop hero of 1972. He was 24 and had been pursuing a dream of stardom since, at thirteen, he'd been photographed as the 'King of the Mods' by Don McCullin.

'I was really into clothes then as an energy source,' he told me. Music had followed as his 'energy source' as he'd gone from one record company to another until he'd finally found his stepladder to success with 'Ride a White Swan' and 'Get It On'.

All that seemed factual enough. But then he began to tell fibs. We often see stars building themselves up with carefully written and well-told stories that make amusing anecdotes on TV chat shows. Sometimes we half believe the tales, and at least they amuse studio audiences. But often we just know that what they're telling us is four-fifths exaggeration. Marc Bolan was five fifths when he got going. So, I asked him if he had really seen someone levitate, as he had told another journalist?

'Yes. It was in Paris. He was standing on the floor, and he raised himself about eight feet into the air. I was with about four other people. I can do it, too.'

Could he demonstrate it for me, I asked.

'No. I don't feel like it. Do you doubt it? You have a very downer attitude which I find disconcerting. I've done magic rites and conjured up demons, too.'

How did he do that?

'It takes time to learn. I've also seen flying saucers. It's based on mathematics. There are certain herbs and incantations that can make you invisible… You don't really become invisible. It's just that the person watching you can't see you.'

So, it went on. How he only had about £100 in the bank but was worth over a million; how he'd written the biggest selling book of poetry ever; and how he'd had no education at school, then gone out, bought a guitar, taught himself to play and written three songs that same day.

All he lacked, was a government paid spokesperson to tell me that they were all alternative facts.

At around this time I made my first appearance on television. Over the years, I'd begun to realise that I could control my stammer if I simply acted out the character of someone who didn't stammer. It took years to get it right, but I got progressively better to the point where I was able to go on TV and do a 10-minute section in a film review show, reading an autocue and showing film clips. I rehearsed it before the show, of course, only writing words I knew I could say, and knowing where to pause and draw breath. Only once at the end of a clip, when I got over-confident, did I stumble on a word. The following day at the *Evening Standard* my friend Julian Norridge expressed amazement. If I couldn't talk to him in the office without stammering, how had I done it on television to millions? The answer was that the Ray Connolly he'd seen on TV had been faking it, pretending to be a TV presenter. And TV presenters don't stammer.

That had been a breakthrough moment. A few months later I was asked to interview Little Richard for *Late Night Line-Up*, and this time I couldn't prepare what I was going to say. Once again, however, I played the part of a non-stammerer. To be honest, Little Richard did all the work. He was magnificently, camply outrageous. I just had to sit there and prompt him.

After the Little Richard episode, I realised that as much as I might stammer in daily life, I had a method that would get me through radio and TV appearances. Of course, as soon as I was off-camera, or off-mic, or when I was at home with my family, my stammer would return. I could put on a performance for the public. But I couldn't do that with Plum and our children. They knew I stammered. They expected me, too.

As it turned out, my speech hadn't held me back as an interviewer, anyway. Marsha Hunt, she of the glorious Afro-hair whose performance on stage in the musical *Hair!* has led to a kind of tabloid immortality (as well as a Roy Jones photograph in the Smithsonian Museum of African American Culture in Washington) reckons that my getting stuck for words prompted interviewees like her to continue talking to cover up any awkwardness.

18.

'I ain't got no quarrel with them Vietcong'
- Muhammad Ali

John Lennon would often describe himself as being working class. He even wrote an autobiographical song about it. But he wasn't working class. He just enjoyed the idea. He also imagined himself as a leftwing revolutionary, but that was just another craze, as, like a cushion, he often wore an imprint of the last person who, intellectually, sat on him. Thus, always restless, he inhabited several different personae as crazes came and went.

Brought up in a pleasant Liverpool suburb, with a strict, but doting, aunt, he'd been to a grammar school then art college. The first home he ever bought was in the Surrey stockbroker belt, and the second was an estate called Tittenhurst Park in Berkshire, where there were donkeys and doves and 70 acres of heath, woods, and oriental trees, as well as an artificially created lake with a rowing boat. That was where he lived when he wrote 'Working Class Hero', which hardly described his own passage through life. He'd been on a primal scream course of psychotherapy in San Francisco in the months after the Beatles broke up, and had brought back from California a concept of pain and repressed bitterness to put in his first solo album, *John Lennon/Plastic Ono Band.* It was the best solo album he made.

'When I wrote "Working Class Hero" I wasn't trying to make a bloody variety show,' he told me over dinner at Tittenhurst one night. (A cook had prepared lamb chops for me: John and Yoko just ate brown rice.) 'I was thinking about all the pain and torture that you go through on stage to get love from the audience. You go up there like Aunt Sally, having things thrown at you. I might just as well have been a comedian getting egg thrown in my face.

'How often do you think the Beatles enjoyed a show? Perhaps once in how many weeks of touring? All this about clubs and gigs is a dream; actually, more like a nightmare. One show in thirty would give us any real satisfaction, and you'd go through all kinds of hell to get that. So, what was I? A performing flea?

'And from that I came out with 'Working Class Hero'. It was an insight into myself. I know that I perform of my own choice, but that's the game. It's like performing for your parents all the time. All people like me start off with this appalling need for love. Why have I made this record? For money? For prestige? For fun? It's bloody hard work making a record. It took six months to write these songs. It's no game. It's bloody tough. At first, I was dying to do it, but, when we've done one track, I just think, "Christ, I wish I'd never started".'

Neither his father nor his mother (who had died in a road accident when he was a teenager) was spared from criticism on the album. Was he worried that his father might be hurt by some of the lyrics, I asked.

He didn't care if he was. 'What did he do for me? He didn't turn up until I was famous. I should get upset. The first time I saw him he was on the front of the *Daily Express* washing dishes. He left me, I didn't leave him. He was down here last week, and I showed him the door.'

His father, Freddie Lennon, or, as John would call him, 'the ignoble Alf', would later privately write that John had terrified him on that visit. According to his father's second wife, Pauline, the couple had gone to visit John and taken him a bottle of aftershave as a birthday present. But John had not been in a birthday mood. Grabbing his father by the lapels he'd said he was cutting off the financial allowance he'd been giving him and saying. 'If you tell anyone about what happened here today, I'll have you killed… cased up in a box and dumped out at sea right in the middle of the ocean…twenty, fifty or, perhaps you'd prefer, a hundred fathoms deep'.

To anyone who knew John this was all wild, angry, Long John Silver nonsense. But the Ignoble Alf didn't know his son very well and believed the threats. Although John later regretted his outburst, the two would never meet again. That had been John, acting and speaking on an impulse, and being sorry about it later.

He and Yoko were an obsessively inward-looking couple. I learned later that John had been using heroin around that time, something I'd suspected when one of his secretaries at Tittenhurst told me that sometimes whole days would go by when 'nothing ever happens here. Nothing at all. They stay in their bedroom all day.'

Are you lonely, I asked John. I was sure he was.

But he insisted he was not. 'I never did have many friends. The Beatles were my friends, but they were also the people I worked with. We were friends, but then the function ended and that was the problem. The friendship had nothing to live on except the memory.'

His new album would, he expected, be criticised for its simplicity, but he had an answer for that. 'With songs like "Working Class Hero" the words present themselves quicker than I have time to write the tunes, and, when the words are good, I don't bother much with the tune. With some of the old ones, like "In My Life" and "Across The Universe", I have the words before the tune, and then almost any tune fits. "Working Class Hero" is derivative of every tune I ever heard. "Mother" is basically the same tune as "You Can't Do That".'

John and Yoko weren't completely in isolation at Tittenhurst Park. For several weeks, during one of John's crazes, a Hare Krishna group lived in one of the outbuildings there. 'They're all ex-druggies,' he assured me one day. 'But they're all right.'

Everything went well for a while and the lodgers decorated their new home as a little temple, as they ghosted around the estate muttering 'Hare Krishna' and 'Peace' whenever they bumped into anyone. On a further visit, however, I noticed that they had left. 'What happened to the Hare Krishna people?' I wanted to know.

John grinned. He'd had to kick them out. 'They were driving me mad with all that "Hare Krishna…Peace, man" chanting all the time. I couldn't get any fucking peace.' There was always a joke with John.

When the Beatles had begun, they'd seen themselves as being in competition with other rock groups, in Liverpool with Gerry and the Pacemakers, then in London with the Rolling Stones. But, after they'd broken up, they saw their main competitors as each other. And, when George Harrison's first solo album, *All Things Must Pass,* got better reviews than his own, John was peeved.

'Have you seen what *Time* magazine said about George's album?' he asked me on one afternoon at Tittenhurst Park.

I had. 'It's got a huge advance order,' I told him.

'Advance orders are all talk. It looks nice on paper. The guy in *Time* is saying George is the philosopher, and that fucking idiot in

The Times (meaning William Mann, *The Times'* music critic who, some years earlier, had written that the Beatles were "the greatest songwriters since Schubert") is saying that Paul is a great musician. Where does that leave me?'

'A nutter,' I suggested.

'Yes. I'm the nutter. Fuck 'em.'

He might have laughed about it, but his competitive instincts had been raised. A few months later he recorded a new album in the studio he'd had built at his home. Because he couldn't get his hi-fi system to work in his bedroom, he played me what he said would be his next single on a small record player. It was a song called 'Gimme Some Truth'.

I was disappointed when I heard it. 'What's on the other side?' I asked.

So, he turned the demo over and played me a piano led ballad.

'Surely that's the A-side,' I said.

He called to Yoko, who was sitting on the bed. 'Yoko, Ray thinks "Imagine" should be the A-side.'

'Oh, good,' she replied.

He smiled. 'I'm glad you like "Imagine". I like that one, too.'

Of course, he must have known very well that 'Imagine' would be the hit. Unknown to me, it was already planned as the album's title. He probably just wanted me to confirm his own opinion, that it was one of the best songs he'd written.

At that time, I'd begun helping suggest occasional guests for the new *Parkinson* chat show on BBC-TV, and mentioned to the producer that I might be able to get them John and Yoko. Michael Parkinson was all for it, but the producer was slightly worried that the pair might do something outrageous, such as taking off all their clothes as they had on the cover of the *Two Virgins* album, or both getting into a bag in front of the cameras. That was then the public perception of what 'looney John and Yoko' might get up to.

In the end, the BBC played safe. John and Yoko went on for the first half of the show, to be replaced by the solid, predictable film actor Trevor Howard for the second part. Big mistake. John was witty and self-deprecating, and Yoko was revealed to the British public as having a sense of humour. I watched from behind the cameras as John kept the studio audience laughing, as I'd known he would.

'We should have had him and Yoko on for the full programme,' Michael Parkinson regretted afterwards. 'We will next time.'

There wouldn't be a next time. A few days later, the Lennons left England for New York. John would never return, nor realise that 'Imagine', the song most associated with him, and a number one hit in many counties around the world in 1971, wasn't released as a single in the United Kingdom until 1975. It must have been more profitable to sell it as an album than a single, although no-one had told John. And, in love with his new life in America, he never even noticed. When, he finally found out, he blamed Allen Klein, and put 'Working Class Hero' on the flipside of the British single.

When Cassius Clay had beaten Sonny Liston to become the World Heavyweight Champion in 1964, he seemed to have reinvented boxing. No longer did it look like legally sanctioned brutality, but a sport of wit, quick hands and dancing feet. So attractive was Clay's physical beauty and charm, a boxing match might almost have become a game of tick, as he ducked and leaned away from those who would do him harm. That was what his admirers told themselves, anyway, as the world fell in love with him.

The love affair continued after he became a Muslim and changed his name to Muhammad Ali (Clay having, he said, been the name of his ancestors' slave owners). We were bemused, but still supportive as he defeated all the other boxers in his class. He was so loquaciously witty and so incredibly likeable. And, after he'd refused to be drafted into the US Army in 1967, claiming that he was a conscientious objector, saying, 'I ain't got no quarrel with them Vietcong', he'd become a new kind of hero. The war in Vietnam was deeply unpopular with young people, not only in the USA, but across the world. So, when he'd been stripped of his title and lost his license to fight, he'd become a martyred hero.

Then in 1971 the Supreme Court overturned his conviction for evading the draft and he was allowed to return to the ring. By now, however, his title of heavyweight champion had been given to Joe Frazier. So, the scene was set for the "Fight of the Century" at

Madison Square Garden, New York, in March 1971. Joe Frazier, who was characterised as a slugger, won.

Over the next few months, I met both men when they visited the United Kingdom. I talked to Joe Frazier first in a small hotel room in London's Lancaster Gate. He had just returned from a run around Hyde Park, and was lying shirtless on his bed. As wide and as deep as a sideboard, he was punching one fist after another, to emphasise what he had to say.

'I recall the time people said to me that I'd never be champ,' he said. 'They said I was too short, that my arms wasn't long enough and that I didn't have the punch to put those big fellas away. But I proved it to them. I did it. And now I'm going to prove that I'm a singer, too.'

That, unfortunately, he was unable to do. Touring Europe as a soul singer with a group called The Knockouts and singing 'Mustang Sally', he was being met with little enthusiasm and bad reviews. He couldn't understand it. Why did reporters write such lies about him? he asked. 'All the time I've been in the ring, I've never done or said anything to hurt anyone, and now these cats are throwing rocks at me in the papers. There are all those bad guys in the world going around doing bad things, but they don't get the bad publicity I do.'

He came across as a guileless, wounded man who put me in mind of the Lenny character in John Steinbeck's *Of Mice and Men*. He was, he told me, the youngest of thirteen children from a sharecropping South Carolina family. 'My father only had one arm on account of how they had to amputate the other after a car accident, so I was always my daddy's left hand. He was a hustler. He'd cut wood or chop cotton or be a junk man, collecting old cars and cutting up the metal. I was his baby, and he took me everywhere. Consequently, I was a mature man by the time I was 13.

'For my Daddy I never could do no wrong. Momma would go fussin' and give him the devil and say he was ruining me, but he didn't mind. He passed away in 1965. He knew I was fighting, but he never got the chance to see me as I am today. I wish he could have lived to enjoy himself and have some fun. I'd like to have shown him what living is really like, and for him to have shared with me the things I enjoy doing.'

He talked very softly with a slight nasal intonation, the result, probably, of a flattened boxer's nose. 'I've always been singing. I'm a Baptist and was in the church choir. My Daddy and me would always sing when we were working together. When I was 14, I volunteered for the army, but I flunked the tests. They give you all these blocks and squares and rangle-tangle triangles, and I couldn't do all of them. In 1964 they passed me 1-A, but by then I had a growing family, so I didn't have to go.'

He'd been married at 15 to a second cousin and moved to Philadelphia where he worked in an abattoir butchering cows, before taking up boxing and realising he could make a good living at it. 'I never feel any pity for any man than I beat. But I respect any man who signs that contract to fight me, because he knows I'm going to go out there to take him apart. When I punch a man and see him crumble and fall in his back, I feel great excitement. There's a great thrill in it.'

That being said, 'the most exciting thing I ever knew was to realise that I could have all I wanted and live a comfortable life. I didn't want to live like Daddy and Mom. I understand that they didn't have the opportunity, but they did for me what they did, and I'm gonna do better for my kids.'

Later in life he had some business problems, and he would die of liver cancer in 1977. Despite their rivalry, Muhammad Ali attended his funeral. In total, Smoking Joe would have eleven children, five with his wife, two of whom became boxers themselves.

I got to Muhammad Ali a couple of months later, on a private London to Manchester railway train that had been hired by Ovaltine for the day. I suppose the message would be 'Drink Ovaltine and become a superman like Ali'. He may not have been a superman, but he certainly was a superstar. In a dark grey suit and pale blue shirt, lying prone across all the three first class seats of an old-fashioned enclosed compartment, he was indeed something to behold. He did not, however, seem to behold me, keeping his eyes firmly closed throughout our entire meeting. While Joe Frazier had been polite and animated, Ali was bored. Stardom was new to Frazier. Ali had been a star all his adult life. And on the day that I met him he seemed a very tired star. Maybe it was the result of the tour of Nigeria he'd just done, during which General Gowon, the head of state of that country at the time, had conversationally mentioned that he, too, used to do some boxing.

'What did you box?' Ali was reported to have replied. 'Apples or oranges?'

Talking to me, Ali first went into his usual routine of mocking his opponents, Smokin' Joe Frazier being his most recent. 'He's dim,' he said. 'And one mo' thing. He's ugly, too.'

So, I asked about his children. Would he like them to be boxers?

At that, he seemed to wake up. 'Nah. Doctors, lawyers, Scientists, engineers. Never boxers. For me boxing was the best thing I could have done. It was the only way I could get rich. But, if I could, I'd have been a great doctor, or something like that.'

Then he fell back into another routine about how he was tired with fighting and wanted to dedicate his life 'to the freedom of the negroes in America… I'll unite them, and free them mentally. We have to build a whole nation for ourselves. A separate nation. We can't live with white Americans. It's impossible. The cultures are too different… We want to be free from the white man… I don't hate the white man. I know the white man. I don't hate snakes and tigers because I know them… Some white people can't live together. Some white Russians can't live with the Jewish Russians, white Englishmen can't live with white Turks. White Scotchmens can't live with white Dutchmens. Black men don't want to live with nobody but ourselves.'

He was on a roll, reciting from a well learned script that ended with one of his poems: 'Better far from all I see, to die fighting to be free…' And so on.

'Did you write that yourself?' I asked, knowing that his corner-man, Bundini Brown, had come up with the phrase, 'floats like butterfly and stings like a bee', which had become part of the hit song 'The Black Superman'. (Primary school children loved the line, 'I'm Ali, catch me if you can'. Not everyone has a song written about them.)

Ali was affronted by my question. 'I'm not only a great boxer. I'm genius. I ain't just a dumb negro boxer. I'm a great writer, too.'

Then he just went on and on again. The interview, such as it was, had finished before it had really got started. A few months later Ali appeared on the *Parkinson* chat show and fell into the same apartheid recitation only for Michael Parkinson to start to argue with him. That didn't go well. Not having debating skills, Ali got angry and began digging himself deeper into his argument. He'd expected a cosy, jokey conversation and he wasn't used to popular chat show hosts contradicting him.

Years later, Mike Parkinson would say that Ali had revealed himself to be a bigot that night. I disagree. Ali had simply been reciting a line that was fashionable with Black Muslims then. He remained a devoted Muslim for the rest of his life, but, by the time of his death in 2016, at the age of 74, he had rowed back from some of the sayings of Elijah Muhammad.

That he should have died of Parkinson's syndrome, thought to be probably the result of a career of too many blows to the head, seemed bleakly ironic for the golden boy who had made boxing fashionable again. But the really sad thing is, despite the ultimate calamity of his life, the 'greatest' of them all, as he proclaimed, young men, encouraged by newspapers and TV coverage, still pursue glory and risk brain damage in the boxing ring.

Ali wasn't the genius he said he was, but he was, for a time, the most famous man in the world, a generous philanthropist, a great sportsman and a globally admired beacon of light for many where light rarely shone. Unfortunately, I happened to meet him at the wrong moment. It's one of my regrets that I didn't talk to him in different circumstances. I don't believe any of his children ever did become doctors or lawyers. And, despite what he told me, two of his daughters did become boxers for a while.

One of the funniest books I've ever read was Spike Milligan's account of what happened to him after, as he put it, he 'received a cunningly worded invitation to partake in World War Two'. The memoir was called *Adolf Hitler: My Part In His Downfall*. It had a huge swastika on the front, and it was so funny I found myself giggling out loud on a plane from Rome to Sicily. This surprised the Egyptian lady sitting next to me, who, seeing the cover, had been unaware that there was anything funny about Hitler and the Nazis. But she didn't know Spike.

As the plane approached Sicily it began to buck and shudder, possibly due to the volcano billowing out of Mount Etna, which I was there to report on. But the Egyptian lady wasn't interested in volcanoes. Panicked by the plane's turbulence, she grabbed my arm and took away the book. A life and death situation might be happening, and she was about to enter eternity with the lunatic next to her finding something funny in a book about the Third Reich.

It struck me as a comedic situation, so I told Spike Milligan the following week when I went to see him at his office at Notting Hill Gate. Instantly, he began adding absurdist details that only he could imagine, laughing until tears filled his eyes.

That was Spike. Give him a germ of an idea and off he would run with it, making it crazier all the time. Poet, comedy writer and cartoonist, his work creating *The Goon Show* in the Fifies had set the compass for British comedy for the rest of the twentieth century.

I knew he suffered from depression, but that morning he was a one-man comedy show, telling stories about him and Harry Secombe, making his own nervous breakdown sound funny, and remembering the first time he played a clown in a children's nativity play. 'They'd given me blue to put on my face, but I thought it should have been black. Then in the last scene, when all the other children were crowded around the Virgin and Child, I wasn't supposed to go on. But I did anyway. It didn't seem fair. So, I went and stood by the manger. I thought the clown has a part in life. That cameo in my early life says it all.'

He was 54, and, as he talked about being wounded by a shell blast, which had left him with chronic anxiety and a stammer when he heard guns going off, a cloud of sadness suddenly appeared. He didn't know why no-one had ever asked him to play a clown in a film. He would have liked that, but maybe it was too late.

My favourite memory of him, though, will always be when he appeared on the *Parkinson* show and listened quietly as Parky recounted all the beautiful women in the life of fellow guest Roger Vadim. 'Brigitte Bardot, Catherine Deneuve, Jane Fonda...' went Parky.

'You can see why they call him Roger, can't you,' butted in Spike.

I never got to know George Harrison very well. That was my fault. After the success of 'Something' on the *Abbey Road* album, George was finally getting recognition as a songwriter. So, when he recorded his first solo album, *All Things Must Pass,* I wanted to talk to him. It could, however, never be arranged. He would have read my review of the record, so perhaps he was hurt that I mentioned 'My Sweet Lord's' similarity to the Chiffons' 'He's So Fine'. Maybe he also thought I was too close to Lennon and McCartney, which I was, or perhaps he thought I should have shown more interest when I'd found him talking to some other journalists about his spiritual journey into Indian mysticism. I should, but I'd known that mysticism was never going to get into the *Evening Standard.*

Whatever the reason, my requests for an interview had always been rebuffed, so when a children's charity Concert for Bangladesh at New York's Madison Square Garden was announced I thought this would be my opportunity. Arriving in New York I booked into my hotel room and put a call into John Lennon who I believed was in the same hotel.

He wasn't there, but, inviting me up to the Lennon's suite, I found Yoko in a quandary. John and George had fallen out after Yoko had insisted on being in the concert with George refusing to allow her on stage. Torn between his old friend and his wife, John had gone off to Kennedy Airport to fly back to Europe, and now Yoko had decided to follow him. There was, however, a problem. Her younger sister, Setsuko, who was in her early twenties, had specially flown from Switzerland, where she was a student, to New York for the concert, and she didn't know anyone in the city.

Then I, the solution, had appeared. Within minutes, Yoko had cancelled my little room, and moved me into one of the several bedrooms in the Lennons' suite, as she prepared to follow John back across the Atlantic. 'You can use the limousine, so ask the chauffeur to take you anywhere you want to go, and here in the hotel just sign everything "Lennon" plus fifteen per cent,' Yoko instructed.

And, as Pan American had misplaced my suitcase on my way over, she suggested I choose whatever I wanted of John's clothes, which he'd left behind in his hurry to leave. 'And if you need any money or anything at all just ask May Pang,' she added. May was a pretty, American girl I'd met in England earlier, who was on secondment to the Lennons from Allen Klein's office.

With that, Yoko was gone. I chose a blue gingham shirt and an expensive French black leather jacket of John's, which, although my suitcase was delivered the following day, I wore all weekend.

Setsuko and I got along well enough that weekend, but I can't remember that we had much in common for conversation as we were chauffeured around Manhattan in our stretched limo the next day, which was a Saturday. Then in the evening we were driven downtown for the concert. I'd expected to be somewhere at the back of the auditorium with the other journalists, but May Pang had arranged two seats in the front row for us.

It was a good concert, a real pop show with plenty of hits, 'While My Guitar Gently Weeps' and 'Here Comes the Sun'. And 17,000 New Yorkers, who'd been restless when Bangladeshi Ravi Shanker had opened, were ecstatic to see George on stage with Eric Clapton, Billy Preston, Leon Russell, Badfinger and Bob Dylan.

Then it was over, and Setsuko and I were being rushed out of our seats, across the stage and down a tunnel at the back to where nine limousines were waiting for the performers. Then, as barriers held back thousands of fans, off we went up a ramp and out into the street, a motorcade of rock limos, police motorcycles holding back the cross-town traffic. For a few minutes as we raced off to the post show party, I got an idea of how it must have felt like to be a Beatle.

'Glad you enjoyed the buzz,' John Lennon teased when I got home.

I had. But, as exciting and well-meaning as the concert had been, it had somehow felt like an exercise in nostalgia, a requiem for the Sixties.

I never did get to interview George Harrison. And whether the children of Bangladesh ever got all the twelve million dollars that the concert and its filming had raised for them, I don't know. I suspect not.

David Bowie had been a star in his own head before anyone noticed him. Fame had always been his ambition, which was true of quite a few people I interviewed. It was certainly the case with Muhammad Ali, Elvis, Mick Jagger and probably Paul McCartney. All of them would do something extraordinary to bring them to public notice, and in Bowie's case it was a record.

'Space Oddity' had been unlike anything else in the record charts in1969, and it captured the moment perfectly. There had been space stories in comics for generations, but space travel only became real for most people when the Apollo 11 moon mission put it on the TV news. To make it personal, however, took an act of extraordinary invention from Bowie with a song that saw the earth from the viewpoint of the lonely astronaut; one in which he described his vehicle through space as 'sitting in a tin can'.

It was a different view on things, but then Bowie was different, from his different coloured eyes to his deliberate taunting of the media about his bi-sexuality. Dusty Springfield had feared that if her sexuality had become known it would have ruined her career. But only a few months later Bowie was confident enough to have no such worries. Attitudes were changing and popular music was changing, too. He was helping that change.

'I think what I've done on stage is to create a kind of neuter state,' he told me during a break in recording at a Soho studio. 'It isn't unisex either, but it does incorporate both masculine and feminine aspects of sexuality. I think androgynous is the best word to describe it. I first realised I was bisexual when I was about thirteen or fourteen.'

Had he been frightened of public scorn?

'No. I was more frightened of football.' He thought about that for a second, then reconsidered. 'That makes me sound really fey, doesn't it? Actually, I've always been an outsider.'

But the outsider had suddenly become the focal point as other rock groups hastened to copy his on-stage sexual ambiguity. The fashion for 'glam rock' or 'rock and rouge', as it was called, bothered him. 'I really don't think they know why they do it. It's all part of a great misconception.'

Unlike the copycat groups, he'd always worn cosmetics. 'I first began to fool around with it when I was a mod. I used to wear ankle swingers and luminous socks. I wore Clearasil and eyeshadow then, too, and I've never got out of it. Elvis wore it, too. I like to change my appearance a lot. I'm narcissistic. My hair has been a variety of colours. Fortunately, it takes dyes well.

'Make-up isn't a new thing particularly. But I think it's become inevitable because of the indifference to long hair now. I mean, the only possible shock factor was that guys began to wear make-up. I suppose I knew that years ago because I've always been involved with shock tactics.'

As a shock tactic it worked to get him noticed. But he was much more than a shock tactic. I never cared for his Anthony Newley voice, but by repeatedly reinventing himself, as a stage actor as *The Elephant Man* in New York, and an extra-terrestrial alien in the film *The Man Who Fell To Earth*, he showed real creativity, while musically he was extremely influential. His early career in different little groups had been fraught with failure, and there was a three year gap between *Space Oddity* and *Ziggy Stardust* and on to 'Rebel Rebel, you've torn your dress, rebel rebel, your face is mess' with that mesmeric guitar riff. He took his time.

Years after our meeting, when he was married with two children and on his way to building an impressive art collection, he would regret the cocaine use that had led him to talk about fascism. Had he ever meant any of it? I don't know. He remained an enigma throughout his life. He died in 2016, a great producer and clever songwriter. For all his hits, such as 'Fame' and 'Let's Dance', there are few song lyrics as dramatic and hopelessly lonely as Major Tom's lines after he's lost contact with Ground Control in *Space Oddity*: 'Planet Earth is blue, and there's nothing I can do'.

Plum and I rented the ground floor of a house with a pool in the Algarve in September 1970. It was a traditional little Portuguese villa outside Albufeira, along a track and by a secluded beach. Louise, aged, four, worried that her grandfather might drown when he went water ski-ing for the first time, Dominic crawled after some cockerels, and I began my first novel on my portable Olivetti Lettera 22.

Many years later we went back to find the house. Its shell was still there, but it was now in the middle of a modern holiday village. The beach was no longer secluded. All that remained of our first holiday there were our old photographs. I was even more glad that I had taken them then.

19.

'A plastic bag half-filled with water titled Napoleon's bladder

When John Lennon left Britain to begin a new life in America in the summer of 1971, it represented something more for him than a change of country. Encouraged by Yoko, it was a decisive step in shedding what remained of his Beatles' skin, and, he hoped, re-inventing himself as a radical chic bohemian. He no longer wanted to be seen as just a rock star.

Assured of wealth for the rest of his life, his emigration was achieved in style as he and Yoko moved into two adjacent suites on the seventh floor of the St Regis Hotel on New York's E. 55th St. From there, John would fall in love with New York as Yoko showed him around what he described as her 'old stomping ground', in the city in which she'd begun her career as a conceptual artist.

A few weeks after they moved to America, they invited me to join them in the St Regis, and to celebrate John's 31st birthday at an exhibition of Yoko's art at Syracuse University in upstate New York. As soon as I arrived at the hotel, John was enthusing about his new hometown. In a grand suite stacked with newspapers, magazines, fan mail, posters, and film editing and early video equipment, he raved about how the jaunty abrasiveness of New Yorkers reminded him so much of the people of his Liverpool youth. Like all his passions, he threw himself into it with high enthusiasm.

'Look at this,' he said, picking up a letter. 'A university in Tennessee is offering me sixty thousand dollars just to talk. *Just to talk!* I don't even have to bother singing! It's unbelievable. Invitations like this come every day.'

The following day we all flew up to Syracuse. With us, among others, was secretary, May Pang, who was now on loan to Yoko from Allen Klein's office. Also with us was Phil Spector, and a young woman companion, who looked, I thought, happily stoned.

When we got to Syracuse, unabashed academics, as much as students, mobbed the ex-Beatle and his wife, which appealed to John's new image of himself. 'I've bet Yoko a thousand dollars that somebody somewhere will write an article which really understands her work before the end of this year,' he said. Then came the inevitable joke. 'If nobody writes it, I'll have to write it myself ...'

The event was called 'This Is Not Here'. Yoko explained it in this way: 'I'm trying to get across the idea that the art is in the people who come to see it. It's like saying, "you are important, not the objects". It's the people's reactions that are important. Everyone is an artist, but some people are more intimidated by art than others. No one can say that Ringo's contribution is less important than that of Andy Warhol or Jasper Johns or John Cage.'

'In fact,' interrupted John, 'some of the ideas sent in by some very big names were very disappointing. The best ones came from those who consider themselves non-artists. Who wasn't an artist as a child? But when you're twelve there's always somebody who says, "now go and do your chemistry".'

As we moved around the exhibition, the theme of which was 'water', John pointed out contributions by Warhol, Bob Dylan, Allen Ginsberg and Willem de Kooning, letting it be known that he wanted to be considered an artist, too. His own piece was inevitably, another joke, a plastic bag, half-filled with water, and titled 'Napoleon's Bladder'.

We were all staying in a Holiday Inn, and, later that day, there was a small birthday party for John in one of the bigger suites in the hotel. There he sat singing 'Give Peace A Chance' and other songs for a group of Syracuse students and lecturers, as Ringo and his then wife, Maureen, Yoko's sister, Setsuko and her boyfriend, ate slices of cake and joined in. John's career as a musician had meant that there had been no college for him after the age of eighteen, so to be lionised at a university was flattering.

It was a happy day, but it ended on a sour note. Accompanying us on the trip up to Syracuse were several tough-looking New York bodyguards. On returning to my own room to get some cigarettes, I discovered some of them were having a party of their own; taking it in turns with the young woman who had accompanied Phil Spector on the flight up from New York.

'Hey, you wanna have a go...?' I was asked by one, as he saw me passing in the corridor. When you are seen to be a friend of someone extremely famous, the hangers-on always address you in a very friendly way.

No, I didn't, I said, and, continued back to the party, where I told John what was happening. He looked puzzled, surprised. Then he said quietly: 'Don't tell Yoko.' Which was something he repeated the following day when he asked for more details.

If John was being protective of Yoko it would have been ironic, because, before she'd met him, Yoko had been a tough and self-reliant person. It was indeed her independence that had attracted him. Or was he afraid that she would have flipped angrily had she found out that behind her back her big day was being sullied?

I'd seen nothing to suggest that the young woman was averse to what happened. But it was a depressing moment.

Although I met him several times, I never got to know Phil Spector. And, in truth, I really can't remember anything positive that anyone ever said about him, other than that he was brilliant when it came to making hit records.

Always liking the idea of being on the side of the underdog, the following day John metaphorically put on his protest hat, and, followed by a caravan of media vehicles, off we went in a limo to visit a tiny Native American reservation. It appeared that the people there were taking on the state of New York which was claiming the right to build a road through their land, so a visit by an ex-Beatle couldn't hurt their campaign.

Whether or not it helped, I have no idea, but, unknown to John, the regular demonstrations with which he was then becoming associated were not going unnoticed. The FBI was already compiling a file on him as an anti-war activist. Had they seen it, the Lennons' suites in the St Regis would have looked to the FBI like the headquarters of a counterculture movement, as arch activists, Abbie Hoffman and Jerry Rubin, had quickly latched on to the ex-Beatle. For John, it turned out to be just another passing enthusiasm.

'It was Yoko who sold me on New York,' he would say about his new home. 'She made me walk around the streets and parks and squares to examine every nook and cranny. You could say I fell in love with New York on a street corner.'

The street corner he most fancied was that at number 1 West 72nd Street, which housed the gothic, millionaires' Dakota apartment building. The block offered a spectacular view across Central Park, and, while I was staying with them at the St Regis, John put on a suit and tie to go and be interviewed by the reputedly stuffy board of residents there. He was not amused when Yoko's choice of dress for the interview was a pair of floral hot pants and blouse with the top three buttons undone. Angrily, he insisted that she wear something more dignified for the visit. 'You look like a tart, a fucking whore', he suddenly raged. And, since I had a friend whom I'd previously visited there, and knew how smart an address the place was, he turned to me for support. 'Tell her, Ray.'

It was an embarrassing moment, but, without a murmur, Yoko left the room to return in something more formal and John's verbal attack was forgotten. That said, it must have been humiliating for her. When it came down to it, John knew very well how to be the well-mannered, middle class young man he had been brought up to be. But he knew how to be a bully, too, a side of him that I hadn't seen before. I expect his first wife Cynthia had.

Despite his artistic pretensions and self-proclamations, John was always a rocker at heart and one day in New York he told me rather regretfully that since his divorce from Cynthia he'd lost track of his boyhood collection of early Elvis records. A quick phone call to a publicist at RCA Records fixed that, and a few days later an entire collection of Elvis's singles (including, sadly, the rubbish film ones) was delivered to the Lennons' suite. According to Sean Lennon, 'Hound Dog' was still on the juke box in the kitchen at the Dakota apartment ten years later when John died.

Relations with Paul were still abysmal, and just before I returned to London, John asked me for a favour. Would I mind being a go-between and ask Paul to get in touch with him without the lawyers, Allen Klein or the Eastmans knowing. It concerned a song writing matter, and he was worried that if he rang Paul, out of the blue, they would 'be at each-others' throats' before they'd even started talking.

Back in England, I delivered the message, but whether the two of them ever resolved the issue without lawyers, I very much doubt. Paul's father advised me not to get involved.

The following February, Plum and I took our children back to Ormskirk to see Plum's father and my mother. We were returning to London when I bought a newspaper at a motorway service station and read about the murder of Gale Ann Benson. The chief suspect was Michael X (aka Michael de Freitas and Michael Abdul Malik) and he had apparently gone on the run to Guyana. I knew Gale Benson, too.

In her mid-twenties, she was the daughter of a Conservative MP and had suddenly turned up at the *Evening Standard* one lunchtime some months earlier, demanding that I interview her boyfriend. He was Hakim Jamal, who she described as 'a black militant author'. She was highly strung and had brought with her some scrapbooks and a stack of documents, which, she said, showed that the 'US Government is engaged in a policy of genocide towards black Americans'.

That didn't sound like an interview for my page. It wasn't my subject. I was more interested in learning how this young English woman, who had been educated at the French Lycée in South Kensington, had become involved with Hakim Jamal. But I promised to read her boyfriend's book, *From A Dead Level,* and hoped that she would leave me to get on with my work.

She did eventually … but then she managed to get my phone number, from, I presume, Michael X, who, I imagine, had got it from John Lennon, and began to pester me at home. Then one night Hakim Jamal rang me himself, and, after berating me as a 'fucking racist' because I wouldn't interview him, he bellowed down the phone. 'I am God. Hear that!' and hung up.

All in a day's work, I thought, and forgot about Gale Benson until I saw the newspaper photograph of her body being exhumed from a hole in the ground in Trinidad.

I never understood why John Lennon had become involved with Michael X. The guy was obviously bad news. On one occasion he'd tried to get me to interview him, too, and we'd talked for over and hour, before he went off the idea when I told him that I would have to ask him about his previous job as a pimp and a rent collector for landlord racketeer, Peter Rachman. An interview with him would never have got in the paper then anyway, as, at the time, he was on bail on a charge of demanding money with menaces.

It seems that shortly after I met Gale Benson, Michael X had jumped bail when someone, almost certainly, I again suspect, John Lennon, funded him to fly to Trinidad. Going with him was his wife Desiree ('You know how Michael is,' she'd told me, 'he wouldn't hurt a fly') and their four children. Once in Trinidad, Michael X set up a commune. Tragically for Gale Benson, she and Jamal went to stay there, where, it was alleged, one morning several men, said to have included Michael X, showed her a newly dug hole in the ground. On asking what the hole was for, she was told it was for her. Whereupon she was knifed and pushed into the hole.

A post-mortem would find that she had inhaled soil in her lungs. So, she had, in effect, been buried alive. Michael X, it would be said in court, had ordered her execution because she was causing Hakim Jamal 'mental strain'.

By the time her body was discovered, boyfriend Jamal had left Trinidad. He would be shot dead in America a year later. Michael X was soon captured in Guyana and returned to Trinidad. Although he was charged with Gale Benson's murder, he was never tried for it, having already been sentenced to death for another killing at the commune he ran.

John Lennon, a long-time public opponent of capital punishment, paid for a defence lawyer and added his name to a plea for clemency for the man who had leeched off him in London. But it was to no avail. Three years later, in May 1975, Michael X was hanged in Trinidad.

20.

'What if our boy runs off to join a fair?'
- David Puttnam

No-one sets out to write a film that might one day turn into a minor cult. But, by accident, I did, when fifty years ago I wrote a movie called *That'll Be The Day.* I'd always been a film fan, but, although I'd reviewed some films for the London *Evening Standard,* I'd never actually seen a screenplay. Then one Saturday in 1972, I went to a friend's house to borrow a book.

He was David Puttnam. We'd met through Mike McCartney, and, as Mike had predicted, we got on very well. After a successful career in advertising and then as a photographers' agent, David Puttnam had recently become a film producer in partnership with Sandy Lieberson, who had just produced the Mick Jagger film *Performance.* As David gave me the book I'd come for, we were having a cup of tea, when he asked me, out of nowhere, if I'd like to write a film for him.

He had an idea that had come from a song by Harry Nilsson. I knew Harry and I knew the song. It was '1941', and was about a boy of our generation, whose father had abandoned his wife and son; and who, when the boy reaches his teens, runs off to join a circus.

'What if our boy runs off to join a fair?' David suggested. To us fairgrounds had been the only place where we could hear rock music played *LOUD*, the way it was supposed to be heard. At the same time, fairs suggested a dangerous glamour that was at odds with the ambitious lives our parents wanted for us.

'Qualifications,' was probably every mother's mantra in the Fifties, but teenage rebellion was more romantic for a movie than qualifications could ever be. So, that afternoon, David and I invented a clever grammar-school boy who, breaking all the rules, spurns the chance to go to university, and pursues a rake's progress before he discovers his real path in life.

What we wanted was to recapture the excitement of our rights of passage years through the music of our youth. We didn't want to make a plucky Brits wartime film, or a kitchen sink, grim-up-north story, and absolutely not a larky 'darling-we're-the-young-ones' holiday jaunt. For us it had to be real, about how our generation had been in that Fifties period, just before the Beatles and the Sixties changed everything. It would be a film, as we liked to remind ourselves, about the day before yesterday.

Over the next few months, as I worked on the script late into the night, I learned how to write a screenplay, with David coming for his breakfast a couple of times a week to see how I was getting on.

Along the way, I learned a few things about movies. One was that no matter how wayward a lead character might be, he has to either have some wonderful redeeming grace or be devilishly good looking and loveable. Unfortunately, the character I created, Jim Maclaine, had all the selfishness of teenagers everywhere and didn't do one decent thing in the entire script. Audiences might hate him, we worried. Then one night David Puttnam took his children to see a West End show called *Godspell.*

He rang me first thing the next morning: 'I think we've found our boy,' he said. The young actor playing the lead in *Godspell* was David Essex, who was so winning and good-looking that a cinema audience would forgive him anything. They did.

A second lesson was to do with research. I'd never worked on a fair, but the boyfriend of our American au pair at the time had; and he gave me a rundown of all the tricks used to rip off the punters.

'On the dodgems, you have to always give them their change when the cars are moving. That way they can't check it,' he told me. 'And wear your pants with the biggest pockets.' That all went straight into the screenplay.

I'd never been to a Butlins' holiday camp, either, but I knew that Ringo Starr had played in one with Rory Storm during his pre-Beatle days. So, David and I had lunch with the ex-Beatle and Neil Aspinall, once the Beatles road manager and by then the managing director of their company, Apple Corps. We struck lucky again. The two amused us so much that Ringo was offered a part in our film, with Neil Aspinall putting together a group to play in our holiday camp, that included Keith Moon and Jack Bruce of Cream. Then Neil got Billy Fury to front it.

What had started out as a screenplay around the life of a clever boy, who writes jokey poetry about Monica's Mouth Organ, Madame de Pompadour and the War of Jenkins' Ear, and who chucks his books into a stream on the day he should be sitting A-level history, was becoming, by degrees, a rock and roll movie.

The third lesson I learned was that a screenwriter had to be, like a journalist, infinitely adaptable. We'd always intended to have a few songs in our film, but, when it turned out that its financing depended on there being a double album of famous hit records, I rewrote sections of the screenplay to fit them all in. In that way we might hear 15 seconds of 'Sealed With A Kiss' if the screen action is, for example, on the big wheel, a smidgen of 'Runaround Sue' when we cut to the dodgem cars and a fragment of 'Great Balls of Fire' by the time we reached the whip. One of my fondest memories of that time was sitting with David Puttnam going through our 'Oldies But Goldies' books and choosing our favourite records. That was how we arrived at the film's perfect title, *That'll Be The Day*. David didn't get the rights to use all the records we wanted, but he got enough. I've seen it written that we got the idea of using Fifties' records on the soundtrack after seeing *American Graffiti*. But that wasn't true. We'd finished shooting *That'll Be The Day* before we saw *American Graffiti*.

Some weeks before our film went into production, I took Plum into hospital for the birth of our third child, leaving Louise, 4, and Dominic, 2, in the care of our au pair. It was a showery day and when I got back, I found the au pair chatting in the sitting room with a boy who had just arrived from Chicago, while the children were outside in the sandpit, crying in the pouring rain. Rushing out, I picked them up, ran the bath and put them both in. The au pair came into the bathroom while I was bathing them and said that she was very sorry. I said, so was I, and sacked her.

So, I was already in a bit of a state when, having now asked a neighbour to take care of Louise and Dominic, I returned to the hospital to see how Plum was getting on.

'She's in the delivery room,' a young nurse told me.

'Really? So soon?' I was astonished. Louise had taken a day and two nights to be born.

'Yes. You're just in time to be with her.' And she led me towards the delivery room.

I stopped outside. 'Actually, I'll wait here,' I said. I hadn't been present when either of our first two babies had been born. Fathers weren't encouraged to witness such things in those days.

But the nurse was a disciple in the modern way. 'Oh, but you must. It's a wonderful moment for you as well as your wife.'

'I'm sure it is but…I think I'll just stay here until it's all over,' I insisted.

'Well, all right. But if you really don't want to go in, you can watch from here,' she said. And, pulling back a flap on the door to the delivery room, she peered inside. 'Oh look, I think the baby's just about…'

'Really…!'

'Yes. It's coming. The baby's coming… See!' And stepping away, the nurse held the flap open for me to peer inside.

She was right. It was indeed an exciting, wonderful moment, with a doctor and nurses surrounding the birthing bed, the mother's legs apart and her feet up in the stirrups, as someone else waited, like a scrumhalf behind the ruck, to take the baby as it emerged.

'Go on, Plum,' I was thinking, 'one last push…' And then: 'Yes, *yes*. Well done, Plum!'

At which point I heard the voice of a senior nurse behind me. 'What's going on here?'

'Oh, Mr Connolly didn't want to be present in Delivery while Mrs Connolly was giving birth. So, he's watching his wife from here,' explained the young nurse.

There was a puzzled silence and then. 'But that isn't Mrs Connolly. It's Mrs Hooper.'

'What? Not Plum?' I closed the flap on the door.

'I thought…' began the young nurse. Then, catching the thunder on the face of the senior nurse, she hurried me away from the Delivery Room.

We found Plum a few minutes later, sitting up in bed in a ward of other expectant mothers, reading *Cosmopolitan*, and eating a small bunch of grapes.

'I've just seen you have a baby,' I told her. 'And, oh yes, I've sacked the au pair.'

Kieron Connolly was born two days later. Once again, I turned up at the moment of delivery, but, when invited again to observe the miracle, I declined and went off to buy some flowers, only arriving back when it was safe to do so. I've never liked anything messy.

Filming *That'll Be The Day* took place mainly on the Isle of Wight, because, in the early Seventies, we thought the island still had a look of the Fifties about it. The cast and crew went by ferry, apart from Keith Moon, who astonished our director, Claude Whatham, by arriving in a helicopter. Ringo arrived in a chauffeur-driven car, choosing to wear, for much of the film, the teddy boy outfit he'd had specially made for the *Magical Mystery Tour* launch party.

It was a happy, busy shoot, with the secondary characters of Rosemary Leach, as the long-suffering but determined-to-cope mother, Rosalind Ayres as the anti-hero's girlfriend and Robert Lindsay, in his first film role, as Terry, his earnest, goody-goody school pal. I've sometimes thought I had more in common with Terry, who goes off to university, than the Jim Maclaine character. But a film about a boy who does all the worthy things, wouldn't have been much fun to go and see at the pictures.

As I was busy working at the *Evening Standard,* I wasn't present during the first week of shooting. But, with the rushes being sent back to London for overnight processing, I remember sitting with co-producer Sandy Lieberson in a viewing theatre and seeing for the first time David Essex and Ringo saying my lines as they walked through the holiday camp. For some reason, I was surprised to hear my words being spoken up there on the screen, although it was much as I'd imagined it when I'd been writing the screenplay.

After that, I got down to the set as often as possible, taking the Puttnams' five year old son, Sacha, to join the unit where he would be playing the young Jim Maclaine in the opening sequence; and writing an extra scene in which Ringo and David Essex play snooker. We'd realised that all Ringo's work would be finished half a day early, and he was so good we wanted more of him. He was happy to do it, but he was also determined to catch the last ferry to Portsmouth, whether or not the scene was finished. As I grabbed a lift with him back to London that night, it occurred to me that while the film was the biggest thing in my career, Ringo had had bigger days.

Meanwhile, as editing followed filming, back at the day job, the interviews, reviews and news stories for the *Evening Standard* kept on coming. Now I sometimes wrote for the *Radio Times,* too. For them there was Morecambe and Wise, Eric telling me how when he had his first heart-attack he'd taken a taxi to the hospital. By the time they got there he'd been clutching his chest in agony.

'Can you give me your autograph before you go?' the taxi driver said.

Then there was a criss-cross tour of America that took me to Sam Phillips (the man at Sun Records who had discovered Elvis and Carl Perkins), and Roy Orbison, who invited me to stay at his house when it was too late to drive back to Nashville. Like nearly everybody of my generation, I'd been an Orbison fan since 'Only The Lonely' so it was good to discover that he really was as nice as everyone said. But he never took off his dark glasses the whole time I was there.

Then, for the *Evening Standard,* there was a long conversation with award-winning photo-journalist Don McCullin, whose pictures I'd first used when I'd been a student magazine editor at the LSE. Don had seen incomprehensible amounts of death and misery in his career covering wars and he described very well what a photograph could do.

'A single shot,' he said, 'can sum up the human condition better than any film. Newsreel fills the hungry stomach of television. When something is going by so quickly, it doesn't give you chance to hold it in your mind. But when people see a single frame, they can look and consider it for much longer, and get to think about what it really means. On television, something immediately follows; frame follows frame, item follows item, programme follows programme, so that the original image is gradually nudged out of your consciousness.'

Born in 1936, the son of an asthmatic street trader, Don had grown up in a Kings Cross basement flat, his parents and brother all sleeping in one room. 'I didn't have it worse than thousands of other people, but, when I now see poor people, I know what it's like to be poor and helpless.' His father had died at forty. Don was 15.

'I can still remember the muffled sounds of tragedy, of the bobby coming round to the house to tell my mum to go to the hospital. Me and my younger brother were ushered into the house next door. To take my mind off it, they gave me a whole pile of *National Geographic* magazines to look through. I've still got those magazines.'

He'd been frightened many times when he was in the presence of butchery, but he came nearest to death when he was hit by a mortar bomb splinter in an ambush in Cambodia. At first, he thought his face was smashed, but his fingers could feel the contours. Then he felt something warm running down his leg.

'I was terrified, I thought my wedding tackle had gone. So, I crawled to a ditch and pulled my pants down to see how badly injured I was. It wasn't that bad. That was the worst battle I've been in. But in the confusion, I'd stopped taking pictures. I was upset about that.'

Another interviewee from North London was a very successful, young commercials director called Alan Parker who had just spent £30,000 on his own TV film. 'Until I did it, I wasn't able to impress on anyone that I could do anything longer than a minute of screen time,' he said.

It was a gamble. Alan would carry a chip on his shoulder for life that he hadn't been to university, but he never lacked self-confidence. Eventually, he sold his film to the BBC, and would go on to make, among other movies, *Bugsy Malone*, *The Commitments* and *Midnight Express*. Then there was *Fame* and that great Irene Cara celebration of youthful ambition in song: 'Fame, I'm gonna live forever, I'm gonna learn how to fly…Fly!'

David Bailey hadn't been to university either, 'nor even a grammar school,' he would say. But, in the days before art college education became a stepping-stone to a career as a photographer, Bailey had begun his career as a dogsbody in a studio, having brought a camera while doing his National Service in the RAF.

As we talked, he'd just found out that a documentary he'd made about Andy Warhol for the BBC had been banned because someone there had been offended. He was merrily scornful. 'You can't make a film about Andy Warhol without having a few transvestites about the place, can you? It would be like making a film about a jockey without having a bloody horse in the show.'

He had become one of the 'faces' of 'Swinging London' and had seen a character based on himself played by David Hemmings in the Michelangelo Antonioni film *Blow Up*. It all looked very glamourous, but success had taken years to arrive. 'I had to work from eight in the morning until ten at night, and then be up half the night developing. Everybody was talking about swinging London, but I didn't know where it was.'

I interviewed footballers, too, Jimmy Greaves, Pat Jennings, Peter Osgood, Francis Lee (who was just starting a business turning recycled newspapers into toilet paper), and Peter Storey. He was an aggressive guy on the field, and the *Evening Standard's* sports editor asked me not to print Storey's comments as they might wreck the paper's relationship with Arsenal FC.

Ann-Margret had seen her character in the script of *Carnal Knowledge* described as a 'tub of lard', but, married to Roger Smith of *77 Sunset Strip*, she was a real bobby-dazzler. The only person I ever met who grew up in a funeral parlour and slept next door to the mortuary with its open coffins, she was perfect eye-candy for Sixties Hollywood. Like so many beautiful women, though, her looks probably got in the way of her talent. She was good.

I always reckoned that I could spot a hit, but when I told Jimmy Cliff that the theme song from his terrific film *The Harder They Come* would be a number one he just laughed. He *knew* it wouldn't be, he insisted. He was right. But, in a way, it did better than that. It became a standard, with a very long life. I loved the lyrics, especially the line 'And they think that they have got the battle won, I say "forgive them, Lord, they know not what they've done"'. Some songs just take a little longer than others to be noticed. 'Too Many Rivers To Cross' and 'You Can Get It If You Really Want', both of which were in the film, wouldn't be instant hits either, but we still know them.

Around that time, I was involved in making a documentary about the BBC's pop music station Radio 1, which involved going out to a hospital at Stoke Mandeville to interview, on film, the disc jockey Jimmy Savile. For some reason he was delayed, so, while we were setting up the camera, I chatted to a young woman who had helped us arrange the interview.

'Jimmy likes young people,' she told me.

Yes, I thought. He's such an odd bloke, so unattractive and silly, he probably likes to big himself up in front of kids to make him feel important.

Then Savile appeared, we did the interview and I forgot all about him. Only years later, in 2011, after his death, when allegations against him of sexual abusing young girls appeared, did I remember the conversation at Stoke Mandeville. Had the young woman been trying to tell me something?

When *That'll Be The Day* was released in April 1973, I had no idea how it would be received. Friends who'd been to screenings told me that they'd enjoyed it, but that's what friends are for, isn't it, to kindly lie when you want them to? The best I was hoping was that it wouldn't be ridiculed, or just ignored by the critics. So, when Barry Norman, whom I'd never met, said a few disobliging things on the BBC's Film'73 the night before our film went into the cinemas, I was devastated. A very kind review in the *New Statesman* lifted my mood, and then dozens of good reviews eventually picked me up again. But Barry's words still rankled. So, when a journalist I knew, Rod Gilchrist, congratulated me on the good notices all I could think to say was: 'Thank you. Everyone liked it apart from that cunt Barry Norman.' That was a word I never used, so it shows how upset I still was.

A few months later at a screening for another film, a familiar face from television approached. 'Hello, Ray. It's that cunt Barry Norman. Good to meet you.'

It was a brilliant way for Barry to introduce himself and defuse any possible rancour. We laughed, had a drink together and I drove Barry back to the station that night, friends ever after. On reflection, he was probably right with a couple of his criticisms. My misfortune had been that I heard them before I read the nice things other critics said.

Only when the movie played to full houses around the country did the marketing strategy behind the *That'll Be The Day* double album become apparent, clips from the film being used to promote the record through TV commercials. The album topped the LP chart for weeks and virtually everyone we knew had a copy. Both David Puttnam and I were given gold celebratory records for it, too, although the only thing I'd done had been to choose my favourite songs.

That month was a double whammy for me in that my first novel, *A Girl Who Came To Stay,* was published at almost the same time as the film was released, as well as my *That'll Be The Day* novella. It was exciting when the magazine *Honey* serialised *A Girl Who Came To Stay* and producer Tony Garnett, famous from *Cathy Come Home*, optioned it for a TV film, though the film never happened. They rarely do. Nor was I surprised when Ken Loach, the other half of the Garnett and Loach team who had made *Kes* (still one of my all-time favourite films) didn't go for it. It was hardly Ken Loach material.

Today when *That'll Be The Day* is frequently shown on television, I watch it with fondness and surprise. Not that I like everything about it, particularly one scene when the David Essex character has sex with a young girl on the grass at the fair, while the Everly Brothers' record 'Devoted To You' plays ironically in the background. When the film's editor, Mike Bradsell, saw the rushes of that scene he sent an angry note to director Claude Whatham saying that the action of the Jim Maclaine character had been much more forceful than had been suggested in the script.

That was true. My thought when writing it had been that the girl had been enjoying some heavy petting which had gone too far, and she'd immediately regretted it. Claude had directed it differently. I always want to apologise for that bit.

The entire film only cost £210,000 to make, which is just over a million in today's money, with all the principals being paid around £5,000 each. That was a fortune for me at the time, but, I suspect, rather less of one for Ringo. I spent some of my money putting a deposit down on a big, classic, white Citroen DS that had headlights that swivelled around corners and a suspension that made it rise six inches off the ground when the engine was started. They don't make cars like that anymore. I'm glad we had one when they did. I wish I still had it.

By the Seventies much of the devastation caused by wartime bombing in London had been cleared away, but I was occasionally reminded of it when, while digging our garden, I would find occasional shards of splintered glass in the soil. They were the result, I assumed, of a bomb having exploded somewhere nearby, that had blasted the windows of our Victorian house. It all seemed a very long time ago, until one quiet Sunday morning, I came across the real thing, an unexploded World War 2 bomb, about eighteen inches long, just across the road.

It must have been unearthed by an excavator on a site that was being developed for the new Kensington and Chelsea Town Hall, and hadn't been noticed when the soil and clay had been pushed to the edge of the pavement.

So, I phoned the police and very soon an Army bomb disposal team arrived and ordered everyone to stay inside our homes. Then, carrying the bomb across the building site to a remaining air raid shelter, they set off a controlled explosion.

In her novel, *Life After Life,* Kate Atkinson, relates a night when such a bomb, along with many others, landed in the streets around our house in Kensington at about the time that I was being born two hundred miles away. In this way, the history of some pieces of broken glass reappear in fiction, and fiction captures history.

21

'Show me a boy who never wanted
to be a rock star
and I'll show you a liar'

Even before *That'll Be The Day* was released, David Puttnam was thinking about a sequel, telling me that the public would be soon 'demanding' to know what happened after that final image of David Essex buying a guitar. Which, by the way, was scripted and nicked from the last frozen frame of Truffaut's *Les Quatre Cents Coups*.

What David wanted to know was: 'Do we do the sequel for the theatre or as a film?' As I knew even less about theatre than movies, I plumped for a film. So, to plan it, I joined David and Patsy Puttnam on their family holiday in Italy that summer.

This time we knew from the beginning that we were going to make a film about rock music. It would be *the* story of young Britain's obsession with pop groups in the Sixties, and to produce much of the music we got Dave Edmunds of 'I Hear You Knocking' fame. I'd never met him, but when I went to see him working on the music at Rockfield in South Wales, I discovered that he was a brilliantly talented one-man band and engineer in the recording studio. Except for our *Stardust* rock opera, *Dea Sancta,* he played all the instruments, did much of the singing and produced and mixed all the tapes himself. He'd left school at fifteen to work as a trainee mechanic in a garage, but then he'd taught himself to play the guitar. Musically there seemed to be nothing he couldn't do.

David Essex hadn't sung in *That'll Be the Day*, but in the gap between the two films, he'd become a teen idol with his record 'Rock On'. So, we now had our very own rock star to play the leading part. What we were not going to get, however, was a Beatle, with Ringo declining to repeat his role. It was his loss, I think. He could have had a decent second career in movies. He could certainly act. But did he feel that some of the script was too close to his Beatles' experiences? We never knew.

Adam Faith got the part instead. Initially, I was dead set against him, and Michael Apted, our new director, who, incidentally, had turned down *That'll Be The Day*, was also unsure. David Puttnam, however, was insistent. Most producers would have pulled rank on me and sent me back to my typewriter at that point. But this producer liked writers and dragged me to meet Adam, who immediately did to me what his character does to all those who stand in his way in the film. He chatted me out of my doubts. He was slyly perfect in the part.

Until a couple of weeks before shooting began, Tony Curtis was expected to play the American rock manager. He was all very chatty and friendly when we met in London to talk about the film. But then his agent, Swifty Lazar (a great name for a Hollywood agent), demanded a fee that was somewhere in the region of a third of the movie's budget, and the film couldn't afford him. So, at the last minute, Columbia Pictures, who had the US distribution rights, replaced him with Larry Hagman, a US television actor whom none of us then knew.

I'd originally written that the part be played as a New York Italian called DiGillio, and, like a good pro, Hagman had prepared for it with a Bronx accent. When he arrived in London, however, and we met him, he and we quickly decided that he would be more comfortable playing the character as a Texan, whom I now renamed Porter Lee Austin, after Larry's birthplace in Austin, Texas. A few years later Larry would be given the part of JR in the TV series *Dallas*, and, when asked by *Playboy* magazine where he got the JR character from, he happily admitted that his performance had come from his role in *Stardust*.

To give the film authenticity, Michael Apted was keen to have some of the smaller parts played by people in the rock or television business, so we got my old friend Marty Wilde as a manager, and American star Ed Byrnes, Kookie from *Sunset Strip,* as a TV presenter.

Nineteen seventy-four was a time of three day weeks and nine hour rota power cuts during the miners' strike, with TV closing down at 10.30 pm to save power, so until the last minute we weren't sure whether shooting on *Stardust* would even begin.

It did on a February morning at a modern church in West London where a few dozen extras had been hired to mob our fictional rock star, Jim Maclaine, as played by David Essex. They weren't necessary. As David Essex left the church in his film role, hundreds of local girls, who must have bunked off school, mobbed him as he fought his way to a limousine carrying his fictional son, who happened to be four-year old Dominic Connolly. 'All these girls were screaming at me,' Dominic told his mother when he got home.

As his own rock fame was growing by the day, it can't have been easy for David Essex to play a fictional rock star. And it probably wasn't easy for Keith Moon either, who would now be central to our invented band. With The Who he was used to fan adoration when he played to stadiums, but to us he was just another actor playing a small part as well as miming playing the drums which Dave Edmunds had pre-recorded. That probably didn't sit well with his ego either.

Desperate, as he always was, to be the centre of attention, and this being the time of the record 'The Streaker', he would wander naked around our hotel car park in Lancashire at four in the morning, just when the crew were returning from a night shoot. On another occasion he 'borrowed' the unit carpenter's tool bag and sawed the door of his hotel room in half, so that he could hang his head out of it like a horse in a stable.

You never quite knew where you were with Keith. Very friendly, amusing and likeable at one moment, he could be a real pest the next, and very irritating. Which he was one night in Manchester when he and I fell out, with him trying to hit me. Naturally, I responded, whereupon a scrum of production assistants descended on the wrestling drummer and writer. 'Don't hit his face,' the make-up artist shouted to me. 'He's been made up.' Presumably, blows to any other part of the drummer's body that wouldn't have shown on camera would have been fine. The following day, Keith and I were good friends again, the little spat forgotten.

Five years later I bumped into him in a bar in Chelsea one evening. He was his usual fond, ebullient, outrageous self, but his chucking pills into the air and catching and swallowing them like a seal was disturbing. He would be found dead in bed a week or so later at the age of 32.

Before filming had begun, realising that we were possibly on a winning run after *That'll Be They Day*, the thought occurred that perhaps we should extend the franchise (although we didn't use that term then) and carry the story on to a third film. We could have easily done that, and, probably, profitably, too. Thankfully, we resisted the temptation. A couple of years' earlier I'd written the obituaries of three young rock stars, two of whom, Jimi Hendrix and Janis Joplin, I'd interviewed. So, it seemed appropriate that the downward druggy spiral of Jim Maclaine should end badly. While the remote Moorish castle, near Guadix, in southern Spain that, along with the associate producer Gavrik Losey, Michael Apted and I chose for the final scenes, insisted on high drama.

We couldn't have got anyone better in the world for the part of Jim Maclaine than David Essex at that age and that time in his career. The last twenty minutes are my favourite part of the film, with the boxing match in the courtyard, the tab of LSD given spitefully to the dog, Jim Maclaine in his bath, fully clothed, and then in his white suit for the final TV interview.

Movies are rarely made in the order that the story ends up on the screen. And *Stardust* was no exception, with the American scenes coming at the end of the shoot, after which Larry Hagman invited all the principals down to his house in Malibu. After six weeks together, we'd got to know Larry and his wife pretty well, but we were all astonished when, after dinner, they led us into a veranda where, without warning, they took off all their clothes, and, standing naked, invited us to get into their jacuzzi with them.

One by one, trying to hide our nakedness from each other by undressing behind the palms and potted plants that peopled the veranda, we quickly climbed into the bubbling water. Mrs Hagman, it seemed, did a side-line as a jacuzzi designer, about which she was telling us, when an internal phone rang close to where Larry was sitting.

'Hi. Sure. Come on in and join us,' he said putting the phone down.

At which point, two glamorous Hollywood wives, big hair and tight jeans, made their way into the veranda, took off all their clothes, too, and climbed into the jacuzzi, one on either side of me.

They were, we discovered, a couple of Larry's neighbours whose husbands were away on location. And, with nothing better to do, they'd come to spend an hour in the jacuzzi at the Hagmans' place. What was surprising was how quickly we all got used to the naked situation, as the conversation soon went from the movie we'd been making to that universal suburban subject, soaring property prices. Malibu, it seemed, was nearly as expensive as London.

That was just about the end of shooting on *Stardust*, but, as I was in California, it made sense for me to begin work on a documentary about someone David Puttnam and I considered to have been almost the first dead rock star. He hadn't been a singer or a musician, but for years we'd seen his face in magazines, on billboards, T-shirts, posters, calendars and postcards. He was James Dean, the star of *East Of Eden* and *Rebel Without A Cause*, who had crashed and died at the age of 24, while driving his Porsche to a racing car event in September, 1955. That had been pre-rock and roll, four months before Elvis had made his first hit record. Apparently, Dean had been driving so fast in his open car that his head had been almost severed from his body on impact.

His moment in the spotlight had been brief. *East of Eden*, based on the John Steinbeck novel, was a Cain and Abel story, with Dean playing the part of a misunderstood teenage boy. As soon as it was finished, he was put into his second film, *Rebel Without A Cause*, along with Natalie Wood and Sal Mineo, which was a study of the post-war American middle-class delinquency, and included its famous chicken run sequence. It was in *Rebel Without A Cause*, too, that the famous red zip-up jacket and blue jeans made their appearance, although they nearly didn't. Originally, perceived as a low budget black and white film, a week's shooting had already taken place in monochrome before, after early reaction to *East of Eden*, it was decided to begin the movie again in colour. By such commercial whims are iconic images created.

As soon as *Rebel Without A Cause* finished shooting, Dean went off to Texas to appear in *Giant*. And then came the car crash. His entire Hollywood career had lasted just eighteen months, but from the moment of his death, fame placed him among the most recognised of American cultural icons. 'Live fast, die young and have a good-looking corpse,' he'd liked to joke.

But who was James Dean, we wanted to know? Was he that good an actor? And why did his image remain contemporary with every successive decade?

David Puttnam and Sandy Lieberson had acquired the rights to Robert Altman's documentary *The James Dean Story*, which, although a poor film, contained a priceless road safety commercial that Dean had done just before his death. 'Drive safely, because the life you save might be mine,' he laughed in it, changing the scripted line from 'might be yours' to 'might be mine'. Thirteen days after filming the commercial he was dead.

So, as *Stardust* began being edited, I set about interviewing on film as many people as I could find who'd known James Dean. It didn't start well. Elia Kazan, who had directed *East of Eden* wasn't interested. 'You aren't bringing a camera in here,' he barked angrily down the phone from New York, and George Stevens who had directed *Giant* wasn't well. Nicholas Ray, who'd made *Rebel Without A Cause,* was happy to be filmed, but he seemed more interested in showing off to a group of film students in his San Francisco cutting room. What I didn't know then was that, not having made a film in over a decade, he had a serious drink and drugs problem. What I also didn't know was that, during the making of *Rebel Without A Cause,* he'd had an affair with Natalie Wood, who, being then only 16, was under age in California. That relationship had upset Dennis Hopper, who had a small part in the film, because he'd believed that he was Natalie's boyfriend.

Of course, that had all been twenty years earlier, and, if Dennis Hopper was still a bit peeved, he didn't show it when I interviewed him. Instead, he gave me a retake of his *Easy Rider* character, just as Peter Fonda had done when I'd met him. We filmed Hopper at a commune near Taos, New Mexico. Out in the desert, in his Levis, boots and cowboy hat, he snapped into character and put on a Dean-like performance for our camera.

'We were out on *Giant*,' he said, 'and there were four thousand people lined up about a hundred yards from where Jimmy was doing his first scene with Elizabeth Taylor. He was so nervous he could barely speak. And suddenly he turned and walked off about halfway between where they were shooting and where the people were watching. And, nonchalantly, he unzipped his pants, peed, dripped it off, and walked back into the scene, and did it first time.'
Later, Hopper said that he'd asked Dean why he'd done that. To which, he said, Dean replied: 'Well, it was the first time I'd worked with Elizabeth Taylor and I was really nervous. So, I figured that if I could go and pee in front of all those people, I could go back there and do anything on film.'

All of which may well have been true, although Hopper didn't actually appear on film in that section of *Giant*, so I'm not sure why he would have even been there. But, even if it did happen, it sounded to me less like a case of nerves on Dean's behalf and more of a demonstration of the actor's habit of attention stealing. Carroll Baker, who was also in *Giant*, told us something similar when we filmed her, Dean having grabbed her under the table while they were filming. She'd thought he'd been trying to steal the scene, although there might, of course, have been another more obvious motive. She was a very attractive young woman. Hollywood composer Leonard Rosenman, who wrote the music for *East of Eden* and *Rebel Without A Cause,* and who had shared a flat with Dean, explained his behaviour in this way. 'Jimmy was narcissistic. But narcissism for an actor is like silicosis for a coalminer.'

Certainly, Dean was a good-looking young man who loved the camera as much as it loved him. In our research we found hundreds of photographs of him, including one, taken some months before his death, where he was lying in a coffin in a funeral home.

We did many interviews for our film, including one with Sal Mineo in Houston, Texas. He'd only been sixteen at the time of *Rebel Without A Cause,* and, having been called for a rehearsal, he and Dean were asked to read a couple of scenes. 'I was very embarrassed, and I told the director I didn't know which role he wanted me to read,' he said. 'Nicholas Ray was very puzzled and asked, "Which role would you like to play?" And I said, "Plato. It's a better part", although Jimmy had a lot more lines.'

Towards the end of *Rebel Without A Cause,* the Natalie Wood and James Dean characters, pretend to be the grown up parents of Sal Mineo in what looks like an improvised scene in an abandoned mansion. In real life none of the three would grow old, James Dean being killed even before the film was released. Nathalie Wood died at 43 in 1981 in a drowning accident, while Sal Mineo was stabbed to death by a thief at 37, a year after our interview.

So, why did James Dean become such a legend? As always, it was the man and the moment. He had a particular ability for displaying neurosis on screen, a talent that just happened to come along at the birth of America's obsession with youth culture. His casting as the confused kid fitted the moment to perfection. After that the advertising industry turned those good looks, the jeans and T-shirt, and that great hair, into a classic style.

It's been suggested that Dean was a one-trick-pony of an actor, only great at playing the confused kid. What would have happened to him had he lived to become too old for those parts? The answer probably lies in the second half of *Giant* when, along with Elizabeth Taylor and Rock Hudson, he had to age into his mid-forties. The two established stars simply added blue rinse to their hair, but Dean grew a moustache and had the studio shave his forehead at the temples. When Sal Mineo bumped into him in the studio as the older man, he didn't recognise him.

For decades after Dean's death, young film actors aped his mannerisms, not least Warren Beatty in *Splendour In The Grass*, while Martin Sheen, a huge fan, based his performance on Dean in the movie *Badlands*. More recently Leonardo DiCaprio, Johnny Depp, Robert De Niro and director Martin Scorsese all admit to studying Dean's performances. Cinemagoers may not have realised it, but they've been watching Dean's influence on film for years.

Documentaries like ours are really made in the cutting room, and having returned from America with our interviews, I spent a year putting it together with editor Peter Hollywood. To me it was an invaluable experience. Every screenwriter would benefit from some time spent working in a film editing suite.

We called our film *James Dean: The First American Teenager*, and, to give it contemporary resonance, we put David Bowie's 'Rebel Rebel', Lou Reed's 'Walk On The Wild Side', the Eagles' 'James Dean' and Elton John's 'Funeral For A Friend' on the soundtrack. It was first shown on BBC-2.

When *Stardust* was released in the autumn of 1974, the censor originally wanted to give it an X-certificate because of some nudity and drug use. But, as nothing in the film encouraged drug taking, we made a couple of cuts and David Puttnam talked him out of it. David and I had worked very closely together on both *That'll Be The Day* and *Stardust*, both of which had been his initial ideas, so I would happily have had the credits of both reading 'Story by Ray Connolly & David Puttnam' and 'Screenplay by Ray Connolly'. But David didn't want it. He never wanted to direct either, falling out with directors from time to time, probably when their vision or enthusiasm didn't match his own. I used to think that perhaps he saw himself in those days as an Irving Thalberg or David O. Selznick figure.

'Show me a boy who never wanted to be a rock star and I'll show you a liar…' was a line I wrote in the sleeve notes for the accompanying *Stardust* album, and then found it immediately added to the poster for the film. It's still quoted at me from time to time, although it might not be if its derivations were known. 'Show me a farm boy who never fucked a sheep and I'll show you a liar,' a young man from Wyoming once said to me. I preferred my version.

When *Stardust* was released, it was another big hit, with another hit album and novella from me. David Essex was now a very big rock star, having written and performed a song called 'Stardust' that played over the end titles. Best of all for me, though, was to win the Writers Guild of Great Britain award for the best British original screenplay of 1974. When the great Carl Foreman handed me the plaque, he said: 'Congratulations, I hope there will be many more.'

'There will,' I joked. 'I've made my mind up.'

There weren't, of course.

Inexplicably, BAFTA didn't give awards to screenwriters in those days, but I had assumed that director Michael Apted would have been at least nominated for one for his role as director. He wasn't. Adam Faith got a nomination, but that was about all in the UK, which, looking back, still surprises me. In April 2020, I was hoping to be joined by Michael on stage at a Q and A after a showing of *Stardust,* but Covid got in my way. The following year it took Michael's life.

Without having seen *Stardust*, but having read the reviews, John Lennon wrote to me from New York in 1975 with a friendly ribbing that I must have used all my old interviews for my screenplay. There was an element of truth in that, because I knew the rock world and the isolation and depression that extraordinary fame can bring. But *Stardust* was fiction, the ending being closer to what would happen to Elvis in 1977 than anything that had already happened.

Having made the break from regular journalism while we were filming, I never did quite get back to my *Evening Standard* page, as one project followed another. The *Evening Standard* editor, Charles Wintour, was very patient with me.

22.

'All it is, is a movie... Moving Pictures. Just like Donald Duck. In fact, we've even got Donald Duck' - Sandy Lieberson

Having a successful movie is all very well. Everyone involved enjoys the plaudits. But a film that transmutes from being 120 pages of script into becoming an expensive, unfinished disaster, with a crew seemingly immobilised on location in Italy, is only amusing for those who weren't involved. *Trick Or Treat?* was such a film. It was a catastrophe, and, after having had two hits with my first two screenplays in less than three years, it brought me crashing down to earth. But catastrophes, of course, make better stories.

In hindsight, the making, or unmaking, as it turned out, of *Trick Or Treat?* now seems like a year-long episode of the French Netflix TV series *Call My Agent.* But *Call My Agent* is supposed to be funny. Nothing about trying to film *Trick Or Treat?* made the director, producers, actors, financial backers or writer laugh. And it was all this writer's idea.

I first thought of it in 1969. I then published the idea as a novel in 1974, and spent all of 1975 trying to help turn it into a movie. When it was abandoned half-way through shooting it was estimated that £400,000 (over £2.5 million in today's money and two thirds of the film's budget) had been spent shooting under forty minutes of usable footage.

At the start everyone agreed that I'd had a good and commercial idea, a story of two girls who fall in love, decide to have a baby together, and who, in doing so, become involved with a sophisticated, sexually manipulative married couple.

I was still hooked on French cinema, and, it was, in my mind, a love affair between four people, a sort of erotic Chabrol piece about sexual relationships and emotional ambivalences. It was set in Paris and was about an American girl, called Kathy, and three Europeans. At a time when English films were unattractive outside Britain, (*That'll Be The Day* and *Stardust* had done well critically everywhere, but their foreign box office had been disappointing), it seemed an opportunity to make a film with international appeal.

Things began to go wrong from the start. The first company to show interest was Warner Brothers, but I turned down their offer to stay with my friends David Puttnam and Sandy Lieberson at Goodtimes Enterprises. There are many advantages in working with an independent production company, but there is one major disadvantage. While the major studios can afford to spend mountains of money in pre-production, the resources of a small company can't stand a large early investment in a film that might not get made.

But this film was going to get made. I was on a hot streak, so my agent, Anthony Jones, negotiated a terrific deal with Goodtimes that included my role as an additional producer, one of those extra credits that star actors like to appropriate for their films. It also meant more money. Director Michael Apted, who was much sort after following *Stardust*, liked my novel, too, and was keen to direct.

I had a first draft of the screenplay ready by July 1975 that attracted the National Film Finance Corporation, EMI Films, and an Italian company called Rizzoli. By then the planned location had been moved from Paris to Rome, and Michael Apted and I found ourselves on a European tour in search of a cast. All kinds of names were bandied about, and then a French casting agent said, 'Do you mean someone like Bianca Jagger?'

'Bianca Jagger! She'd be worth talking to,' said Michael.

I knew Bianca, and, through a mutual friend, I tracked her down and arranged to meet her in Rome. David Puttnam and Sandy Lieberson were cautiously interested but wanted her to do a screentest. This was arranged and after it was viewed it was agreed that she had cinematic presence. By now, however, the sexual nature of the film was beginning to concern her. She wanted the script to be more faithful to the novel, which was surprising since the book was more sexually explicit than the script. During the next six months the question of nudity would be a point of endless discussions between Bianca and the rest of us. We wanted to make a serious film about a sexual relationship between two women and a man and his wife. To us that involved nudity. In Bianca's mind it seemed there was some movie baron who wanted us to make a dirty film. That was not the case. Bianca never said she wouldn't do the nudity scenes. She just worried a lot about them. And mostly she now complained about the screenplay, which I hadn't yet got right.

In a rational world, at this point, we should have put the film aside until I'd worked out the problems with the script. But we weren't in a rational world. We were in movieland. And everything that could go wrong was going wrong.

Both EMI and the NFFC liked Bianca's screentest, but when the National Film Finance Corporation were presented with a revised budget upwards of a further £50,000, they backed out. Another source of finance had to be found. It turned out to be Hugh Hefner's Playboy film division, but only on condition that the picture was to star Bianca Jagger. Even so, Heffner's people didn't have any say in the script or the film. But, from being just a vague casting idea a few weeks earlier, Bianca had now become the most essential ingredient in the making of the film.

So, Michael Apted flew to Hollywood to choose someone to play the part of the American girl, and David Puttnam went, too, to clear up the Playboy deal. Then Bianca arrived there. Having read the book again, and the latest script, she now wanted a woman writer on the project. Looking back, the climate of today has changed so much that I wouldn't now dare to even think about writing about a love affair between two women. But this was then.

Michael's choice for the girl to play Kathy was a photogenic Californian called Jan Smithers. The next problem to be solved was that of the woman writer with whom I was now to work. Michael knew someone, but we had to see if Bianca liked her.

Now I was in Los Angeles, too, and picked Bianca up for lunch where a very nervous Michael was waiting with my new screenwriting woman partner. After lunch I asked Bianca if she liked the new writer: 'Darling, it's your script. If you like her, that's all that matters.'

A few weeks later in London that wasn't all that mattered: 'It's shit,' said Bianca upon reading the new writer's efforts. She wasn't wrong. A new plan was then made. Robert Altman's film *Nashville* was a hit that summer, on which, it was being said, the actors had made up their own dialogue. As Bianca didn't like what I'd written, or what the new writer had come up with, 'Maybe improvisation is the way to go,' Michael Apted began to wonder.

The moment I began writing scenes without dialogue (to be presumably invented by the actors) was the moment that I should have walked away. But it was my baby. I didn't. Instead, I suggested that the way to do it was for Bianca to work with me. She agreed. The next day I waited at home for her. She didn't come.

That night I spoke to Michael, who was now in Rome looking at locations. 'Be very firm with her, Raymond,' he insisted. So, the following morning, I wrote out all the things I thought Bianca should hear.

'Listen,' I told her over lunch. 'You are being employed on this picture as an actress ... If the story needs changing, I'll take ideas from anywhere and anyone. If you want to help on a new draft of the script, come to my home... We start shooting on November 3. My job is to get the script right by then ... I know you're terrified.'

'No, I'm not,' she replied, and then said that she no longer wanted to be in the film.

I went home. As I walked through the door the phone was ringing. It was producer Sandy Lieberson, chastising me for jeopardising the whole film without consulting him first. Sandy was right. And it was his company's money I was jeopardising.

A few nights later, Sandy and Michael saw Bianca in Paris. This time, however, she decided she was not going to withdraw from the film.

October was spent fighting Equity. They didn't want Bianca: we did. Unfortunately, we won when a compromise was reached. Soon Michael was in Rome setting his locations, and Bianca was in London arguing about the frocks with Marit Allen, who was Sandy's wife, the film's costume director. Jan Smithers was meanwhile also in London getting tense and catching flu.

On November 11 most of the crew moved to Rome, along with Jan Smithers who came bearing a suitcase full of jars of vitamin pills, yeast and health foods. In our hotel, Michael Apted and I then continued to work on the screenplay. When Bianca arrived in Rome, she was accompanied by a bodyguard. There was, she thought, a danger of her being kidnapped. 'Nonsense,' said Gavrik Losey, the associate producer. 'Who would want to kidnap you?'

Shooting started on November 17. Unfortunately, a rainstorm hit the city as the first clapper was about to go down, and the entire morning was spent getting two shots. A deal had been done for Valentino to exclusively dress Bianca for the film, so, straight after lunch, she and Jan Smithers went off for fittings, only to return when it was too late in the day to do more than rehearse the next scene. 'It seems that Valentino is getting more time with the leading lady than I am,' complained director Apted.

For a week, filming struggled on. By the second week, Sandy Lieberson was doing his best to keep everybody happy, but the tension was beginning to tell on everyone. Then, one morning, Bianca told the second assistant director that she was too ill to leave her room. The doctor was called, and influenza and exhaustion were diagnosed. Now, however, Jan Smithers was breaking into tears with increasing frequency. 'You're the writer, he's the director and we're the actors,' she would sob. 'Why can't we just make the film and stop all the bullshitting?'

On the eleventh day Philip Collins, a representative of EMI Films, arrived, alarmed at the film's slow progress. Whatever he said to Bianca, it worked, because she was at the location by 10.30, but still not ready to shoot until four o'clock. Instead, much of the day was spent discussing whether it was possible to replace her.

Filming Jan Smithers walking down the Via Veneto in an evening dress at dawn the next day went well. But, later, Michael was met with Jan Smithers' tears, amid accusations that he was making a pornographic film. He now decided that there was no way he could carry on knowing that he didn't have the confidence of either of his leading ladies.

Dinner that night was a sober affair: shooting for the next day had been cancelled. Sandy Lieberson, who had quite as much (if not more) to cry about than the rest of us, came up with the most philosophical comment: 'For Christ's sake, you guys, all we're doing is trying to make a movie. It isn't the end of the world. Nobody's dead. Nobody's even dying. All it is, is a movie … moving pictures … just like Donald Duck.' He paused for a moment: 'In fact we've even got Donald Duck.'

The next day, while I worked on a scene to be shot later in the week, Michael Apted and Sandy Lieberson went into secret session with the leading ladies. By now the argument about nudity had turned into a full-scale attack on the script by Jan Smithers, which was a surprise because when she'd been cast, she'd had hardly any comments. Ironically, I was told that Bianca defended me.

Back at our hotel, Michael was in despair. 'I don't think that you and I can carry on and make this film together, Raymond,' he told me. 'One of us has to go.'

I went home that afternoon with Philip Collins. It was, Philip said, the worst few days of his entire life. 'Thank God you're out of it,' said Plum when I arrived home.

Shooting was then abandoned in Rome and the crew returned to London for filming. Over Christmas, Michael Apted and my writer replacement, Kathleen Tynan, worked on yet another version of the screenplay but it was to no avail. On the Friday before shooting was due to restart, David Puttnam got a message from Los Angeles to say Jan Smithers would not be coming back. Bianca, meanwhile, resorted to her lawyers. When it was sorted out, it seemed that both actors, through their lawyers, were saying that they wanted to alter the terms of their contracts to include more money and what amounted to an approval of the final cut of the picture. No director can work in that situation. The picture was cancelled.

The last time I spoke to Bianca was at five minutes to one on the morning of January 14, 1976, a day or two before the movie was cancelled. I was at home, when the bedside phone rang.

'Don't answer it,' said Plum. 'It's that woman again.'

I did answer it. She was right.

'You could say that *Trick Or Treat?* gave you a very expensive education in film-making,' film producer Tony Garnett would later say to me when I metaphorically cried on his shoulder. He was right, too.

At the time, I wanted to blame Bianca for the collapse of *Trick Or Treat?* But it was our fault, too. She wasn't an actress. She knew that, although she probably enjoyed being courted. I now think her behaviour was due to fear of being found out. We should never have cast her.

As I say, the story of the making of *Trick or Treat?* could have made a whole series of *Call My Agent.* But we all got over it. Sandy Lieberson went on to become president of Twentieth Century Fox, Michael Apted had a terrific career in Hollywood, and also in Britain, where he produced the *7-Up* series for television, and David Puttnam made many films, won many prizes and honours, and eventually became Lord Puttnam. As for me it all provided useful background information for my novel *Shadows On A Wall*, which tells the story of the making of a movie when things go even more wrong, and when the writer, of course, gets sacked.

One thing that we often asked ourselves throughout those unhappy months was, 'Where is Mick?' Sandy Lieberson had produced his film *Performance*, but never once did Mick Jagger make contact with him on behalf of his wife. Bianca was on her own. Shrewd fellow that Mick Jagger. As for Bianca, she never made another movie. Wise decision.

'This day my Daddy might play football with me,' Dominic Connolly, then aged five, used to regularly say. Sometimes, I did kick a ball around the garden with him, although too often I didn't. I was always busy working. So, I left it to Plum to take the children to playgroup, then primary school, and to organise what they ate, what they wore, their birthday parties, days out, family holidays, Christmas, doctors, hospital appointments and everything else... to, in effect, run the entire home and family. That was how it was in our house in the Seventies, how I assumed it always was and always had been in everyone's homes.

It wasn't until the abandonment of *Trick or Treat?* when I found myself at home with nothing to do, that it struck me that a busy career can be a terrible thief, robbing fathers or mothers of some of the great joys of family life. Harry Chapin wrote and sang a terrific song on this subject called 'Cats in The Cradle'. With horrible irony, having put into song the regrets of the busy father who misses seeing his son grow up because of work, Harry Chapin was killed in a road accident when his own son was only nine years old.

I can't say that I became a modern father after I arrived home from Rome that night. I didn't. Singing songs and playing games was more my style of fathering. Like film writer William Goldman, I liked to make up stories to tell my children instead of reading to them.

Perhaps I should have written them down and tried for a second career as a writer of children's stories. But I didn't, and at a time when the British film industry was not doing well in the Seventies, I concentrated instead on writing novels and plays for television.

But one thing changed. Since then, I've always enjoyed working from home, where our children constantly fed me information from fields through which I no longer walked.

23.

'A male millipede has his sex pouch on his eleventh ring and he takes out the sperm with a feeler-like hand' - David Attenborough

Mal Evans was a really nice guy. One of that ensemble of people who had come down from Liverpool with the Beatles, he was huge, six feet three, with horn rimmed glasses. But his story became the stuff of tragedy, when, in 1976, he was shot dead during a confused encounter with the Los Angeles Police Department.

I met him during the filming of the *Magical Mystery Tour* in 1967, but he'd been with the Beatles since 1961. Before that he'd been a Post Office engineer and used to eat his lunchtime sandwiches with his girlfriend, Lil, at Liverpool's Pier Head. Then, one day, he took a different route on his way back to work, which led him down an alley of warehouses. There, as he told me, 'I heard some music coming from a basement and thought it sounded like Elvis'.

What he found, as he stepped into that basement, was the Beatles making one of their early lunchtime appearances at the Cavern. After that he went back during most lunch hours. Because he was so tall, he was noticed, and, at George Harrison's suggestion, was offered a part-time job as a bouncer. Soon he was the group's road manager and their ever-faithful retainer, the man they called their Gentle Giant. He never had to fight to control the hysteria. He was so big and smiling in his horn-rimmed glasses that it was never necessary.

With the Beatles on the cusp of fame, he left the Post Office and joined them. Driving them up and down the country through fog and snow, his life was spent lugging amplifiers and speakers in and out of their van, which he also drove.

His 1963 Post Office Engineering Union diaries, with everything written in capital letters, makes a fascinating primary source for Beatles' chroniclers, in its attention to the mundane details of dinners with the Beatles at motorway service stations and breakfasts at transport cafés. His only wish was for better headlights for the van. Then there are the expenses, everything noted to the last penny: 'April 9, 1964, £11-17s-6d.' He was as honest as a ruler.

So, when, in 1963, the Beatles moved to London, Mal went, too, driving home to Liverpool every weekend that he had off to see Lil, who was now his wife, and their baby. He was immersed in the Beatles' world, present at every single recording session, gig, and TV and radio broadcast. At £25 a week he was being paid slightly more than he'd earned at the Post Office. But Beatles' manager Brian Epstein was fussy about appearances and insisted that Mal wore a suit instead of jeans. Epstein didn't offer to pay for the suit and Mal didn't like to ask.

Naturally, Mal enjoyed the glamour of being at the Beatles' sides. When they made movies, he had small roles in them (he was the fellow who keeps swimming in *Help!),* and, when they met famous people, such as Muhammad Ali, he also met them. In Hollywood when they visited Elvis, Mal was there, too. Throughout the Sixties, he was the ever-helping hand in the studio, even suggesting occasional words or lines when a song was being written.

Gradually, though, Mal found himself being seduced away from his family. And, when the Beatles broke up, he wanted to be more than just their much-loved servant. He wanted to be a songwriter and a record producer. In his quiet way, he wanted some of the glory. The young married man from the Post Office had disappeared. The new Mal had begun to manage a little Liverpool group called the Iveys (later to be renamed Badfinger) on behalf of the Beatles. But gentle Mal wasn't cut out for management. In April 1969 his diary reveals he had to approach the Beatles' new American manager, Allen Klein, for a loan of £1,000 for the band. It worried him.

'Situation with Iveys getting a little too heavy for me,' he wrote in his diary. 'Had to tell George I'm broke. Really miserable. I'm in the red and the bills are coming in. Poor old Lil suffers as I don't want to ask Apple for a rise.'

What he didn't know then, and from which he would never profit, was that two of his little group would write one of the classic songs of the time. It was 'Without You', which would become a very big hit for Harry Nilsson.

As the Beatles went their separate ways, Mal, in his early forties, was facing a mid-life crisis. He still went to the Beatles'

Apple office but there wasn't much for him to do. In the end, Mal told them he was leaving. He didn't, however, only leave the Beatles. He left Lil and their two children as well. 'I was devastated,' Lil would tell me years later. 'It still hurts.'

Without the Beatles, Mal was rudderless. He couldn't go back to being the Post Office engineer he'd been and had once expected to be for the rest of his career. But could he go forward? In 1974 he went to Los Angeles and worked for a time as a record producer. There was a girlfriend, too.

On January 4, 1976, two years to the day after leaving Lil, he became depressed and picked up an air rifle which he had in his apartment for shooting at lizards. On seeing the gun, his girlfriend called the police, allegedly saying: 'My old man has a gun and has taken Valium and is totally screwed up.'

When the police arrived, Mal was told to put the gun down. He responded, it was alleged, by pointing it at them. They shot him dead instantly, four bullets hitting him. Only afterwards did they discover that the gun wasn't loaded.

Lil wonders, but will never know, if there was a chance that she could have saved Mal and their marriage. 'A few months before he was killed, he rang up. I think he was depressed, so I assumed he'd had a row with his girlfriend. He asked me if I'd have him back if he came. I was dying to say. "Yes, like a shot!" But my pride wouldn't let me. So, I said, "Ring me in two weeks' time and ask me again". But he never asked again.'

Mal Evans was a good man, for whom everything went wrong when the Beatles broke up. Those closest to the cauldron of fame often get burned the most.

Plum and I were watching Sharon Tate screaming in Roman Polanski's *Dance of the Vampires* on television, when the bomb exploded at the end of our road. The Troubles in Northern Ireland had become increasingly bloody by the mid-Seventies and had now spread to the mainland. So, here in London, we'd almost been expecting it. But it was the sheer, fat, loudness of the bang that shocked.

The explosive device had been left seventy yards from our house in the front of a jeweller's shop on Kensington High Street, and, as I ran down to the scene, other neighbours were coming to see if they could be of any help. There actually wasn't much to see, other than a shocked passer-by in a lake of broken glass, who was already being tended to by two other people. A burglar alarm was howling and within a couple of minutes a police car raced to a stop.

There was nothing I could do to help, but I hung around as more police and neighbours arrived, before, returning home, where I followed the instincts of the journalist and rang the BBC to report the bomb.

Incidents like that stay lodged in one's mind, so that was the moment that I opened on when I began my next novel, *Newsdeath,* the story of a newspaper reporter who narrowly misses being blown up in an attack by a right-wing terror group. It would take me over a year to write it, because, without an advance, and no longer wanting to be tied to regular journalism, I needed to earn a living at the same time.

Commissions for three 50-minute BBC TV plays, that would be transmitted to coincide with the Queen's Silver Jubilee the following year, filled the income gap. Today none of the current TV channels offer much in the way of single drama pieces, as series and serials are almost always about cops or hospitals. That's the current fashion, and it's a shame, because throughout the Sixties and Seventies the BBC's 'Play For Today' attracted massive audiences, giving writers, directors and actors, not only the chance to tell short stories about everyday life, but also, most important of all, the opportunity to risk failure. From that chance sprang some spectacularly successful careers.

The Jubilee plays, as the BBC season was collectively called, wanted a story for every second year of the Queen's reign, and I wrote the opening one, set in 1952, a plot about a family firm saved from bankruptcy by a daughter who commits her life to it and its staff. It was called *Almost Tomorrow* and was a thinly disguised parallel with the Queen's own commitment to the country. I had no strong feelings about the monarchy, but I always admired the Queen for doing that most thankless of jobs. Hannah Gordon played our lead, and, although I couldn't be present, I was thrilled when years later she told me that she'd broken down with emotion at the read-through. Reactions like that are one of the perks of being a writer.

Probably foolishly, I turned down the opportunity to write a series based on *Almost Tomorrow,* and instead wrote a second play about sibling rivalry set in the mid-Sixties. It starred the young Martin Shaw as a photographer in a David Bailey type of role, with an unknown Midge Ure as a rock star. It was called *Our Kid.* The third play was the last 50 minutes in the life of a newspaper based on the closure of the *Daily Sketch* in 1971, which gave an early television part to an actor just out of drama school called Fiona Mollison, who has remained a friend ever since.

It was good to get plays on television, but the videotape cameras used in those days, and the studio lighting, was primitive, while rehearsals in Ealing didn't really compare with taking over a fairground as we had done in *That'll Be The Day,* or a castle in Spain like the one in *Stardust.* So, when my agent, Anthony Jones, suggested me as a writer for a Roger Vadim film, I was quickly on the plane to Paris.

Vadim (his real name was Roger Vladimir Plemiannikov, the son of Belorussian immigrants to Paris, but only ever called Vadim, and never Roger) was an almost heroic figure of my teens. Not only had he written and directed *And God Created Woman*, he'd discovered and then married its young star, Brigitte Bardot.

In the Sixties, Bardot defined French female sexuality, so she might have been enough for most men. But Vadim had a wandering eye and beautiful women wandered his way throughout his life. By the time I met him he'd also been married to Annette Stroyberg and Jane Fonda, while Catherine Deneuve had had his baby. He was then in his late forties, married for the fourth time to Catherine Schneider, whose inherited wealth, he told me, came from her ancestors who had made cannons for Napoleon, and with whom he was living in a super fashionable Paris house that looked out over the Champ-de-Mars.

The working title of the proposed film was *Vadim's Dracula,* which was to be set in modern-day London. And, after an exploratory meeting, it was suggested that I join Vadim and his wife on a ski-ing holiday in Avoriaz, where I would discover from his wife, when he was out ski-ing, that the two were getting divorced, but hadn't wanted it to spoil their holiday together.

The rich French are so cool about these things. And Vadim was the ultimate in cool. Good looking and quietly spoken, he was the exact opposite of the confident Casanova of his legend. He was, in fact, almost motherly, worrying, when we went out to dinner that my steak wasn't *bien cuit* enough for an Englishman and fretting that the cheese would be too ripe for me.

When he came to see me in London, where Plum was all but speechless as he smiled at her, he was staying with an old girlfriend who happily chauffeured him around. She was very attractive. Well, of course she was. And, when I went to see him in Paris, he would politely break off talking to me when Brigitte Bardot's mother (whom he still called 'Maman', despite her being his last mother-in-law but three) rang. Then he would listen kindly to her problems. You could see why women loved him, and children, too. One day he told me gleefully how he and his daughter with Jane Fonda would steal money from Jane's purse to go to the cinema. Jane, the star of his film *Barbarella*, 'counted the centimes', apparently.

Vadim never talked about having 'affairs', only of having 'adventures', one of which probably began one afternoon in Paris when he suggested we go for an ice cream to the Hilton Hotel. Inevitably, two very attractive young women were waiting for us. One worked for a film company on the Champs Elysees, with whom, he later admitted, he'd once had 'an adventure while in the mountains'. The other was Polish, and for some reason she followed us back to the house, where, before long, she was sitting on Vadim's knee at his desk as they chatted.

Feeling a bit spare, I stepped outside into the small garden and pretended to consider the view that took in, to the left, the Ecole Militaire, and, in the distance, to the right, the Eiffel Tower. When I looked back the couple had begun snogging. Then, unknown to the girl, Vadim noticed me outside and gave me a big, happy wink. His next adventure was beginning.

That was Vadim, the lover of women, and a man who liked to gossip: 'Warren Beatty sees every woman he wants as a challenge,' he told me. 'Sometimes he will phone me in the middle of the night when he's been successful'. I never asked him what it had been like being married to Brigitte Bardot. But he told me anyway. It seems that, in bed, she was 'very bourgeois'.

Vadim's Dracula never got made, of course. After I submitted my screenplay to Warner Brothers I was replaced by another writer, but Warner Brothers didn't like whatever he wrote either. At which point they lost interest in the idea. That was the way it went in Hollywood.

When Vadim died in 2000, at the age of 72, four of his ex-wives turned up at the funeral and Catherine Deneuve went to his memorial service. History doesn't recount how many other women with whom he'd had adventures were there, too, to shed a tear at a happy memory.

The shy awe that Plum had felt when Vadim visited us was nothing compared to the numbed gasp that our cleaner, Shelia Rampton, exhaled when she answered the door to Dennis Waterman. Sheila was a big fan of *The Sweeney* and would soon be a fan of *Minder*. Dennis had come to see me to talk about *Newsdeath,* which, after good reviews, had been optioned for a film for which I was writing the screenplay. As it never went anywhere, either, that day would be the highlight.

Friends who don't know the movie business would sometimes chide me about my unmade film scripts and look disbelievingly when I would explain that most scripts never made it to the screen. But it's true. I'd had beginner's luck. I hadn't realised when I'd begun writing films how lucky I'd been to have David Puttnam's energy pushing our ventures forward.

In truth, unless writers are very rich or extremely successful, or are prepared for their families to suffer the privations of their devotion to their art, none of which I was, they tend to knock on lots of doors in varied writing careers. So, I next wrote a radio play, *An Easy Game To Play,* about an inter-generational Liverpool love affair; then followed it with a trilogy for ITV called *Honky Tonk Heroes,* about a country and western music club in South London. The inspiration for that had come initially from first hearing Dolly Parton sing 'Jolene' while on a plane to America. My first thought had been to wonder at the guitar playing, but then I'd begun to think how we all know a Jolene, and how wives and girlfriends are always wary of them.

Country and Western music, with its perpetual tales of cheating, drinking, misery and more cheating and drinking, was always a rich seam for small town drama and failed ambition. So, when it became popular for a while in Britain, it seemed to me the ideal setting for a TV series with music. The band was good, and the songs were popular down to earth stories of you, me and her. I'm not sure I got the scripts right, nor was the casting perfect, not helped when our leading actor, who was playing the owner of the Western styled night club in South London that was the centre of our series, fell off his horse while filming and broke his leg. That had never happened to Clint Eastwood in *Rawhide*.

So, the idea was probably better than the plays, but the viewing figures were pretty good, and one night in the Central Lobby at Westminster, Labour MP Joe Ashton positively raved about it to me. There's no accounting for taste. Herbert Kretzmer, of *Les Miserables* fame, may have been right when he told me it should perhaps have been written for the stage, a thought that had never occurred to me. The series did me one favour, though, by introducing me to an actor called Philip Jackson, who, thirty years later, would play another kind of part in my life.

Writing interviews for newspapers was always a more certain livelihood for me, because I enjoyed asking questions, but whether they were good pieces or not depended on the subject's attitude. The classically trained pianist Billy Joel, was very open, telling me how he'd discovered that playing the piano was a great way to get off with girls. His hit songs, 'Uptown Girl' and 'She's Always A Woman', sort of tell you that, but it had been a surprise for him, because he'd never thought of himself as a looker. His subsequent litany of beautiful girl friends and five wives would suggest he was right. His piano was his magnet.

Tony Bennett, on the other hand, in between rhapsodising about Jerome Kern and Cole Porter and the songs of the Forties, with which I didn't disagree, dismissed most modern popular music as 'a commodity built on obsolescence and the trash can for the Coca Cola society'. I suspect Billy Joel, like me, wouldn't have fully agreed. It was probably a generational thing.

The notion of generation doesn't seem to have ever crossed the mind of David Attenborough, in that his TV series are made for the entire family, even to the point of his occasionally showing us creatures in moments of pro-creation.

'Yes, yes!' he beamed at his home in Richmond one Boxing Day morning. 'They're always at it in my programmes, aren't they! I order it on my shopping list now. I write down in my script "Frog enters SHOT. Copulates. Then exits under leaf". And then, blow me, some cameraman from Brazil sends me just what I wanted.'

Warming to the subject, he thought millipedes were among the most fascinating copulators. 'You see, they are a group of animals who have come out of the water relatively recently, in an evolutionary sense, and aren't yet used to living on land. When they were in the water it was easy for them because they just had to squirt the various stuff into the water and leave nature to do the rest. But now there's a terrible business where they are trying to find their sexual openings.

'A male millipede has his sex pouch on his eleventh ring and he takes out the sperm with a feeler-like hand. He then has to bung it into the female's genital opening which occurs on her fifth ring, and you can see him counting, looking for the opening…one, two, three, four, five. And, if he misses, he's got to start all over again. It's absolutely fascinating.'

As was Tom Stoppard with his wry reflection on being a playwright. 'When I started, I wrote a play because I wanted to be a playwright. Now I write plays because I am a playwright. It's not quite the same thing.'

We were on holiday in Corsica when I noticed that a German couple close to us on the beach were reading different newspapers but with similar headlines over big photographs of Elvis Presley.

'Excuse me, but…?' I began to ask.

They anticipated my question: 'Yes, he is dead. Yesterday. A heart attack.' He'd only been 42.

I went back to Plum and the children and lay back on the sand. Without a typewriter or a phone in our villa it was too late for me to consider writing anything. And, in some strange way, I felt relieved. At least, this sad, lonely man wouldn't disappoint anyone anymore.

We took our children to New Zealand for a Christmas holiday the following year. Plum's sister, Ruth, and John from Swanpool Lane, my best friend from boyhood, lived there with their four children, who were then Abba mad. I think ours had preferred the Bee Gees songs that had filled the airwaves when we'd spent a couple of days driving around Los Angeles on the way there. But it was nice to see was how free the New Zealand children were when they played in their large garden.

Plum and I had both grown up in houses with big gardens, and, lucky as we were to have a garden at all in central London, it always bothered us that our children weren't enjoying the benefits of the space that we'd had. So, the following summer, we sold our house in Kensington and moved out to a detached house behind Wimbledon Common. It had a huge garden of wisteria and rhododendrons and a lawn that swept right around one side of the house where a swing hung from the branch of a high oak tree. The house had been built in the late twenties on a patch of land then known as Bluebell Wood. The bluebells were still there, and, among them, we would find the occasional old tennis ball, presumably left behind by one of the house's former owners, British tennis star Roger Taylor.

Altogether it was a terrific place for the children to play and for me to play with them. Best of all was a game of soft tennis we invented. That was the year when son Dominic, then aged 9, asked me if I liked the Police, only to look at me with incomprehension when I went into a little homily about the need for the Metropolitan Police.

'I mean Police, the pop group, Dad,' he said at last. 'Like Sting.'

I was losing touch.

24.

'Dear Ray, Glad you've learned to talk proper. It could hinder yer kreer' - letter from John Lennon

After John Lennon went to live in New York in 1971, I really thought that the Beatles' part of my career was finished. I hadn't seen Ringo since we'd made *That'll Be The Day*, and although I interviewed Paul McCartney a couple more times, my contact with John in New York, had, in those pre-email days, been down to a couple of calls and a few letters. 'Glad you've learned to talk proper. It could hinder yer kreer,' he'd joked about my stammer at one point in written Scouse. After which had come a silence when, as Yoko told me on the phone, he'd left her and gone off to California with the assistant May Pang. That was a surprise. Eighteen months later had come a postcard from Yoko telling me that not only were she and John back together, she was expecting a baby, too. Then, another silence as John became reclusive in their Dakota apartment.

Five years later in 1980 came word that he was recording again. I picked up the phone to call him. Yoko answered. She aways did. Could I speak to him? He was busy. How would John feel about an interview? Yes, but not yet, was the answer. I tried again two weeks later and got a similar response. So, I gave up. I was freelancing at the *Sunday Times* and had other stuff to do.

Then on December 7, Yoko rang me. Why wasn't I in New York interviewing John and her, she wanted to know. They'd been expecting me. The BBC had been there that weekend and John had told them I was coming over.

So, I agreed to go to New York the following morning.

Our children, who were then 13, 10 and 8, were excited that night as I packed my case, played the new John and Yoko album again, checked my tape recorder and cassettes and made some notes. I was excited, too. The *Sunday Times* had agreed to give my Atticus column the whole back page of the paper for my interview, so it was going to be a pretty big deal.

The last thing I did before going to sleep that night was to phone the Dakota to tell them I would soon be on my way. I got an assistant, who told me: 'John and Yoko have gone down to the studio to remix one of Yoko's tracks. But John said to tell you to come straight here when you get into New York tomorrow. He's looking forward to seeing you again.'

The phone at our bedside woke me at 4.30. At first, in the dark, I thought it must be that the taxi I'd booked to take me to the airport had come too early. It wasn't. It was the features editor at the *Daily Mail* who had just been woken himself by a call from their New York office telling him that John Lennon had been shot.

Still half asleep, I didn't understand what he was saying, and began telling him that I was going to see John in couple of hours and…

He interrupted me. 'He's been shot, Ray.'

'Shot! Shot? Is he hurt? I mean, badly hurt?' I asked.

'I don't know. They didn't say. It only just happened. But I called because I might need you tomorrow.'

By now, Plum was wide awake at my side. I didn't know what to do, what to think. Those were the days before 24-hour news, so, just before 5am, I went downstairs to the kitchen, put the kettle on and tuned the radio to the BBC World Service.

The lead sentence of their first item said it all: 'Former Beatle John Lennon has been shot dead in the street outside his home in New York.'

I took Plum a cup of tea and sat on the bed as we both tried to take in the news.

Ten years earlier, knowing that journalists are often asked to prepare obituaries for the very famous, John had said to me: 'Have you written my obituary yet?'

I'd told him that I hadn't. We'd both been thirty then and the idea of his death had seemed remote.

'Well, when you do, can you show it to me. I'd love to read it,' he'd replied.

At about six thirty the phone rang again. It was an old friend, Roy Wright, the deputy editor of the *Evening Standard,* saying, 'Sorry to wake you, but…seven hundred words by eight o'clock? Is that all right?'

It was. I was upset, yes, but I was a journalist. I did what I had to do. Going downstairs to my study, I began to write.

As in millions of other homes that morning, when our children came down to go to school, our house was filled with the sound of John Lennon's voice as every radio station was playing his records.

When they'd gone to bed, they'd been excited because their dad was going to see John Lennon. Now, here he was, just one sleep later, dictating the Beatle's obituary over the phone.

With my flight to New York cancelled, I spent the rest of the day writing for two more newspapers before going to Capital Radio for a studio discussion.

Yoko rang a few weeks later, wanting to know why I hadn't flown out to see her when I'd heard the news, implying that I didn't care about the widow.

'There were thousands of people outside the Dakota,' I told her. 'I saw them on TV. I would never have got through.'

'Yes, you would. Ringo came.'

'I'm not Ringo,' I protested.

Some months later, while I was in New York editing a novel, I phoned her, and she immediately invited me up to the Dakota. She was sitting in the kitchen with her son, Sean, who was then about six, and a man called Sam, whom I assumed to be an assistant. For a while Yoko and I chatted about old times, then she asked Sam to take Sean to watch television.

When we were alone, she explained. Sam was her new lover. After John had been murdered, she had obviously been very upset, but: 'I need sex. I'm not a nun, not a virgin. So? There was Sam. John liked him and Sean likes him. So, why not Sam?'

Worrying slightly that Sean and Sam, in the next room, might be able to hear her, I asked if she should be telling me this.

Misunderstanding, she said: 'Oh, that's okay. I talked to John while you were in the cab on the way here and he said I can tell you anything.'

I learned later that Sam was Sam Havadtoy, an interior designer and artist who had done some work at the Lennons' home. He and Yoko would be privately together for the next twenty years, which was eight years longer than Yoko was with John Lennon. I saw, not for the first time, the two sides of Yoko that night. In public she was the most famously grieving widow in the world. In private, something different.

As they were both artists, Sam might even have been a better match for her than John, but they never appeared together in public. It has been suggested that their affair began a year before Lennon was murdered, but I don't know. That wasn't what Yoko told me that night.

The two broke up in 2001 when Sam went to live in Hungary where he has an art gallery. He has never spoken about his relationship with Yoko.

That she should so quickly have had another man in her life astonished me at the time. But, on reflection, it was consistent with the way she had always lived, going from one husband to the next with hardly a backward glance, even leaving her daughter Kyoko, to be looked after by her second husband when she met John Lennon.

Paul McCartney must have been one of the last people to hear about John's death. Always in the habit of switching off his phone at night, it hadn't been until Linda returned from taking their children to school the following morning that he found out.

'I was looking through the window and saw her car draw up. The expression on her face told me something terrible must have happened,' he told me.

It was terrible: for John who was planning to come back to Britain, for Yoko and Sean, and for John's other son, Julian, and John's ex-wife Cynthia. But it was terrible for Paul, too, in all kinds of ways. He and John had been friends since he'd been at school, and together they had changed the shape of popular music. At the time of the Beatles' break-up, a decade earlier, they hadn't been speaking to each other, but time had softened them both, with Paul even inviting John to join him at a recording session. For years fans had dreamed of a Beatles reunion. That was never going to happen, but the possibility of Lennon and McCartney working together as songwriters occasionally was becoming increasingly likely as the years passed and the wounds healed.

Then John was murdered, and that possibility disappeared from Paul's life forever.

As a writer you sometimes find yourself doing things, or being in a situation, you never expected. One of these happened to me in Memphis, Tennessee, while I was researching a film called *Hoochy*

Coochy for Columbia Pictures. My idea was to tell a *Huckleberry Finn* story of a white piano-playing boy from Minnesota, who in 1954 drops out of college…

I know the beginning was a bit like that of *That'll Be The Day,* but it was always a good opening, and *Hoochy Coochy* soon went off in another direction as our hero travels south down the spine of America on Highway 61, which pretty well follows the Mississippi River. I liked that: going north to south across America as opposed to the more usual east to west. On his journey, our dropout hero soon meets and is accompanied by a black friend called Homer, with whom he discovers the various regional seeds of rock and roll music, black and white, just before it happened.

The movie never got made. Once again, that's Hollywood. They invite you over, give you a hire car, put you up at the Beverly Wilshire Hotel, and then sort of forget all about you and your project in the steeplechase to find the next 'go-project'.

By this point in my career, I knew all that, but I enjoyed doing the research which, one Sunday morning, took me to a Pentecostal church on East Trigg Drive in Memphis Tennessee, where I'd read that a teenage, pre-fame Elvis, used to stand in the porch there to listen to the choir.

It hadn't really hit me before going into the church that day that I might be the only white person there. But I was, and I was enjoying the singing from people who looked like the Blossoms or the Four Tops, when, during a break, the pastor, the Dr Reverend Vernon Brewster, addressed the congregation, welcomed newcomers and asked that they introduce themselves.

So, I made my way up on to the altar, took the microphone, and, admitting that I didn't go to church anymore, said that I was a lapsed Catholic, but had always loved hymns and church music. Then I told them some of the plot of the Hollywood film I was writing, and they showed me the side door and porch where years earlier white people had been able to come to listen to the music. And, yes, the Reverend Brewster remembered Elvis being there.

Everyone, apart from me, was, of course, dressed in their Sunday best, and before I left a couple of matronly mothers came forward with some advice. If I'd parked my hire car outside, they said, and especially if it was a new one, I shouldn't leave it there too long because it wouldn't be safe in that neighborhood.

I'd been given that advice once before. Back in Liverpool. Near the cathedral.

While I'd been travelling around America on my Huckleberry Finn tour, Michael Apted had traced me and asked if I'd like to write a film about the young John Lennon for him to direct. David Puttnam would be the producer. My immediate worry was that we wouldn't be able to get any Lennon and McCartney music rights, but Warner Brothers had assured Michael that we could. And, as our film would be about John's pre-fame days in Liverpool and Hamburg, when the Beatles mainly performed rock standards and very little original material, three or four of their early songs were all we would need. Our working title was *Working Class Hero*.

So, as soon as I finished a first draft of *Hoochy Coochy*, off I went to Hamburg and Liverpool to write what I still reckon was a terrific screenplay. Michael Apted and the head of production at Warner Brothers liked it, too, and I was flown back out to Los Angeles to discuss a few minor points with her and Michael. Everything pointed to *Working Class Hero* being a 'go' movie.

It wasn't. A couple of months later I got a call from Michael to tell me the project was dead. He didn't know the exact reason, but it seemed that there might be a problem with Yoko. She wouldn't have been in the film, of course, in that it would have ended before the Beatles left Liverpool. But she was very controlling, and, at the time, she seemed to be repainting John Lennon's legend as that of a peace-loving feminist, which he never was. Nor, for that matter, was he ever a 'working class hero'.

So, if Yoko was the fly in the ointment, it made sense. And as she and I weren't friends any more I never discovered the full story. Years later another writer did get a film made about the young John Lennon, but without any Lennon and McCartney songs, of course.

I was disappointed that *Working Class Hero* wasn't made, because, like all screenwriters, the film now already existed in my head. That old trope that the first time a film is shown is in the mind of the screenwriter is dead right. No screenwriter could ever write a movie without seeing the images and hearing the dialogue in his mind as he cuts and writes and rewrites and cuts and rewrites again. His or her job is to present the structure and shape of the film, to invent the characters and to visualise and hear every scene. If the script is handed to a good director he will add his input, and along with the director of photography, the editor and the actors, and hopefully they will make the film even better than the writer originally imagined. If the screenplay ends up in the hands of a lesser talented director, at least he has a good map to follow. Michael Apted was a very good director. He would have made a very good film.

I've heard it said that Hollywood could pave the entire 21 miles of Sunset Boulevard with unmade film scripts. Well, maybe not the *entire* length, but talk to any screenwriter and you'll discover that he or she has a shelf of unmade movie scripts at home. I've got a few. One would have starred Cher. It was her idea, but we just didn't get on after I'd waited for weeks for her to even talk to me. Then there was another about a couple of buskers who win the Eurovision Song Contest. I always liked that one. But nobody else went for it. Maybe it will one day make a novel.

But why is there so much waste of effort, so much pointless writing and rewriting in movies? There are numerous reasons, but, basically, it's simple economics. Although screenwriters may seem relatively well paid, the cost of a first draft screenplay is the least expensive part of any movie. Without the screenplay that sets out the story, the characters and the dialogue, there is nothing to convince the movie's financiers to back it, nothing to attract a director, and nothing to tempt the big stars whom the public like to see.

But top directors, big stars and big budget movies cost scores of millions of dollars. They won't want to be involved without reading a screenplay they like. So, without the screenplay there is nothing, as without the acorn there is no oak tree.

But which acorn will develop into an international billion dollar blockbuster? No-one knows for sure. So, to cover themselves, the major studios have traditionally spread their bets by commissioning lots of screenplays in a system of payment in which the screenwriter gets more, bit by bit, in stages until the film is finally made. For the executives who back the right projects it can lead to great fame and fortune and everything that goes with it. For those who plump too often for the wrong ones, it can be a one-way ticket to Palookaville.

So, why do many terrible films still get made?

God knows.

I always come up with *The Third Man* when asked to name a perfect film, a miracle that happens when all the principles in its making are at the top of their game. In this case the screenplay was by Graham Greene at his most brilliant as he invented a story of cynicism, corruption, friendship and betrayal in war shattered Vienna. Then there was producer Alexander Korda backed by David O. Selznick, cinematographer Robert Krasker's monochrome images of the pudgy white face of Orson Welles grinning in the darkness, the zither music of Anton Karas, Joseph Cotton as the everyday American writer of pulp fiction and director Carol Reed's masterly control of everything.

The ending wasn't as Graham Greene had written it, and he worried that the final shot of Alida Valli on that long walk from the cemetery to, and then, past Joseph Cotton wouldn't work. He was wrong, as he realised later. It's become one of the most famous scenes in cinema history and it was director Carol Reed's idea not Greene's. Like I say, great teams make great movies. Oh, and by the way, remember that famous cuckoo clock dialogue in the ferris wheel scene that Orson Welles always said he wrote? He did, but only after he'd nicked it from somewhere else.

I'd spent a lot of time with rock groups, but I'd never been on stage with one, until Freddie Mercury suggested that I come out from the wings and stand behind a speaker when the crew turned the lights on Queen's audience in Sao Paulo, Brazil. 'That way you'll be able to see what we see,' he said. I did what he said and for the first time understood the extraordinary high that rock stars must get when they stand before an ocean of adoration. No wonder ovations for simply existing go to performers' heads.

This was the first time a major rock group had toured in South America and Queen were performing for 130,000 fans stretched right across the pitch and up the terraces of the Morumbi Stadium. After the show, a thrilled drummer Roger Taylor told me: 'It was extraordinarily moving that in a city where very few people speak English, well over a hundred thousand joined in the chorus of "Love Of My Life"', which was a song that had been relatively unsuccessful in Britain and the United States but which had become Queen's anthem in South America.

It was a bizarre night of different elements. There were the fans, not over-excited as those in Britain and America might be, but polite and on their best behaviour. Then Queen themselves, looking almost fragile amidst the lights and billowing clouds from their smoke machine and the roar of their music. And all around them, heavy, plain-clothed policemen in bomber jackets and T-shirts, hip guns ready, proudly showed off the bullet holes fore and aft in the tonnage of their bodies.

That was my only visit to Brazil. A few days later I watched Rio de Janeiro's Copacabana Beach evolve in a 24-hour cycle from being, in the early morning, the biggest gymnasium in the world, to becoming a maze of junior football pitches when the schools let out at lunchtime. Then came the languid afternoon beauty bikini fest, to be eventually followed in the evening by the appearance of hundreds of tiny lighted candles paying homage to Iemanja, the goddess of the sea. All of which would be cleared away at dawn to leave the beach spotless to begin another day.

And, all the time, music was playing somewhere.

25.

'Oh dear. This is unbearable. McEnroe is clearly very much out of sorts with himself ' - Dan Maskell

One of the reasons I've always liked journalism is that it gave me the chance to meet people whom, in the ordinary course of a life, I wouldn't ever have run into. But there was something else, too. It often afforded me the chance to have my say, to have my words published. Thus, when I wrote a daily TV review column for the *Evening Standard,* I knew that many people would read me, because we all like to read reviewer's opinions to see if they agree with ours. As my column ran at the same time as the Falklands War, letters poured in, and because letters had to be written and posted, they were generally more considered than today's snap online comments.

The sinking of the *Belgrano* and the loss of the *HMS Sheffield* occasioned the biggest response, when viewers were moved by their own impotence as they watched Ian McDonald, from the Ministry of Defence, break into the BBC evening news with his litanies of casualties.

On a lighter note, were the merry letters we got after my TV review of the John McEnroe-Jimmy Connors final at Wimbledon in June,1982, when I referred to Connors as behaving like 'a mad axeman in some demonic possession' and suggested that John McEnroe was 'a teenage werewolf in some equal state of mental unbalance…screaming and shouting to himself as though conversing with unheard voices'. The game was, I wrote, about as sporting as the Battle of Borodino, and marked a moment when tennis became gladiatorial.

Dan Maskell, that most polite and gentlemanly of commentators, who once got me to pluck a few blades of grass from the Centre Court to take home and show my children, had been, for him, almost hysterical with rage at McEnroe's on court behaviour. 'Oh dear. This is unbearable,' he'd murmured as he'd watched the tantrums. 'McEnroe is clearly very much out of sorts with himself.'

That voice and those impeccable manners were what Wimbledon tennis was all about.

When I wasn't reviewing television programmes, I was writing a TV film for a Channel 4 series that David Puttnam was producing. I think my story was rather good in a sad way, about how the past is never just the past, and how hurts can return to be inflicted on the innocent of the present. I'd had the idea after seeing a photograph of Simon and Garfunkel when they'd been a schoolboy duo; and had then wondered what might have happened to two other gifted boy musicians if they'd fallen out in teenage and only met again when one had become a priest and the other a college lecturer.

I'd wanted to call it *Blue Suede Shoes Backed With Tutti Frutti*, which was an answer to a sort of strip poker question in a game that the duo had played when, as rock nerds, they'd tried to persuade a girl to undo her bra. Elvis fans will know the title's derivation. But the late Jack Rosenthal, a friend who was the script editor, didn't get the association or like the title. To be honest, I don't think he liked the script at all. That was okay. I didn't like everything Jack wrote. So, I changed the title to *Forever Young*, and Jack withdrew from the project.

A Peter Maxwell Davies theme, 'Farewell to Stromness', was lying on a disc in David Puttnam's office at the time, having perhaps been submitted as a possible theme for *Local Hero*. But, as Mark Knopfler's wonderful 'Going Home' rightly got *Local Hero*, I took the Peter Maxwell Davies theme for *Forever Young* and wrote some lyrics for it.

Ours was a little 90 minute film, for which I wrote an accompanying novella. David Drury directed and Nicholas Gecks and James Aubrey played the two leads. I just wish we'd kept the original title.

My next film project was *Defrosting The Fridge* for the BBC, which was about American football, which was then becoming, for a short time, popular in England. BBC producer, Terry Coles had the original idea and title and then asked me to think up a story and write a screenplay. After a weekend in Rouen with a coach full of young Englishmen pretending to be Americans who were there on a trip to play a team of young French men also pretending to be Americans, I set our story on the Suffolk coast not far from the US Air Force base at Mildenhall. The film was how an

American football coach, who had just got out of prison, comes to train a little English team and becomes involved with the local community. Sandy Johnson was our director and Joe Don Baker, who'd had a great BBC TV success a couple of years earlier in *Edge Of Darkness,* was cast as our football coach.

Joe Don Baker is a good actor, but I couldn't stand him. At the read-through he ignored the lines written and made up his own version of the script, presumably in the belief that the writer was just a glorified typist. I told him, probably rather pompously, that was not the way we worked at the BBC.

What really maddened me was a stunt he pulled one morning when his character was supposed to cook something in his trailer for an eleven-year-old fatherless boy who hero-worshipped him. The scene was based on a moment in my own childhood when my farmer friend, Joe, had cooked lunch for me when his wife was in hospital. In a sense Joe had been a surrogate father for me on that day.

But Joe Don didn't want to do the scene like that. The thought of food made him feel 'sick to my stomach', he said. Instead, he wanted to teach the boy to play poker, thus making their relationship a buddy-buddy one rather than father and son. What I'd written tapped into a personal memory. That's what writers often do. What Joe Don wanted was to tap into a Western cliché. He was such a prat.

The film was to end with a sort of mock Eve of Agincourt dressing room speech by the coach to the players, all of whom knew they were going to be soon soundly thrashed by the visiting US Air Force team. Joe Don had already said he didn't like the original version I'd written of the speech, so I'd rewritten it. That wasn't American enough, he said. So, I copied out a speech I found in an American college football memorial book. That wasn't American enough either. This 'you can't write American dialogue' stuff really irritated. Larry Hagman had never complained. He'd always been word perfect in *Stardust.* English writers grow up hearing as much American dialogue as they do English dialogue through films and television.

The trouble was that Joe Don had no suggestions of his own of what he wanted to say. All he knew was that he didn't want me to be present when he said it. He was like a big baby from Hollywood, wanting to show us all how they did it on the backlot at Warner Brothers.

Despite Joe Don's appalling behaviour, *Defrosting The Fridge*, which was a look at English life in the old Ealing Comedy tradition in which we laugh at ourselves, wasn't bad.

The late Peter Bowles was the opposite of Joe Don Baker in that he was a professional dream to work with when we did two series of *Lytton's Diary* together. After the success of *To The Manor Born, Only When I Laugh, The Bounder,* and, best of all for me, *The Irish RM,* Peter was, at the time, the most successful TV actor in the country. So, when he came up with the idea of playing a gossip columnist on a daily newspaper, Thames TV listened, and, eventually, I was approached.

My first task was to make it clear in the scripts that few reporters get emotionally involved in the stories they are writing. They don't usually fret and worry about the people they are writing about unless they know them very well. At the same time, although they may sometimes seem uncaring, they aren't all manipulative, uncaring bastards, like the Kirk Douglas character in *Ace In The Hole.* Some are. But not many. Their main aim is to get their story right, get it past the lawyer and into the paper. For 95 per cent of the time our pretend journalists in *Lytton's Diary* got the tone dead right, so, only a couple of times did I find myself murmuring to the director, 'Could So-and-So do a bit less acting. She's sounding a bit upset. It's only a story she's working on, you know.'

The other thing was to get across the idea that a newsroom was just like any other organisation. Rival newspapers were the main competition, but other reporters on the same paper were the bigger competitors, none of which had to be said openly in dialogue but shown in the characters. To get all this right, we, like the brilliant *All The President's Men*, with Robert Redford and Dustin Hoffman, put our cast in a specially built set of a newspaper office. Our location was an empty Victorian building that was dressed with heavy old typewriters, and busy noise and activity. The designers and set dressers did an excellent job, while Chris Burt, the producer, even got Rick Wakeman to do the theme music for us. It was classy all the way.

Coming up with the stories was a joy to do. Peter Bowles, who soon became a good friend and was a very intelligent reader of a script, had some ideas as starting points, and I mentally dived into my hundreds of interviews looking for moments, characters and trains of thought that could be useful. The terrific thing about a newspaper series is that, unlike police and hospital narratives, the writer can go anywhere with his plot. One of my favourites was an episode in which Lytton gets information seeming to suggest that a highly respected, medalled and knighted old soldier murdered two of his platoon in Malaya in the Second World War. It was a story of moral ambiguity. Then there was a thinly disguised episode about *Private Eye*, featuring the very funny John Bird, and an even thinner disguise for one about a Rupert Murdoch type of figure, wonderfully played by John Stride in full Aussie rant.

I learned a lot about plotting in *Lytton's Diary*, some episodes having three stories in 52 minutes, meaning that each show could take anything up to six weeks for me to write, after which would be the shooting. So, all in all, it was two years' work to come up with thirteen hours of television, all of which were enlivened by Peter Bowles' often funny stories against himself. There were stacks of them, but I particularly liked the one about when he and Albert Finney were both at RADA and were asked how they would prepare if they were asked to play Macbeth. Peter went first, saying that he would study some Scottish history so that he could get properly into the role of a Scottish king.

Then it was Albert Finney's turn. He said: 'I'd learn the fucking lines. Say them. Then walk off the stage.'

Lytton's Diary was, for me, particularly rewarding in that I felt that I got Fleet Street right. So, along with Peter Bowles and the Thames TV head of drama, I was already planning a third series which would take newspapers into the digital age, when I was told that the series had been cancelled.

I was astonished. We'd been prime time viewing on Wednesdays at 9 pm, an intelligent, articulate, sometimes amusing, extremely well-acted, starry, popular show that regularly brought in ten to twelve million viewers. We'd got everything right. To cancel it seemed to me to be an incomprehensibly stupid decision. It was for Peter Bowles, too, and he lived next door to the guy responsible for putting us all out of work.

Which is what happened. I was suddenly unemployed. Plum and I had just bought a house in Central London where our children were at school. One minute I'd been planning the stories and plots for our future year, and the next I was wondering how I was going to pay the mortgage. It would have been the same for all the actors, producers and directors working on the series. As viewers, we always forget that when a programme that we enjoy (or even one we don't enjoy) is summarily scrapped, it can be tough on all those freelance people creatively involved.

I can see that a series like *Lytton's Diary,* that had twelve regular actors and many smaller parts, and a huge set to build, must have been expensive to produce. But an explanation wouldn't have gone amiss: a phone call of some sad regret. But we never got one.

Luckily, because Thames TV had an excellent foreign sales department, royalties for *Lytton's Diary* from around the world kept Plum and me afloat. Financially, though, it was a setback, and I didn't see the series again until 2019 when it was shown on Talking Pictures TV. Peter Bowles and his wife, Sue, watched it, too, and we all had a jolly lunch and told each other how clever we were. Certainly, we were cleverer than the clot who'd cancelled us.

Our children were all teenagers by then and we spent just about all our family holidays in an old house in a forest in Provence in southern France. Plum found it through a tiny agency. The first time we went there we arrived at night, turning off a little hillside road and making our way down along a track through the trees to what looked like a forgotten farmhouse. It was so remote that I thought we'd made a terrible mistake.

We hadn't. In the morning we walked out of our bedroom on to a terrace and found that we were in our own untouched Garden of Eden. Except that it wasn't ours. It belonged to an American academic who lived in Paris and who, some years earlier, had bought an entire valley of forty hectares up in the backwoods. He hadn't wanted so much land, because it was all forest and all he could ever do with it was look at it, but it came with the house. Take it or leave it. So, he'd taken it, after which he and his family had spent years renovating the property.

It was perfect. Nestling at the side of a little valley, with butterflies besieging the lavender, marmots in the shutters, and sometimes a litany of baby striped boars trotting after their mother, it looked down through an uncut meadow to its own stream. There was even a small circular swimming pool. But, best of all, there were no other houses to be seen, no cars to be heard, no people to pass. Generations ago it would have been farmed, and the remains of terraces, now massively overgrown and lost in the forest, could still be found. Our whole family loved it, with son Dominic writing a thesis on it for his geography degree as an example of rural depopulation.

It would remain a central part of our summer lives for the next twelve years. My mother and aunt came one year, and my sister, Sylvia, and her husband, Ermanno, drove down from their home near Geneva several times. My old university friend, Ian from Taunton, and his wife Lyn would come, too. We would usually take the house for about a month at a time, when I would take my work. Several chapters of two novels were written there. We all have a favourite place and time that lives on in our minds years after we leave it. That was mine. I wanted to buy it, but, when it eventually went up for sale, I couldn't afford it.

26.

'I never thought I looked good enough to go to discos. So, I sat in and ate and played the piano' - Victoria Wood

When I first began buying records, I always looked very carefully at the names of the songwriters that were in tiny parentheses under the title of the song. In that way I began to realise that some names cropped up on hits by a number of different singers. Apart from Carole King and Gerry Goffin, there were Jerry Leiber and Mike Stoller who wrote Ben E. King's 'Spanish Harlem' and the Coasters' 'Yakety Yak', and Barry Man and Cynthia Weil who wrote 'You've Lost That Lovin' Feeling' and 'On Broadway'. Then there were Doc Pomus and Mort Shuman with 'Teenager In Love', 'Can't Get Used To Losing You' and lots of Elvis hits. Mort Shuman was for me a name to be revered.

I'd interviewed Morty in the late Seventies after he moved from New York to Paris and brought his show about Jacques Brel to London, so when I was asked to work with him I was excited. Canadian producer Chris Malcolm wanted to turn Morty's old hits into a juke box musical, and, when I joined them, we decided to set it in 1962 during the time of the Cuban Missile Crisis. That was the period when Morty had had his biggest hits, and I remembered that the street on the Lower East Side of New York City where I'd lived that year was continually humming with music from open windows. The street would be our setting.

We decided to call our show *Save The Last Dance For Me*, after Morty's biggest hit, which would be a blackly ironic title when the characters in our story are afraid that New York is about to be vapourised by Krushchev's Soviet Union. It was wonderful working together, and, over several months, Morty would come around to our house, play the piano and talk about the people for whom he'd written hits. He was just a lovely guy.

Unfortunately, no-one seemed to remember the Cuban Missile Crisis, and nobody wanted to put on our show. It was probably my fault for trying too hard to be different. Perhaps if I'd written a boy-meets-girl type story about a youth club in Luton we would have got a better response. Always more of a film man than a theatre type, this was the first time I ever wrote for theatre, so I imagine I was a bit green about it.

We had all moved on to different projects, as is the nature of failure, when in 1992 Morty died. He was only 52. A decade later, Chris Malcolm suggested that we try again with our show, but, by that time, New York had suffered the 9/11 attack. Fear of a missile attack in the Cuban Crisis could be covered lightly because it hadn't happened. But there was nothing light about the attacks on the World Trade Centre.

Childhood always fascinated me when I was doing interviews, discovering the child before he or she became an adult, as it were. Roger Waters, of Pink Floyd, had told me about his mother being a member of the Communist Party, for example, and that his father had died in the battle of Anzio in World War Two. It was possible, therefore, to see links there to his later political affiliations. While Ringo Starr, patiently learning to play the drums while for months a patient in a TB sanatorium as a boy, painted a picture of a quiet little drummer behind the two superegos at the Beatle microphones.

So, when in 1989 *The Times* accepted my suggestion that I have a weekly page interviewing people about their childhoods, I found myself working with my old *Evening Standard* friend, Andrew Harvey, and taking the opportunity to throw my net as wide as possible. All told there would be over fifty childhood interviews. I began with Victoria Wood.

'I'd look at the other girls and wish I could be like them, meeting in the Wimpy Bar on Saturday mornings, and going to discos. I never thought I looked good enough to go to discos. So, I sat in and ate and played the piano. And I got bigger. I hated being fat, but I didn't do anything about it. I just felt wrong. And I had glasses which didn't help, and spots because I ate so many sweets. And really greasy hair.

'But I think it was all going on inside. I was biding my time. I don't think you can write unless you've been in a position where you're isolated. You can either take part in things or observe. I think if I'd been thin and gone out with boys, I wouldn't have had anything to write about. If you're fulfilled you've nothing to say.

And it's a joy to me now that all that happened because it got me where I am. I wouldn't change any of it.

'I believe we all have a certain time in our lives that we're good at. I wasn't good at being a child. Some girls at 14 are terrific, but, by the time they're 18, they're finished. It must be sad to be 18 and to know that all your best years are behind you.'

At 18, all of Gary Lineker's best years were just starting. He always knew he wanted to be a sportsman, his only decision being whether it would be playing cricket or football. 'I wasn't outstanding like some kids. I didn't get into the England Schoolboys team or anything,' he told me. But he was good, so good that when he passed the 11-Plus his family moved house so that he could go to a grammar school that played football rather than rugby.

When he was 13, he was training twice a week with Leicester City FC, except on Fridays and during the summer, when, in a change of sport, he trained with Leicestershire Country Cricket. He had a choice to make. In the end he chose football. It was in the family. His grandfather had been a skillful player in the army, but, because of the family fruit stall on Leicester Market, he'd never had the opportunity to pursue football as a career.

'There was no money in it in those days,' Lineker said. 'My grandad would always come and watch me from when I was eight. Both my parents came, too. My dad would often take our entire team to the fixtures in his fruit van.'

Performance poet Benjamin Zephaniah remembered his youth as walking along streets in Birmingham and London with his mother knocking on doors asking complete strangers if they had a room for them. 'We found rooms, too, with a Pakistani family who looked after us,' he said. 'My mum was always trying to get away from my dad. When he found us, we always moved on.'

Then, in his teenage years, came approved school and finally jail for a number of burglaries. 'About fifty,' he reckoned. He was dyslexic and would write poems in a rap metre about life on the streets, fantasising about life as a writer while he was in jail. He didn't think what he wrote was poetry; it was just something he'd always done. But others thought differently. People listened to him. He has now published over thirty books and received honorary doctorates from seven universities.

Paul Daniels found his Damascene moment while on holiday in the rain in a cottage in the Yorkshire Dales, when he picked up a Victorian home entertainment book that showed him how to do card tricks. And Terry Pratchett put his career as a writer down to someone giving him an old copy of *The Wind In The Willows,* which he read 'by the light from the street lamps on London's Western Avenue' as his father drove him home. 'Until then, I had no idea that books like that existed,' he remembered.

Interestingly, considering his later career, Michael Palin fondly told me about his father and the faded gentility of his parents' life when they got their first black and white television set in 1958. 'It was quite a handsome set. But my father, who loved church music, kept it covered up all the time with a sort of knitted antimacassar. He'd go through the *Radio Times* and circle the things he wanted to see.

'Watching television was a big production. He'd turn the armchair around. And then there would be the warm-up time, about a minute and a half, and he'd wait. And then, finally, the programme wouldn't be on. That always used to throw him. The previous programme had obviously over-run. "What's this? This isn't 'The Festival of Nine Lessons and Carols', is it?" he'd say, when it palpably wasn't, probably someone showing their bottom on a nature programme. "Mother! Get the *Radio Times*."

While Mary Soames had a unique childhood. One evening when she was a little girl her father, Winston Churchill, told her that if she looked into the drawing room at their home, Chartwell, she would see an Arab prince. What she saw was Lawrence of Arabia dressed in cream-coloured Arab dress, with a long, curved sword at his side.

'He would arrive as Aircraftman Shaw on his motorbike dressed in his Air Force uniform. My father had great admiration for him. I always had to feed my animals and milk my goats before I went to school, and on my way back I would come across him walking on the lawn.'

At 17 she left school on the day war was declared. Then at 18 she joined the Auxiliary Territorial Service and was posted to an anti-aircraft battery, where bunks were three tiers deep. 'The Army was a great leveller,' she said. 'My whole life has been as a daughter, a mother and a wife. I'm not whingeing about that. Actually, I'm extraordinarily proud of it.'

I'd always been in awe of the film *The Sting*. It was so perfectly plotted, as the good-looking small-time conmen, Robert Redford and Paul Newman, con the big bad villains, and, in so doing, fool us, the viewers, too, with a couple of terrific twists that we don't see coming. It was just a very clever and well-written film. So, when, in 1989, Peter Bowles stopped me in the street and told me that he and his co-star in *The Irish RM* , Bryan Murray, wanted me to write a new series for them about two likeable conmen, my initial reaction was to decline. I was flattered, but I didn't think I had the right kind of crooked mind for that. Apparently, I had.

The series was called *Perfect Scoundrels*. I wanted to call it *Bad Penny Blues*, after the Humphrey Lyttleton record, which I suggested for the theme music, too, with Humph even bringing me a copy of the record. I lost that battle. That was all right, getting the cons right was my real job.

If the conman just wants to steal from the unsuspecting, cons are not difficult to plot. But our *Perfect Scoundrels* conmen had to be likeable. So, my role in writing the series was to devise cons in which our heroes only took on villains more crooked than themselves. Which, inevitably, would put them in jeopardy, because conmen can't go rushing to the police if a vicious criminal whom they've conned turns nasty. Peter and Bryan were good friends, but to make it even more fun to write, and more fun to act in, I arranged it so that the two didn't always get on, or even trust each other.

We had a great director in Ian Toynton, who has since done many of the big Hollywood series, and it was terrific fun to do. The myth is that you can't con an honest man. Well, as many of us have discovered to our cost, you obviously can. But the notion that conmen play upon the greed of the 'mark' (the victim of the con) served us well when we convinced a dodgy property tycoon that secret geological research showed that there was oil in Killarney. Then there was the one about a multi-millionaire who sold phony health remedies to the gullible, and another where we faked a previously unheard Elvis Presley record, for which I even got my friend Mort Shuman to write a new song for us. My favourite story, though, was about a preacher who was running a money-making religious cult and who had sexual designs on our heroes' very pretty accomplice, played by the late Arkie White. The fact that the Bryan Murray character was also keen on her, made the implied kompromat pulled on the preacher all the more delicious.

I dropped out at the end of the first series in a disagreement over what I was being paid. The episodes were so difficult and time consuming to devise that I wanted more money. I didn't get it. But that was all right. I had a novel to write. Peter, Bryan and I all remained good friends.

When he reached 18, our elder son, Dominic, decided that he wanted to take a gap year before university. And off he went, just a few months after leaving school, to teach in a Shona village in the bush in Zimbabwe, a place that, just eight years earlier, in 1980, had become a new country at the end of the civil war in Southern Rhodesia. It's tough on parents when any child leaves home for the first time, so, four months later, Plum and I went to see how he was getting on. It turned out to be a pivotal moment for my new novel that would be called *Sunday Morning*.

I've never started any fiction, whether a novel, film or TV play, with a story mapped out. My technique is to have an idea of what I want to write about, then muse on it until I see in my mind's eye what will be the opening image or scene, after which I begin to explore it, dress it with characters, and discover where it takes me.

I knew that *Sunday Morning* was going to be about the growth of a media conglomerate from being born as a tiny news magazine. That was an area I knew well. It was also going to be mainly about London in the Sixties to Eighties, which I also knew a bit about. But it wasn't until Plum and I went to Zimbabwe, that I realised it would also be about the end of empire.

Thirty years earlier I'd studied Central Africa as part of my social anthropology degree, so I knew about the main tribes, the Shona and the Ndebele, but only in an academic sense. Visiting Dominic in his room in a prefab near a tiny African village, where he taught in a school that the local parents had built 'with our own hands' after their country had gained independence, and then setting off with him to travel across Zimbabwe, began to fill in the background of my story.

There were the mountains and forest of the Vumba that lie along the Mozambique border: they look and smell like Scotland. Then there was the albino child trying to hide her eyes from the glare of the sun, the remote, grand colonial house on a hill, the lingering paternalistic attitudes of some white Rhodies towards their black staff, and an African father on a lonely hill having a picnic with his son while reading *Far From The Madding Crowd* out loud to him. These were the images in my mind and on my camera as gradually *Sunday Morning* took shape, a story about four young ambitious people, like me, and so many of my generation.

When I got home, it took me a year to write *Sunday Morning*, and, although it was fiction, it was strangely like writing the story of a life I'd never lived, just as exhilarating in some parts, and just as upsetting in others.

27.

**'I thought that to be a composer I would
have to speak like someone on the BBC'
- George Martin**

Do you remember foreign? It used to start at Calais with a stamp on your passport. In those days everywhere else was foreign, and everywhere else was foreign to everywhere else. The varieties of human behaviour, language, culture and style among our few nearest European neighbours was bewildering. That's how it was in 1955 when I first encountered foreign on a school trip to Lourdes. It was very exciting. Soon, though, France and most of Western Europe became less foreign as our holidays in the sun became cheaper, until eventually only the Iron Curtain countries of Eastern Europe were out of bounds, with Europe seeming to end at Austria.

We obviously knew about all those other countries beyond the Iron Curtain. But they were, in my schoolboy imagination, darkly coloured by a *Biggles Flies East* adventure in which he was, post-war, fighting Communism. Beyond West Germany was, apparently, the cold, joyless, Soviet empire where East German guards shot people who tried to escape, and where Russian soldiers put down uprisings in Hungary, East Germany, Poland and Czechoslovakia. Listening to radio sports commentators when our plucky football teams played away on European nights at the seemingly joyless Dresden, Budapest and Warsaw stadiums added heroism to our football fantasies.

Then, suddenly, Gorbachev and glasnost were upon us, and in 1989 the Berlin Wall came tumbling down and that changed everything. Overnight Europe seemed to double in size, and we realised how near was Eastern Europe and how much there was to see there.

Sunday Morning was finished and soon to be published, so I was already musing on another novel, when Plum and I took our car for a ski-ing trip to Austria in 1992; after which, we just carried on driving to Prague with its cobbled streets and ancient tramlines.

Czechoslovakia, as it was then, was still what I would call a 40 watt country in that there wasn't much to buy in the shops; but forty odd years of Communism had done it one enormous favour. Modernisation had hardly spoiled it. It wasn't just foreign. With its towers and steeples, it was also architecturally medieval and romantic. No wonder they'd filmed *Amadeus* there.

The notion that foreign was already in retreat and change was on its charger was clear, as on the Charles Bridge touts sold surplus Red Army uniforms alongside pirate cassettes of Western rock groups. Today Prague is an EasyJet weekend for boys and a hen night for girls, but in the early Nineties it was a place in transition.

I dropped Plum off at the airport after a couple days, and, as she flew home, I drove on down the fishbone back of Czechoslovakia and into Poland. The new novel that I was planning was about the making of a hundred million dollar movie concerning the love affair between Napoleon and the Polish aristocrat, Maria Walewska. But before I began writing, I wanted to see Poland, and to find my way into my story. Cracow, historical and blackened, as it was then, where no restaurant served after nine o'clock, and where Steven Spielberg's *Schindler's List* was due to soon start shooting, didn't present any ideas, so I drove south into the Tatra Mountains.

By now, I knew what I was seeking, and, as I turned a steep corner in the forest covered hills I found it. Below me was a flooded river. That would be my opening scene, where a young Polish boy out fishing with his father sees a large car emerge from the water as the flood level drops. But it wouldn't be any car. It would be a huge, flashy American limousine containing three dead bodies, one of whom would be dressed as Napoleon, and another his mistress Marie Walewska. That would be the beginning of *Shadows On A Wall*.

With that settled, I set off for home to start writing.

On the couple of occasions that Paul McCartney had invited me to see the Beatles recording at Abbey Road Studios, I'd always been rather afraid of George Martin. To me, as a young journalist, George was the boss, and, although he was friendly enough, I'd kept my head down in his presence. So, I was flattered when, in 1994, I was asked to co-write, with director Alan Benson, a BBC-2 documentary series for George to present. It was called *The Rhythm of Life*, and I learned more about music in our months on that series than I did in all my years being, as Alan Benson would tease, 'an enthusiastic amateur'.

In the early Sixties, George really must have seemed the most unlikely musical collaborator for the Beatles. There were they, four cheeky, idiosyncratic, ambitious young boys from Liverpool, obsessed with rock music; while George Martin, already 36, with a wife, children and a mortgage, was classically trained and had the voice and demeanour of a middle to-high ranking civil servant.

Yet, George Martin's relationship with the band, was an association which was to change not only his and their lives, but also the nature of popular music. In later years, though some of them might not have wanted to admit it, but getting George Martin as their producer had been the Beatles' second biggest lucky break after Lennon's meeting with McCartney.

George Martin wasn't a performer and was little appreciated by the general public during the Beatles early years, but his contribution to their records, and the overall sound of the time, was immense. Modestly, he told me that the Beatles were so good that any competent producer could have recorded them. That may have been true, but only up to a point. Yes, the Beatles would probably have been successful had George Martin never existed.

But would they have sounded the same? Would any other producer have had the technical and musical expertise, combined with the patience and the diplomacy to translate their whims into the music they were imagining? I don't think so. While they bubbled with radical creativity, George Martin's musical know-how put that creativity on record and embellished it.

There was something else. The Beatles knew everything there was to know about rock music. But, when they met George Martin, he didn't even much like it. Instead, he was steeped in classical music, jazz, swing, even Scottish country dance, stuff the Beatles knew hardly anything about. Their coming together, the eager rockers from Liverpool, and the cultivated arranger from London, was a marriage made in musical heaven. Another producer might have encouraged the Beatles to stay a brilliant four-man rock band. But George Martin realised what else could be done with their songs.

Would anyone else have thought of laying a string quartet behind Paul McCartney on 'Yesterday'; or used an octet of violins, violas and cellos on 'Eleanor Rigby', that spikey sound that George Martin borrowed from Bernard Hermann's arrangement for Alfred Hitchcock's *Psycho*? And then there was the piccolo trumpet on 'Penny Lane' and the Victorian steam organ on 'For The Benefit of Mr Kite' for the *Sergeant Pepper* album, revolutionary ideas for pop music, and made to work because of George Martin knowledge of music and skills in the studio.

Nor was he just their producer, he was also an arranger, and, although largely uncredited, he was the pianist and harmonium player on thirty-five of their recordings, about a sixth of everything they recorded. The John Lennon song 'In My Life' is a classic but may well not have been if George Martin hadn't written and played a Bach influenced bridge for it, which, when speeded up, made it sound like a harpsichord. If anyone deserved to be called the 'fifth Beatle' it was George Martin. His musicianship was all over their records.

Most of all, though, he was both their musical editor and teacher, and like a good teacher, he encouraged, thus making it possible for the Beatles to express themselves to their fullest. The inspiration worked both ways. While he helped bring out the best in them, they stretched the musicality in him.

While we were planning *The Rhythm of Life,* I went out to visit George a couple of times at his Georgian house in the Wiltshire countryside, where I discovered a quite different man from that of his public image. He'd been born, he told me, in 1926 in the Holloway district of North London. His father worked as a machine carpenter, and his mother had gone out scrubbing floors when his dad was out of work for nearly two years during the Depression.

'We were,' he said 'very, very poor, living in a rundown four storey house with a family on each floor. There was no great musical tradition in the family, but my uncle was a piano tuner and started a business with a friend making pianos. Unfortunately, they went broke, but they had a number of pianos lying around so we managed to get one. I can remember reaching up to play the keys when I was very small. I can't remember not playing. I can't really explain it, but I was born with an understanding of music and perfect pitch.'

At the age of ten, he was sent for music lessons, until his mother fell out with the music teacher. Then, when he was in his early teens, his life was transformed when, as part of a musical education programme, a symphony orchestra visited his school and played a piece by Debussy. Most of the other boys were probably bored, but George was captivated that music could paint such pictures in sound. He'd already taught himself to play the piano by ear, and, at sixteen, he began running his own school dance band.

With the possibility of university out of his parents' economic range, his ambition was to be an aeronautical engineer. So, when, in 1943, he was called up, he entered the Fleet Air Arm as an observer, where, as he rose to the rank of lieutenant, the first of the changes in his life occurred. His accent changed, from that of a London lower middle-class boy, to that of the cultivated schoolmaster, which he was to keep for the rest of his life.

'I wanted to be a composer like Rachmaninov,' he explained. 'But I thought that to be a composer I would have to speak like someone on the BBC.'

After the war, it was to music that he looked for a career, via the Guildhall School of Music, with the lessons he learned there one day being heard on some of the most popular records ever.

'I was playing the oboe in orchestra pits and afternoon bands in London parks in the late Forties,' he said. 'Then I was taken on as the assistant "artistes and repertoire" man at Parlophone Records in the Abbey Road studios, where I produced everything, from classical music to Jimmy Shand's Scottish country dance records, jazz, comedy, and what was then known, somewhat disparagingly, as "popular music".'

Initially, pop was not even his strongest point, his first successes being 'Barwick Green', *The Archers* theme tune, 'Nelly The Elephant' by 12 year old Mandy Miller, the Goons' record 'I'm Walking Backwards To Christmas', and the *Beyond the Fringe* album. When rock and roll hit Britain in the late-Fifties, he more or less missed it.

'Rock music was alien to me,' he admitted. 'I was never a great Elvis Presley fan.' Nor did he have much respect for the Everly Brothers, which was surprising, as they had provided much inspiration for Lennon and McCartney. In truth, he was just that little bit too old to love rock and roll.

Even though he gave the Beatles a recording contract, he didn't at first have huge enthusiasm for them, allowing them only the lowest royalty possible on their records. Only when, at his suggestion, they upped the tempo and reshaped the song chosen for their second record, 'Please Please Me', did he begin to see how good they could be.

Within a year their lives had changed forever, as had his, when he found himself also producing hits for Cilla Black, Billy J. Kramer and the Fourmost, as well as Gerry and the Pacemakers. Indeed, it was Martin who suggested that Gerry Marsden record 'You'll Never Walk Alone', which has since become the football anthem of Liverpool Football Club and other clubs. He didn't realise his role in that until I told him.

He was the man with the golden ear, but by the end of the Sixties his relationship with the Beatles had changed, they becoming the masters in the studio and he the hired musical boffin. By nature, and sheer working practice, he had more in common with Paul McCartney, whom he considered to be a genius, than either John Lennon or George Harrison. And, though he continued to work with McCartney on and off for the next thirty years, none of the other three asked for his expertise when they became solo artists. 'After John died, Yoko said to me that she wished I'd worked with John once more,' he told me. 'If he'd asked me, I would have jumped at it, but he never asked.'

He was always interesting to listen to when he talked about the Beatles. Paul McCartney, for instance 'never knew his best songs. He'd come in with four or five and you'd always have to tell him which was the best.' As for John Lennon: 'He hated his own voice. When we were recording, he was always asking me to distort and disguise it by putting different sorts of echo on it. In that way when he heard it through the headphones, he could forget he was listening to John Lennon. I loved his voice.'

The Rhythm Of Life was a successful, interesting TV series. But, as with sport, so with music, not much that musicians can say and explain is as exciting as listening to them playing and singing. That was why they'd become musicians.

28.

'There was a flicker of light in the already sunlit cockpit, and we turned to see a ball of fire above the ground' - Leonard Cheshire

I'd been born during the Second World War, but, although it had a profound effect upon my mother's life, and probably mine, too, I have no memory of the war ever being talked about in our home. Apparently, that wasn't unusual, as most families seem to have put the war behind them once it was over. So, only in my mid-career did I find myself having conversations with people from the generation before mine who had vivid wartime memories.

The first came when the *Radio Times* sent me to Stuttgart, with a former pilot from Bomber Command, to meet a man who had been a fighter pilot in the Luftwaffe. The three of us had a very convivial afternoon and dinner as the two old foes joked together and wondered whether they had ever met as combatants in the skies over northern France or Belgium. The shared view was that they probably hadn't, and the two old airmen shook hands as they said goodbye to each other.

It was quite a moving moment, until, on the way back to our hotel, the former RAF pilot suddenly said: 'Nice chap, wasn't he. But every time I looked him in the eyes I saw "Fritz" grinning on my tail through my rear-view mirror'. Memories like his lay deep in his psyche.

A special day in July 1944 would remain in Barbara Castle's memory. Over twenty years later she would become the first woman to have a seat in Cabinet in Harold Wilson's government, but she was then a journalist and it was her wedding day. 'Ted and I had got married that morning. It wasn't a white wedding, but in a time of clothes rationing I wore a little cocktail dress instead. We were going for our honeymoon to Cornwall and Ted had bribed a porter to get us into a compartment on the train. As soon as we got in, the porter locked the door because other people were standing in the corridor wanting to get in, too. Then, suddenly, the air raid sirens went off and V-1s started dropping, and there we were, locked in a train at Paddington, a supreme target. You could have been in your coffin, so to speak. A hundred of these flying bombs were being launched on London every day. Six thousand people died in three months.

'Finally, the train started. It seemed such a relief, a sense of escape, to be getting away. I've always had this image of V-1s falling around us on my wedding day. But nobody ever had a better wedding night.'

One of Group Captain Leonard Cheshire's wartime memories changed the course of his life. After a gilded youth and a Victoria Cross for bravery during 200 bombing runs on Germany, he was chosen, at the age of 27, to be the Prime Minister's official observer when the atom bomb was detonated over Nagasaki in 1945.

This was how he relived the flight for me: 'Because of some confusion and bad weather, the plane I was flying in was about 40 miles from the explosion, but, still, there was flicker of light in the already sunlit cockpit, and we turned to see a ball of fire above the ground which became a cloud reaching upwards, and then a finely sculpted column of smoke. At the base it flattened out into a three-mile-wide pyramid, absolutely black. It was a horrendous site. I had mixed emotions. One part of me was thinking in relief, "That's it. The killing of six years is finished". And another part was thinking about the people who had just died.' He would devote the rest of his life to creating over 200 homes for the disabled.

Harry Secombe would remember first meeting Spike Milligan in the North African desert during the war. That was inevitably a funny story. Others weren't. On the night Mussolini declared war on Britain, sculptor Eduardo Paolozzi, who had been born above his family's ice-cream shop, in Leith, Edinburgh, found himself being woken by the sound of the family's shop windows being smashed and the shop's contents looted. He was Scottish: others saw him as Italian.

'A few days later, all the Italian men in the city were rounded up,' he remembered, 'and put on a ship for internment in Canada. But the ship was torpedoed and my father, grandfather and uncle, who were among them, all died. I was 16 and was jailed. In some ways, it was a relief from the hard work at home. I had my own cell, and the door was open ten hours day. It was very humane, and I was sent books by my school. After three months they released me, and I went back to school and selling ice cream. The insurance company paid for the broken windows.'

Paul Raymond, of soft porn fame, and who would leave his granddaughters a £75 million pounds Soho property empire in his will, admitted that during the war years he'd been 'a bit of a spiv. You could always get by…a bit of black-market here and bit more there. I was into all kinds of things. Eventually, I was called up and sent down a mine in Swinton as a Bevan Boy. I left after a couple of days. I didn't like it at all down there. I wouldn't have minded the Merchant Navy, but the mine was terrible.' He turned instead to running market stalls in Oldham and Rochdale. It took the police two years to catch up with him. 'I could have been jailed, but they sent me to join the RAF instead, where I became a drummer in a marching band.'

Tony Benn's memory was that while stationed in Alexandria he'd been given permission to visit a kibbutz in what is now Israel. And it was while he and some colleagues were fishing in the Sea of Galilee that he heard that the war (in Europe) was over. 'So, we spent the night in the kibbutz where all the different Jews from different countries performed their national dances. Then someone said, "The three British officers will now perform their English dance". After some consultation, I think we performed "Hands, Knees and Bumps-a-Daisy".'

And then there was the German avant-garde composer Karlheinz Stockhausen who told me how his mother had been committed to an asylum when he was four, and how, when he was twelve, his father, a member of the Nazi party, had told him that she'd been killed. 'They would kill people who were in institutions for the mentally ill because food was so scarce during the war,' he said. 'My father was asked if he wanted my mother's ashes, but he didn't take them.'

Everyone had a story… even if they didn't always want to tell it, and that was lingering in the back of my mind when one day in 1994 I found myself on a ferry to Ouistreham in Normandy with BBC-TV producer, John Coleman, and his small team. A national celebration was being planned to mark the fiftieth anniversary of D-Day, and, as I'd suffered the death of my father just a few months after that day, it seemed a good idea for me to be involved in a counter intuitive documentary that remembered the losses that inevitably accompany victory. It was called *A Day To Remember*.

We were taking with us a couple of old soldiers who had been among the first ashore on that first morning of the invasion, one of whom, Bill, had been a professional soldier for much of his career. After that, he'd retired to be a gardener in the New Forest. Then there was a former Free French fighter who'd escaped to England when France had been invaded by Germany in 1940. I learned a lot about the realities of war during that week of filming.

On the first day, Bill showed us what he believed to be the spot where he'd come ashore on the morning of June 6, 1944. 'There was a sort of watchtower up there,' he told me, pointing to what was now a promenade. 'A Gerry was shooting at us and we were pinned down and couldn't move forward. So, I managed to work my way around the side. And… I got him!'

So, it went on all day as we left the beach, filmed the war memorial, and moved to the town and then the little lanes towards Caen.

'What did you do if the enemy soldiers surrendered?' I asked at one point.

Bill was matter of fact. 'We shot them. You couldn't risk it. While you're dealing with him, his mate could shoot you.' That didn't go in the film.

'What was the worst thing you saw during that time?'

Our Free Frenchman knew exactly. 'The young boys in the German army. Even when the odds against them were impossible, they wouldn't, just *wouldn't* give up. They seemed to have some crazy idea of the valour of fighting to the last. When we got to Caen we were being held back by a sniper at an upstairs window. So, a couple of us managed to enter the building and creep up the stairs. There was a lot of noise going on. When we reached the door, I threw it open. As the guy turned, I shot him and thanked God that I'd killed him, and he hadn't killed me. But, when I went across to his body, I discovered that he was only seventeen. Since then, I've often thought about his mother.' After filming our old soldiers, we sent them home and moved on along the north coast of France.

Over the years, I'd always promised myself that one day I would discover what had happened to my father, but, in the end, it had taken a producer, John Coleman at the BBC, to do it for me. That I was unsure of the precise date of my father's death, and more, that I didn't know the exact circumstances or even where he was buried, he found astonishing. It astonishes me now. As a journalist all my working life, it has been my job to ask questions, but all I then knew of my Dad was that he'd been lost at sea. I'd assumed his grave to be among the hundreds in one of the war cemeteries in Normandy.

Intrigued, John Coleman had asked if he might make some enquiries on my behalf, and within an hour he had a date and a place, and the details of the convoy my father had been on. Far from his body lying with thousands of his fallen comrades, he was buried alone nearly two hundred miles away, the only Commonwealth grave in a small cemetery in a village called Servel in Brittany. Obviously, my mother had been told fifty years earlier. But her sadness had been silent. She'd last seen my father at the end of his leave in September, 1944, as he'd walked away up the road. A month later, on October 18, he was dead.

Before going to France, I'd approached the naval records department of the Ministry of Defence in Whitehall for information on the fate of the 9th Flotilla. I'd found it in the Admiralty War Diary. It stretched to several pages and said how on the night of October 17, 1944, as the convoy O.S. 92/K.M.S. 66 pulled away from Land's End, autumn gales had blown up, dispersing the vessels and causing at least eight large transport landing craft to lose their tows. Two sloops, two frigates, four corvettes, a destroyer and an aircraft had been sent to their aid.

The landing craft on which my father was serving, HMLCT 7015, was last seen at three o'clock on the afternoon of Wednesday, October 18, about two hundred miles due west of Land's End. For five days there had been an air and sea search of the area. Two days later, the surviving commander of a sister transport landing craft, HMLCT 7014, who, with two thirds of his crew had been plucked from the sea, described in a report how, after their tow broke, water got into the engine. Then virtually all the buoyancy drums were ripped away in the gale, the cargo became unstable, an auxiliary pump became inaccessible, and the hold covers could not withstand the weight of the water. Slowly their vessel was flooded and sank. Three other landing craft and their entire crews had been lost.

The night before we went to the cemetery in Servel, I sat on my hotel bed and took out my father's wallet that had been returned to my mother from the Admiralty fifty years earlier. She'd shown it to me a couple of times when I'd been a boy, but I'd been too young to appreciate its emotional significance for her. Throughout all those years she'd kept it in the manila envelope in which it had arrived and had given it to me the weekend before we began filming.

It had been in a pocket of my father's uniform when his body had been found. Its contents were still intact as he'd last seen them. There were some personal items: a National Service medical card, an invitation to the Union Jack Club in Asbury Park, New Jersey, (where he'd been stationed as an instructor for some of the war), and a shopping list of measurements, shoe sizes for my sister, Sylvia, and me. And then, wrapped in a kind of primitive plastic, there were some professionally taken photographs of Sylvia and me in a container, slightly discoloured by weeks in the sea, but otherwise astonishingly well preserved.

There were also two other items. One was a sheet of paper in my father's handwriting listing spare parts and tools required for the guns of the eight different craft of the 9th Flotilla. Virtually everything, even such everyday items as screwdrivers, had been crossed out and underlined 'N.A.' Not Available. Wartime shortages. The other was a scrap of faded blue paper, tucked into one of the small leather pockets, on which he'd written the titles of two songs that I imagine my mother must have asked him to buy as sheet music for her to play. They were the wartime favourites, 'You'll Never Know' and 'You Are My Sunshine'.

His grave lay in a small alcove against the church at Servel. Arranged on top of it was a jar containing laurel leaves, a geranium in a plant pot, and some floral plastic mementos of the type popular in France. I have no idea who might have left them. On the plain, white Commonwealth Graves headstone was the inscription: *'J. CONNOLLY, ORDNANCE ARTIFICER, 4th CL.R.N. D/MX 90406. H.M.L.C.T. 7015, 18th October, 1944. Age 33.'*

It was an emotional moment. I don't know if I expected some flash of recognition or perhaps new memories, but none came. I thought of my children and of how my father had never been able to enjoy his family as I enjoyed mine.

The past is a fitful friend. Happy memories are always welcome; sad ones creep up unannounced. All it takes is a fragment of music and, uninvited, the past rejoins us. For me the song 'You Are My Sunshine' had always pricked a tear. Now I knew why.

We were visiting the tiny hamlet of Servel on a cloud-washed day. Beyond the churchyard, a yellow ribbon of gorse ran across the cliffs and down to the beach. It was there that the local people would have discovered my father's body. Part of the Bay of Lannion, it remains unspoiled, cleansed by the same heavy Atlantic waves that would have carried him the three hundred miles from where his vessel sank in the Western Approaches. Although he is buried there, in his lifetime my father never visited France. Now he lies between two French families.

Up to that point, my mother had never visited my father's grave. Immediately after the war it would have been impossible for her. Brittany would have seemed like the other side of the world from Lancashire. And, as the years went by, there was for her, I imagine, a fear of re-opening the wound. Then, the year after I first went there, my sister, Sylvia, took her.

I first wrote about that day in Lannion in an article for the *Readers Digest*. Then, several years later, I received a letter from a Foreign Legionnaire who'd read a translation of it in the French *Readers Digest* and now wanted to meet me. The extraordinary thing was that he was English. As a young man, he'd left his home in the north of England thirty years earlier and had spent an entire career with the Foreign Legion in parts of Africa, France and the Caribbean. Now he was looking forward to living in a retirement home for ex-Legionnaires in France. 'The *Legion Étranger* looks after its old soldiers very well,' he wanted me to know.

The next time he came to England, to visit his family, we met at London's Victoria Station. He'd come especially to London from Yorkshire on a return bus ticket bringing me presents of a Foreign Legionnaire's combat T-shirt, a medal, a beret and two bottles of *Legion Étranger* wine. He was a sensible, direct and very proud man, a soldier through and through, who had been moved by my article and simply wanted to know more about my mother, my sister and me, and how life had turned out for us.

So, I filled in as many details as he required. 'And your mother, did she marry again?' he asked. No, she hadn't. He nodded.

His own career had been fascinating, as he told me about life in the Foreign Legion. Did he ever shoot anyone, I asked.

'Well, they said I was a good shot, and I aimed at a few,' he said with a shrug.

Remembering stories of men who had sought anonymity in the Foreign Legion, I most wanted to discover the trigger that had caused him to make such a radical change to his life. But none of his first replies seemed to quite explain his sudden decision, until I asked him if a girl had been involved.

'Well, yes,' he said after a hesitation. 'There was a young lady. She got engaged to somebody else.'

Then off he'd gone, speaking no French, to join the Foreign Legion.

29.

'Have you seen the old man in the closed-down market, kicking up the papers with his worn-out shoes...' - Ralph McTell

It's invigorating to get good reviews. My novel *Sunday Morning* was well received and there was a race to option it for a TV serial. But, partly set in Zimbabwe, it would have been an expensive production. So, when the winner of the option race left the TV company who'd optioned it and went off to eventually produce *Mamma Mia,* I could sense the tide of interest receding.

Success can be a very narrow window, and every novelist knows that feeling as something he or she has invested years in creating is gradually orphaned. The *Sunday Morning* sales, which for hardback and paperback had totalled just under 45,000, weren't bad, but not great, either. I'd had too large an advance from my publisher, so my next novel for them, *Shadows On A Wall*, which was my movie-making story about Napoleon, would have to sell extremely well. It didn't, the British reviews being good but few.

In America, a country where movies have a much bigger cultural profile, the notices were terrific, the best of my career, and, over the next few years, *Shadows On A Wall*, would be optioned by Hollywood four times for a TV series. But, once again, the TV series hasn't yet been made. So, although the American and Japanese publishers made a profit on their investment and sent me royalties, the British publishers lost money, as *Shadows On A Wall* didn't come close to repaying the advance I'd had to cover the time it took to write it.

If I'd been clever, I would have written a sequel to *Sunday Morning*, which was the story of a group of the people who come of age in the Sixties and end up running a media empire. I've often been asked what happened to those people? How did it turn out for them?

I tell them I don't know. At the time a sequel just didn't occur to me, and I had a living to earn. So, I turned to radio and adapted a BBC play from a memoir by producer John Houseman. It was about Raymond Chandler's time in Hollywood, and we called it *Lost Fortnight*. It was set in 1945 when Chandler had been employed to turn an unfinished novel he'd written into a screenplay for an Alan Ladd movie, who had just been called up by the US Army. The film would be *The Blue Dahlia*.

The radio play was a good project and involved meeting John Houseman, who had been Orson Welles's producer on *Citizen Kane*. To me, Houseman was Hollywood royalty, and, as a screenwriter, I enjoyed his story of how Orson Welles had tried to steal a sole writing credit for *Citizen Kane* from writer Herman J. Mankiewicz. 'Orson's contribution to the writing of that movie was no greater than what any director does on any movie,' Houseman told me firmly. Whether that was completely the case or not, and it's now a Hollywood legend, I don't know. I wasn't there. Houseman was. But I loved hearing movie gossip. Apparently, Raymond Chandler loved gossip, too. But, as a recovering alcoholic, he also yearned for a drink.

Insanely, in the haste to get *The Blue Dahlia* into production before Alan Ladd had to leave for the US Army, Paramount began filming. Chandler, however, hadn't finished the script, and the problem he'd encountered while writing the novel (basically, whodunnit?) hadn't been resolved in his mind. He didn't know whodunnit, or how they were going to end the film, which he finally admitted to a nervous Houseman. How he and Houseman resolved Chandler's writers' block was the stuff of *Lost Fortnight*. It was produced by Martin Jenkins and we had the terrific Peter Barkworth playing Raymond Chandler.

Radio might be the poor relation in terms of drama, and the BBC don't put enough muscle into promoting their Radio 4 plays. But, when they cast a piece well, the connection with the listeners can be total. It's just the radio and you. And you provide your own pictures.

I've made my living for the last fifty years as a jobbing writer. A freelance. Usually, it's paid pretty well. Sometimes wonderfully. But now and again it hasn't. I'm not complaining. It was the life I chose. The drought years never much worried me because times of plenty had invariably followed, but they worried my bank manager something awful. So, in the late Nineties, worn down by his mithering, I let him talk me into the benefits of selling our house in South Kensington. It was the daftest thing I ever did. A year later, after I'd had my finances investigated by a money expert whom I'd read about in the *Sunday Times*, the bank repaid me £35,000, with an admission that they'd been charging me way too much interest on my overdraft for several years. They apologised, as well.

I suppose, having been educated at the London School of Economics, I ought to have been more canny with my money and noticed that I was being ripped off. But my degree hadn't been in finance. It had been in social anthropology, with my special area being the tribes in the grasslands of Africa where a man measures his wealth by the number of cows he owns; rarely more than three or four. There was a difference. There are no cows in South Kensington.

By this time, I'd reached my mid-fifties, and had begun seeing some of my friends taking early retirement. So, I wrote a column for *The Times* about an invented character of my age who is made redundant. I called it *Tim Merryman's Days of Clover*. It didn't really work that well in the paper, but then I was asked to do it as a BBC radio series. It was better there, as directed by Dirk Maggs, though I wish they'd stuck with Paul Nicholas, the actor who had played Tim Merryman in the pilot episode. I'd known Paul, though not well, from our days doing *Stardust,* and he was very good. But I had no say in the change of actors, and it could be frustrating.

When I'd begun writing drama with *That'll Be The Day*, David Puttnam had included me in all the major decisions. But in radio and television I sometimes felt like 'just the writer', my job ending when I handed in the final draft of my script, with little say in the casting and none in the editing. I never liked that and railed against it. There were always things to be changed, and edits to be checked. Some producers and directors have it in their heads that writers will always want to save their lines from being cut. I don't think that is true. It certainly isn't for me. Writers are editors themselves. Every day of their lives they cut their own material. That's what they do, write and edit, write and edit. And they want the film, TV show, radio drama or whatever they've written to be as economically and skilfully told as possible. Without getting in the way, I believe that the writer should always have a say, especially in the editing. Sorry about the rant, but it's something that has always bothered me.

Funnily enough, although I know that newspaper sub-editors have a notorious public image for cutting and chopping pieces without recourse to the writer, I can honestly say that after a lifetime in journalism, and thousands of articles, I can count on one hand the number of times that has happened to me.

Travel writing was something I did for a while, taking the Hurtigruten boat cruise along the coast of Norway, cruising in the Caribbean, becoming marooned in a hotel in Hue, Vietnam, during a typhoon and its resulting flood when the Perfume River broke its banks, and riding an elephant in Thailand. The trick, by the way, is to sit on the elephant's head, make sure you grip with your thighs like mad because it's slippery, then kick the back of its ears to tell it which way to go. The elephant gets the message.

Then one day I came up with a better idea for travel writing. Travelling back in time. For a couple of years in the 1990s, regressive hypnotherapy was a regular feature on daytime television, with people constantly cropping up with accounts of how they'd been hypnotised and discovered that they'd been present when Mary Queen of Scots had been executed or had been a Roundhead in the Civil War. So, vaguely wondering if there was a novel to be written around the subject of two lives colliding, generations apart, something like the Leslie Howard Thirties' film, *The House in Berkeley Square*, I went to South London to meet a hypnotherapist.
He was a little, middle-aged man with dyed black hair. He collected me in his car at the local station, and then drove me to his semi-detached home. What was I getting into, I wondered, as he led me up to an attic that he called his consulting room. Was I really about to discover who I used to be a hundred years ago?

I'd found him through a magazine for psychics, and the fee would be £35 for a successful regression. It was certainly cheaper than the Delorean car and flux capacitor device that Michael J. Fox had needed in the film *Back To The Future*, when he'd gone back to the Fifties and almost snogged his mother while she'd still been at high school.

So, there I was on a divan, as the hypnotist got me to talk about myself. Name, age, place of birth, profession, religion. He frowned when I said I was a journalist, and even more so when he learned that I was a lapsed Catholic. He'd had trouble with Catholics, because the Pope had outlawed any ideas about reincarnation in thought fifteen hundred years ago.

Nevertheless, we proceeded, and he told me his explanation of regression. It seemed to me he was saying that although the physical body may die and decay it might not be so with the mind which has a different invisible source of energy. He didn't explain why the mind didn't die along with the brain, but said, 'you just have to take some things on trust in this life'. Or in other lives, too, I supposed.

At this point, he suggested I lie down on the divan. Curtains were then drawn around me, and, although it was summer, and an electric fire was on, he wrapped me in a very thick banket. It was very hot in the room.

Then he switched on a tape recorder and asked me to stare at a silver orb suspended above me. My eyelids would soon become heavy, he said, whereupon a recording of a Reginald Dixon type of theatre organ began to play 'Air On A G-String'.

By this time, I was, he said, in a deep sleep. Actually, I wasn't, because I'd suddenly remembered the schoolboys' joke about the nudist with the 'Hair On Her G-String'.
I tried to concentrate. I wanted this to work. There might be a best-selling novel in it.
The hypnotist then began my journey into my past. 'You are now twenty. Where are you living?' he asked.

'In a bed-sitter in Bayswater.'

Further back he went. 'You are now sixteen. What are you doing?'

'School.'

'Are you happy?'

Come on, I was thinking. Is anyone happy at sixteen? 'Relatively,' I answered.

'Back to five years of age,' he continued. Next came prebirth. '1935, 1910, 1880. You are going to go down ten steps. I will count them for you, after which you will find yourself in a warm, comfortable cellar.'

The counting began. From somewhere I was aware of the smell of cat urine. Was that in the cellar in 1880, I wondered, or was it on the blanket that he'd spread over me?

'Now you are walking down a long tunnel. When you reach the end of the tunnel you will find a door. When you open it, I want you to tell me what is the first thing that you see. Now. Open the door. What do you see?'

'I can see this isn't working,' I said.

'What?'

'I'm not hypnotised.'

There was a moment's hesitation. Then I was told to close the imaginary door, retrace my steps along the imaginary tunnel, go up the imaginary steps, back through the decades of the twentieth century…until I was back in a South London attic on a warm afternoon.

The hypnotist was silent for a while. Then he made his diagnosis. 'Your trouble is a case of chronic analysis. Perhaps being a journalist makes you question everything. If you'd seen something when the door opened, we would have been away. I could have asked you if there was anyone else with you, what year it was and what your name was. But without somewhere to start there was nowhere for me to go. To experience past lives you just have to let yourself go. About one person in fifteen cannot be hypnotized.'

I was disappointed. Perhaps I should forget about the past and think about the future, I suggested, as he gave me a discount on the failed regression and wrote out a VAT receipt for me.

He looked doubtful. 'You could try a clairvoyant. But if you do, make sure you see about ten, because a lot of them will just take your money and tell you anything.' At which point, he drove me back to the train station.

I suppose I'd always been sceptical about the idea of being able to regress to a past life, romantic though the notion was. But the hypnotist believed in it. He really did.

I never wrote the intended novel, so I never got the big American bestselling paperback I'd hoped for.

After the break-up of the Beatles, I'd assumed that I would never much write about them again. I was wrong. The public's fascination has just kept on growing. Perhaps it was because the Beatles bowed out as a group when they were at the top of their game, rather than carrying on, with each album probably selling fewer than the one before, as has happened with the Rolling Stones. Or maybe it was because their songs became standards and they seemed to represent, in some people's minds, a golden age.

Whatever it was, it meant that I had to accept that I'd been tarred with the Beatles brush, which I suppose wasn't the worst brush in the world with which to be smeared and was therefore still on call to interview Paul McCartney for the *Daily Telegraph*. Then when Paul's wife, Linda, died of breast cancer, I wrote a series about her for the *Daily Mail*. I covered the stabbing and then the death of George Harrison, too, and when the twenty fifth anniversary of the murder of John Lennon came due, I wasn't surprised to get the call from the BBC asking for a play about the day John died. We called it *Unimaginable*. As with the death of President Kennedy and 9/11, everyone over a certain age can remember exactly where they were when they heard the news.

The Best Day Of My Life was our daughter's Louise's idea. It was perfect for a first-person column, so I sold it to the *Daily Mail's Weekend* magazine. Almost every one of us has a 'best day' that we smile to ourselves when we remember, so the job was to find different kinds of people who could tell us the details. And the importance of any interview is always in the detail.

One of my favourite stories was Ralph McTell telling me how he wrote his brilliant song 'Streets of London'. He'd been a student at Croydon Tech when he'd become obsessed with the sound made by a certain kind of guitar, a Harmony Sovereign. Saving up to buy one, he'd just reached £29 in his savings account when he saw a *Melody Maker* advertisement for one at Mairant's Music Centre in Soho for exactly £29. Buying it, and with it on his back, he had the confidence to hit the beatnik trail and go busking across Europe. He was 17.

Then one night in Paris he saw an old man sleeping out. 'He had his boots under his head, and I had this tune in my head and wrote the line, "Have you seen the old man in the closed down market, kicking up the papers with his worn-out shoes..." It was "Streets of Paris", at first, but I changed it to "Streets of London". It might have happened with another guitar. But it happened with this one because of that day when I bought it.'

Terry Wogan, as expected, told me a funny story about when the *Eurovision Song Contest* was held in Jerusalem: 'The winner from the previous year was Dana International, an Israeli transexual. And as she stepped forward to present the award to that year's winner she tripped in her high heels, and three members of Mossad threw themselves on top of her thinking it was an assassination.'

Peter Bowles told of another side of being an actor. By 1970 he was 34, had been married for ten years and had three children. 'I was getting the odd part in television shows, such as *The Avengers* and *The Saint*, but I didn't have a regular income. We were living in a rented flat in Hammersmith and couldn't get a mortgage because we had no money. I never earned more than £7000 year, but usually it was more like £3000. Then one day I read in the local paper that the council was encouraging people by offering them100 per cent mortgages in houses by the Thames which were derelict. We went to the council office early the next morning, the first in the queue, and they took us to a large, four-storey house in a Victorian terrace. It really was totally derelict.

'We bought it for £7000, with Sue, my wife, borrowing £100 from one of her aunts as a deposit. Three months later we moved in. There were no carpets or curtains, and we had very little furniture, just boxes. But I remember going to sleep on that first night knowing that our three children were asleep in their bedrooms and that this house was ours. It was a feeling of extreme happiness, which happens very rarely.'

Then there was Sir Ranulph Fiennes who, while attempting to navigate the world on its polar axis, found himself and a colleague floating around on a disintegrating ice flow in the Arctic and having to fend off a polar bear with bullets.

'We'd been told by the Royal Canadian Mounted Police that you aren't allowed to shoot polar bears unless they've started the final charge at you. We'd seen nineteen adult bears in three months, then one became very aggressive and our efforts to frighten it away had no effect. Finally, when it exhibited all the Mounties' listed signs of aggression, and it came to within about 15 yards of us we decided to shoot it.

'My colleague lay in the snow with the rifle, although he only had two bullets. I was behind him with my pistol. The agreement was that I would fire my pistol bullets at it, and, if it still kept coming, he would fire the rifle. I aimed at the bear's chest with the first bullet I fired and hit it in the ankle. The bear stopped in mid-charge, turned around and left, hardly even limping.

'But we still had to get home. With our rescue ship stuck 17 miles away in solid ice, we had to try to get to it by travelling through melting sea ice. Then one evening I saw what looked like two match sticks on the southern horizon. It was our ship. I was not given to tears but I found my eyes smarting as I jumped up in the air and found myself waving like a madman.'

Ranulph Fiennes was already in his late thirties by that time, but Lenny Henry was hardly more than a child, when at fifteen he passed an audition for the television talent show *New Faces*. 'On the big day I went to Birmingham with my mates, Mac and Greg, and we had lamb chops at Rackhams department store, and then I went to the ATV studio. It was like being in heaven for me. I saw the rickety *Crossroads* set, the guy who played Sandy and the girl who played Jill. And I couldn't wait to tell my mum about the canteen's long fat sausages, egg, chips and beans for about 5p.

'In the rehearsal the producer said, "I think you should start with your back to the audience. It'll be a surprise". I was so innocent and naïve I couldn't think what the surprise would be. When it was my turn, I crouched over a pram with my back to the audience and the camera and started to do a bog-standard Frank Spencer impersonation saying, "Hello Betty, Hello Jessica", like Michael Crawford in *Some Mothers Do 'Ave 'Em*. Then I turned around and there was this massive intake of breath from about 300 people. They laughed and laughed. It was fantastic. The show went out on my mum's birthday and a few weeks later I was on a bus in Leicester being driven by a black man, and he shouted, "Hello, Lenny". And I realised that my life had changed for ever.'

The Best Day Of My Life was the ultimate feelgood column, with almost every person we spoke to coming up with a story that was special to them. Many happy memories came from childhood, but some, like Barry Norman, told of how being made redundant forced a new direction to be taken in life. He became a famous TV film critic.

I didn't ask Tory grandee Lord Hailsham, who used to be known by his birth name of Quintin Hogg, what his best day might have been, but he once told me of what surely must have been one of his worst. Born in 1907, at the age of seven he was due to go off to his prep school when his parents decided to rectify an inept circumcision that had been performed at his birth.

'No-one thought to tell me what was about to happen, nor was a local anaesthetic administered. I was just flung across the doctor's lap, and snip-snip. There it was. All I remember is the humiliation, the pain and all this blood. And then when I went to my private school there was this horrible, little ritual I had to perform every night of sponging the thing with this special sponge which caused a good deal of interest from my fellow scholars.'

30.

'It looks as if it's going to be a nice day'

One day, when I was 59, our daughter, Louise, got married and I found that the old saying that time becomes increasingly condensed with age was true. Days that had felt like decades when I'd been in double maths at school were now skipping by. One by one, our children left home, and our house became less busy and less fun; the record player didn't play Dominic's Tears For Fears' albums anymore. Every family recognises those suddenly silent days in the home, and Louise's approaching wedding turned a key to open the memory door. There I found Louise, aged five, on her first day at primary school, wearing a yellow dress, blue cardigan and sandals and carrying a red satchel 'for my books'; there she was in Portugal learning to swim, and then later in Crete on water-skis. All parents are in love with their own children, every father is in love with his daughter.

And every daughter knows her father. 'Better take your Valium now, Dad,' Louise told me as, alone together, we waited for the car to take us to her wedding. 'Give it chance to kick in before we get to the ceremony, or you know what you'll be like.'

My mother cried at the wedding. She always did cry at weddings, although she thoroughly enjoyed them. But it was a turning point in her life, too, watching, one by one, as her grandchildren, who now numbered seven, went their own way and began producing children of their own. 'I'd like to go on living for quite a while to see what happens to everybody,' she told me once. But five more years was her limit.

I wore my Elvis socks on the day she died. Made of black cotton with the name *Elvis* embroidered in silver thread across the ankles, I showed them to her when, waking on the morning of her death, she found me at her bedside. The sight of them made her smile through the pain. Elvis was a joke we'd shared for fifty years since she'd pretended to despair of me as a teenager.

It was a sunny May morning in Lymington, Hampshire, and, as a nurse opened a window behind her, she looked back and saw white apple blossom on a tree in the hospital garden. 'It looks as if it's going to be a nice day,' she said, as the morphine gave her some moments' respite.

In fact, it was a terrible day. 'Am I dying?' she asked me a couple of hours later. Hiding my tears, I told her I didn't think so, that she'd been ill, but that the doctors had given her some Lazarus pills, so she would soon be better. That was my last joke, the last time I made her smile. Then I went to phone the priest.

I'd like to be able to write that it was a pain-free death. It wasn't. But the presence of the priest gave her a comfort I would never have thought possible. After lying speechless for long periods, a silence broken only by gasps of agony, suddenly my mother was making the responses as the priest gave her the last rites, and she recited the Lord's Prayer with him.

I don't believe in God. I wish I did. I wanted to believe then, but I couldn't. My mother did, though. And that faith made the pain and her departure so much more bearable. Suddenly, a while after the priest had left, she opened her eyes, saw me and called out: 'John! John!'

John was the name of my father who had died in 1944. Did she think she'd already died and gone to heaven and was meeting him again? Was she disappointed when it was pointed out by Maureen, her carer, that it wasn't her husband John, just her son Raymond? I don't know.

My sister, Sylvia, and niece, Francesca, arrived from Geneva to share her last hour. As our mother was slipping away the nurse suggested we both say something to her. My sister did, comforting her, but I couldn't think of anything to say. I just held her hand. Then she was gone.

Later that night I wished I'd reminded her of another day in May, when I was a small boy and she'd taken Sylvia and me to a bluebell wood. And how we'd sat on the top of a hill, a little family of three, and had a picnic of orange squash and jam and bread.

She was nearly 92 when she died, so I'd known the end would come fairly soon, but, somehow, I hadn't expected it. She'd had so many bits and pieces of illnesses over the years, but she just seemed to go on and on, living alone, refusing to go into a care home, struggling through everything, as she and her entire generation had always struggled.

The dream life she'd anticipated in 1936, when she'd married and bought a brand new home with a big garden had been ended with a telegram in 1944 from the Admiralty. There was never another man, never even a date. Not many mums worked in those days, but, after my father's death, she worked hard to make everything possible for my sister and me. And, even though she must have been worried stiff when my school report told her that at the age of fourteen I'd got 6 per cent in arithmetic, 2 per cent in algebra and nothing at all in geometry, she never showed it. Instead, she encouraged me in subjects I was better at. I learned a lesson there. Don't nag, encourage.

Her death changed me. I'd witnessed the power of faith, and, though not reconverted, I now find myself irritated by the sneer of fundamentalist atheists who mock believers of all faiths. I also learned that it's possible to be more generous if you're thrifty. In her later years she didn't want for anything, but she didn't buy much either. She preferred to save her money so that she could give it away, either to her family, and you had to fight not to take it, or to the various children's charities she supported.

Looking back, I find I admire her now more than I realised when she was alive, when her obstinacy could irritate. Many people from her narrow background might have had some latent prejudice towards those of another complexion. By the end she just didn't see colour, admiring immigrants for their ambition to improve their lives and those of their children.

And, this may sound trite, but I do think that her generation, men and women whose lives were forged by the adversity of two world wars and the Depression, were honed into grittier stuff than my own. My mother was just one of millions of ordinary people who took on what life threw at them and got on with making the best of it. Then they gave that best to us.

She's now a part of my memory, no longer the gasping old lady I saw die, but young again, running after me up the road as she taught me to ride a bike, cycling with me to the farm to see Daisy, the horse I loved, and laughing at me as I played 'Heartbreak Hotel' again and again and again.

31.

'Sorry, Boys, You Failed The Audition'

I've loved the discipline of short stories since I was at school. No flim-flammery allowed, no need to explain too much, just a captured moment and reflection on the human condition, with 5000 words the maximum. Usually, fewer. So, when BBC Radio 4 asked me to come up with a story about Liverpool, as part of their Queen's Diamond Jubilee celebration with stories from different cities around the country, I already had the starting point in my head. It came from a line in the film *Citizen Kane.* In it, a journalist is trying to uncover the meaning of Kane's last word, 'Rosebud', when he interviews an elderly employee who tells him that one day in 1922 he'd seen a girl on the Staten Island ferry and there hadn't been a day since then that he hadn't thought about her.

We all have moments like that, and I began to wonder what would happen if an elderly man, now a widower, looked up a pretty girl he saw for just one night fifty years earlier at the Cavern club. The rest was the story, and I called it *I Saw Her Standing There.*

When it was broadcast, I was as satisfied with it as with any TV play. The BBC should do more short stories. All it takes is a script and someone to read it. It could hardly be cheaper.

Women's magazines are often a good outlet. When our son Kieron was a little boy, he fell in love with a pretty girl called Abbie at playgroup and was desolate when she didn't want to play with him anymore. I called that story *Love In A Sandpit.* A lot of mothers wrote to me after its publication. It was, it seems, a common occurrence. Then there was the story about a boy of eight who goes to a fancy-dress party in a very realistic chimpanzee suit and finds himself mistaken for a real escaped chimp, captured and taken off to the zoo. So it was a trading places encounter, told from both the viewpoint of the boy and that of the chimpanzee. I called it *Sam and The Monkey Suit.*

I liked *Penelope As Nevermore,* a brief love affair between a beautiful, bossy academic and a young Indian technician who is hired to fix her computer. And it was a nice surprise when in 2021, the *Daily Express* ran *Let Nothing You Dismay*, which was about a middle-class dad who, having been made redundant, secretly takes a job as Father Christmas in a shopping mall.

My novel *Love Out Of Season,* was really a collision and intertwining of separate love stories that take place in a hotel in the lead up to St Valentine's Day, where a musician and a novelist meet. Then there are two teenagers on the staff, an elderly couple, a pair of reporters taking the chance of a spot of tabloid adultery and a middle-aged nun and a priest who had left their orders so that they could marry.

The arrival of Amazon on our home computers threatened to spell doom for bookshops, and I'm sure it did for some. But, while sales of books being read on Kindles and other tablets, was initially feared, publishers fought back with better designs for their wares. A mooch around Waterstones is now like a tour of Aladdin's cave, so dazzling are the displays of books. An elegantly crafted book cover gives an extra aesthetic value to an author's years of work. It can make it a beautiful present, too.

But Amazon did something else, too. It made self-publishing possible and easy. Self-publishing has traditionally been sneered at as the recourse taken by authors when they can't find a publisher for their book. Well, maybe. But that's to forget that Beatrix Potter first published *The Tale of Peter Rabbit* herself after it was rejected six times by publishers, and that *The Martian*, which became a big Matt Damon film, started life in episode form on author Andy Weir's website.

So, I was hardly charting new territory when, in 2011, I collected all my Beatles interviews and associated articles into *The Ray Connolly Beatles Archive.* It sold from the first day I put it up and is still selling, not in huge quantities, but, steadily, week by week, often to American and European readers. I never tried to find a publisher for it. It wouldn't have been financially worthwhile for an agent or publisher to become involved. Instead, I became a publisher myself and it pays me a small, regular monthly pension, as it will continue to do for as long as anyone is interested in the Beatles. At the same time, it has the historical benefit of having been written as an ongoing project when I didn't know what the Beatles' futures might bring.

With the Beatles still in mind, I then wrote a radio play for the BBC in which I imagined what might have happened to them if they'd been turned down by producer George Martin in 1962, and then broken up as a band. I've always enjoyed hypothetical interpretations of history, what playwright Alan Bennet called 'subjunctive history', such as 'what would have happened to Britain if Hitler had won the war'. And the Beatles was the story of my generation. My problem was, where was the focus?

Then I remembered Freda Kelly, the Beatles Fan Club secretary. I'd first met her in 1967 when we were both on the *Magical Mystery Tour*. But it was only when I interviewed her for the *Daily Mail,* after she'd been asked to appear in a documentary about herself, that I realised that Freda, or someone like Freda, the loyal secretary, who stayed at home in Liverpool when the Beatles went off to London and the world, was my perfect focus.

I called the play '*Sorry, Boys, You Failed the Audition',* and the action took place in Liverpool in the eight years between 1962 and 1970, during which Paul McCartney fictitiously goes off to university and then becomes an English teacher, George Harrison becomes an itinerant guitarist with different groups, John turns into a local Liverpool wit, and Ringo wins the pools and buys the Cavern.

It was produced in Manchester by Gary Brown who cast the brilliant Sara Bahadori as Freda Kelly. When I asked Sara why she had such a good Liverpool accent, when she'd been brought up in the Midlands by Iranian and Scottish parents, she said: 'I used to go home and watch *Brookside* after school.'

I later rewrote and extended '*Sorry, Boys, You Failed The Audition'* as a novella and self-published it on Amazon. It, too, sells regularly.

Very few people can honestly say that they have the luxury of planning their careers. Freelance writers never do. So, when something like the world banking crisis of 2008 comes along, making ends meet without a steady income can become tricky. Ever since I'd been writing, I'd saved a copy of, not only every published word I've ever written, but hundreds of letters from both readers and friends. Inevitably that included some forgotten Beatles stuff. Our children were intrigued and amused when, one day in 2008, by which time they were all in their thirties, I showed them some surviving letters from John Lennon, and the typed lyrics to the songs on his *Imagine* album, complete with John's scribbled changes.

'I'm thinking of selling some of this stuff,' I told them. 'What do you think?'

'Do you think John Lennon saved your letters to him?' Dominic and Kieron both teased.

John Lennon had been a part of my life, not theirs. They hadn't even seen John's letters before. The following day, I contacted Christie's auctioneers and put my little Beatles collection up for sale.

Plum and I had never been to an auction and were surprised to find that the fourteen items I'd recovered from the back of my cupboard had been given the very grand title of 'The Ray Connolly Collection'. It was an exciting morning as we watched a guitar once owned by Brian Jones go for £65,000 and a Hofner bass that Paul McCartney had played fetch £7,000. Obviously, I hadn't owned either of those, but all kinds of bits and pieces of memorabilia were being snapped up by dealers and fans.

My collection came last of all. A test pressing of the *Imagine* album went for a thousand pounds.

'Won't you need it?' I'd asked John Lennon in 1971 when he'd given it to me at his home, Tittenhurst Park.

'No. I've had the gaps between the songs changed slightly,' he'd replied. 'I've got another one now.'

Christie's told me that had it been signed, it would have been worth considerably more to collectors. But a thousand pounds seemed fine to us.

Our big surprise came when bidding for the *Imagine* lyrics began. It was exciting because very quickly it became a two-horse race between someone on a phone in Switzerland and someone else on another phone in New York. The New York bidder won at a price of £20,000. We were astonished. Who on earth would pay so much for shiny old Xeroxes of typed lyrics with just a few squiggles that the singer/songwriter, admittedly John Lennon, had added for me when he'd changed the lyrics?

I got a hint a few years later when I ran into Yoko at a publishing launch for a book by Hunter Davies. Seeing me for the first time in many years, she murmured sharply to me, 'You sold John's letters'. Which, from someone who had monetised her husband's memory many times since his death, seemed a bit rich. But only in 2018, with the publication of Yoko's lavish coffee table book, *Imagine John Yoko*, which contained the song lyrics and squiggles that I'd sold at auction spread across two pages, did I realise who the successful mystery bidder had been. Thank you for the £20,000, Yoko.

I've often been asked if I had any regrets about selling the letters. Not for one second. I kept photocopies, of course. But I've turned down every request to sell any surviving recordings of my interviews. They were conversations between me, the interviewer, and the interviewee. They weren't recorded to be part of someone's podcast.

Time and again I simply went through the door that opened, as I moved from films to radio, television and books, but, throughout everything, I always kept a foot in journalism. Now my cuttings books are a minor trove of social history. Rod Stewart was amusing when he remembered how his view over a railway shunting yard from his bedroom window as a child had led, in his millionaire life, to building a vast model train set over an entire floor of his current home. That train set paints a vivid picture of how his working-class childhood has never quite left him.

In the same way, Catholicism still peoples Edna O'Brien's memories of her upbringing in an Irish convent boarding school, where she formed a secret attachment to one of the nuns. 'I was so in love with her, as in love with her as I've even been with any man, and I haven't been in love many times in my life. If she knew, she didn't let on, but sometimes she would shout at me, and that's a form of love. And she gave me little presents, some holy pictures, things like that.'

Then there was Sir Peter Hall, who in his career, ran both the Royal Shakespeare Company and the National Theatre, and who described himself as very much of the Richard Hoggart generation. 'I was a working-class boy from Suffolk, elementary school, grammar school and university, who found myself absolutely separated from my parents and my family... It wasn't so much a class gap as an education gap between us. My parents were terribly proud of how far they'd come and how far I might go. The result was that I came to feel like an outsider in my own family.'

The child was father of the man in every story.

I enjoyed interviews as much as anything I ever did, but opportunities became increasingly rare as public relations companies took over rationing their stars' media appearances; thirty minutes with you, thirty minutes with someone else, with TV always coming first. That way of doing interviews wasn't for me. I needed time with my subjects. So, when I wasn't working on bigger projects, I found myself enjoyably reacting in 1,400 words of print to whatever stories were in the news, most frequently for the *Daily Mail.* There was a trip to Cornwall to cover the total eclipse of the sun, as I stood with a multitude on a beach at Newquay while the world turned from full colour to monochrome; and then there was David Bowie at Glastonbury.

I liked my advice on A-level results ('Don't dismay if you don't do as well as you hoped'), another piece on 'Why we give things up for Lent', and even one on the hollyhocks in the front garden of our present house in Fulham. All told there have been hundreds of articles, many about music. That's what feature writers do. They respond to current events in little essays. And then they move on to the next subject and the next essay. It's like writing compositions at school.

By this time, Plum and I were reaching that stage when it seemed that the milestones in life were getting closer together as friends and relatives began having health problems, which is something that rarely crosses your mind when you're young. We'd always been sparklingly well, so the day I came down from my study and couldn't wake her terrified me. Our GP had put her being unwell down to a kind of flu. It wasn't. She had a heart infection which she'd probably caught at the dentists, and which resulted in six weeks in the Royal Brompton Hospital. After six months of antibiotics she recovered, but it was a frightening wake-up call.

In popular culture the beginnings and endings of careers are the bits that stay in the public's mind longest. So, it always seemed unfair to me that Elvis Presley was so often ridiculed, after his death, as the fat King of the Cheeseburgers. Yes, he wore terrible, white, rhinestone peppered outfits on stage, had become musically irrelevant and died while sitting on a lavatory at the age of 42. I couldn't do anything about those details because they were all true.

But it seemed to me, history can often be a distorting mirror, and his was a tragedy that deserved more investigation. I wanted to know how and why this blessed, revolutionary, young man with all the God given talents, and who at 21 had become world famous, allowed himself to plunge so low? So, I wrote a biography on him, *Being Elvis: A Lonely Life*.

The answer to my question was, of course, in the title of my book. By the very nature of his fame, Elvis was destined to be always lonely. He was shy and unworldly, who had become imprisoned behind a wall of impossible fame. His talent had been intuitive and cultural, but he'd mortgaged it to a manager who knew nothing about music, and whose understanding of fame was based purely on money. Elvis wasn't the first rock singer, but he was the first rock superstar, who set the template in his musical style for all who followed. John Lennon once told me how difficult it had been for the Beatles during Beatlemania, then added: 'But there were four of us to handle it. Elvis was on his own.' Lennon and McCartney, Bob Dylan and Paul Simon knew how good they were. But I suspect Elvis never knew, believing he had simply been, as he would say, 'lucky to come along at the right time', and that he owed his success to his manager, 'Colonel' Tom Parker, who made sure his boy was never disabused of that fallacy.

When Elvis died at the age in 1977 it was of a heart attack, a condition that was probably the result of years of addiction to prescription drugs. But his death, as he'd become increasingly cocooned inside his Graceland mausoleum, surrounded by toadying yes-men and doped by private doctors, had been years in the making. By the end, he was unrecognisable as the young man who, by dint of his own, largely unknowing, cross-cultural talent half a lifetime before, had changed the world of popular music. The pilgrims who still go to Graceland to see the garish stage clothes that their hero wore in his final years, and to be dazzled by the walls of gold records are missing the point. That's all just show-biz glitter. Elvis was better than that.

John Lennon would, I know, have agreed with me on that. But then John was a more interesting man than image has allowed him since his murder. A year after his death, Yoko Ono sent his fans a message saying that, 'John prayed for everyone'.

It was well intentioned. But, for those who knew him, it's difficult to imagine John Lennon praying for humanity, no matter what he sang in his most famous song. His memory has been sanctified, and he would have hated it. He'd been a joker and a loud-mouther, and he made no secret of the fact that he hated the veneration of dead stars. 'I don't believe in dead heroes,' he would say. That he became one himself was the direst irony.

As I wrote in my biography on him, *Being John Lennon: A Restless Life,* 'he was a collision of contradictions. A natural leader, who could so easily be led, he saw himself as a chameleon, being at various times, a clever, witty, angry, funny, sharp-tongued, far-sighted, impetuous, talented, guilt laden, preaching, sardonic, exaggerating, gullible, aggressive, unfaithful, obsessive, self-absorbed, outspoken, jealous, sometimes cruel but often generous man.' His former wife, Cynthia, put it more briefly. 'He was certainly no saint, but he wasn't the worst'. To his friends, he was hard not to like.

32.

'It isn't funny, Dad. You weren't there'

And then came Covid. Like many people, I was afraid of it from the very beginning. That was in January 2020, when I first began to read reports of deaths in China. If that ever comes to the UK, I'll do everything I can to avoid catching it, I said, as Plum and I watched the news of the pandemic as it reached Iran, Italy and then Spain. Why were planes still being allowed to come into Heathrow from infected areas, I wondered? Why had the Cheltenham races and the Liverpool game against Atletico Madrid gone ahead? What was our sleepwalking Government thinking? It didn't make sense.

So, when Covid did arrive, Plum and I immediately went into virtual isolation. She cancelled her choir; I avoided any meetings. And, because, after her heart infection, I was worried about her, I did all the shopping during the first part of April. There were no big crowds in Sainsburys, but there were no masks anywhere available either.

The first suggestion that all might not be right for me came when I developed a cough. Then I found I couldn't eat anything other than ice cream. Plum phoned our GP and he recommended a course of antibiotics. A day later my niece, Francesca, and my friend Ian from Taunton both phoned and my speech was, apparently, incomprehensible. I can't remember either call. Then Louise phoned and Plum dialled 111, the NHS helpline.

I'm told that an ambulance was at our house within 20 minutes, and I was driven away. That was the last time I would see my home for five and a half months. The date was April 15, 2020. I have no recollection of the events of that day, nor of the few days before, nor any other days until the end of July. Those three and a half months remain a blank in my mind.

Apparently, within a few hours of being admitted to the Chelsea And Westminster Hospital, which is a mile from where we live, it was confirmed that I had Covid-19, and, as I was moved around the wards, it became clear that I had it very seriously. When I was occasionally fitfully conscious that day, and with Plum not allowed to see me, I'm told that I began phoning our children telling them that I'd been kidnapped by the NHS, and pleading with them to 'get me out of this place'. The doctors and nurses were, I told them, 'all dressed as monkeys, with shaving foam on their faces'. They were, I now know, all wearing full PPE, but my mistake was just the first of many terror deliriums.

An unhappy episode followed as the hospital staff struggled to convince me to wear a CPAP mask to help me breathe, with one doctor waking Plum at ten past four in the morning, asking her to try to reason with me. She tried, but she couldn't, so I had to be moved to the intensive care unit and put into an induced coma and kept alive by a life-support machine.

I know all this now because Plum kept careful notes of every conversation with the doctors and nurses at the hospital so that she could tell our children. My lungs were the first target for the virus, and then came pneumonia and kidney dialysis and a tracheostomy, which was basically a hole put in the front of my throat through which a ventilator did much of the breathing for me, while rendering me speechless. Then there were two heart attacks, after which a couple of stents were put in place. Before Covid, I'd never had any indication that there was anything wrong with my heart, my lungs or my kidneys. At 79 I'd been perfectly healthy.

The month of May was the worst time when on three occasions doctors told Plum that I was so weak, that, if my heart stopped beating, no attempt would be made to resuscitate me, because it would be of no use.

Of course, deep into my coma, I knew nothing of the struggle the doctors and nurses were facing to keep me alive. And, unaware of their efforts for my body, my brain was conjuring up a series of hallucinations. What passed through my mind during those months was so realistic that months later I believed that the incidents I'd imagined had really happened.

Some of these mental adventures were bizarre and disturbing. One had me in India facing a frighteningly angry mob when I upset a wizened, dirty minded old guru. Another starred a group of NHS nurses, some of whom I recognised as the people who were taking care of me, taking over our house to make a comedy film in which they ripped out our bath and replaced it with a juke box. In my mind I was lying on the landing unable to stand up or stop them. Then there was one in which I was dossing down in the bar of a West End hotel, when a stranger approached me and said: 'I know who you are. You're Ray Connolly, and you've been very, very poorly. What you don't know is that you're still very poorly.'

I don't remember the moment when I first woke up. But I do know that during my time in intensive care, my bed became surrounded by, as well as much technical equipment, photographs of my family. There were also images from my career, too, an A4 printout of the poster from the film *That'll Be The Day* here, a cover of my biography of John Lennon there and photos of the hollyhocks in our front garden. And, all the time, music was being played to me, songs I liked. All of this had been arranged by the nurses who wanted to know more about me, and who thought that if I could see and hear familiar things again it might help me regain consciousness and remember who I was.

It did. One afternoon our son Kieron was watching me on a video link as Del Shannon's 'Runaway' was being played on my tablet. I was believed to be still in a coma, but he then saw me become energised, mouthing the lyrics, and playing an imaginary organ keyboard break with my fingers as I aped the sound on the record. On another day the nurses played me a Simon and Garfunkel album, probably 'Live in Central Park', and Plum sat with me as, still with my eyes closed, and unaware that she was there, I mouthed all the lyrics to every song. That night when she got home, she emailed to our children: 'Dad didn't know I was there, but it was lovely to see him happy in his own little world…wherever that was.'

I can't remember any of those incidents, but popular music, my boyhood passion, was coming to my rescue and reconnecting me. I remained speechless, but a little later I would smile when Plum and Kieron sang the Everly Bothers' 'Devoted To You' down the phone. That had long been a favourite in our family.

When I finally became fully conscious, I was still very muddled and got it into my head that we had sold our house and bought another in Holland Park. But Plum insisted that we still lived in Fulham. When Dominic came to visit me, I apparently told him: 'I'm worried about Mum. She doesn't know where she lives anymore. I think she must have Alzheimer's and is trying to hide it, like they all do. But she might get lost. Can you see that she gets home safely?'

'Don't worry, Dad. I'll make sure she's all right.' said Dominic.

Of course, it was me who was doolally, not Plum.

So, as the summer of 2020 crept on into August, little by little my medication was changed. Then the ventilator was taken away, my speaking voice began to be restored, though less so my singing voice because my vocal chords had been scratched by the tube that had been shoved down my throat in order for me to breathe. Plum visited me every afternoon, but it was only, as I spent more time awake, that I realised that the months of lying in bed had left me unable to walk.

The true nature of my illness was finally getting through to me, so, I imagine that I was feeling sorry for myself when one day I told a consultant: 'I had a lucky life until now. I was lucky to get into an excellent university, lucky to get a job that I was good at, and lucky to have a decent career. I was lucky, too, to marry the only girl I ever loved and to have a long and happy marriage, and to have three wonderful children… Then I got Covid.'

'Ray, you're still lucky,' the consultant replied.

'I am?'

'Yes. You survived.'

After 102 days in Intensive Care, I was moved to a general ward, and by September I was looking forward to going home, when, having been transferred to a rehab clinic, I began to vomit blood…lots of it, just like a scene in a Quentin Tarantino film. Hastily, I was rushed back to hospital for more tests. Did Covid have one final unkind trick to play on me? Apparently, not. I recovered.

Finally, the transport came to take me home and on September 28, with the aid of crutches, I managed to walk a few paces up the path back into my house to 'Welcome Home' balloons in the hall that Louise had put up. Weighing more than a stone and a half lighter, it was an emotional homecoming, not least because of a secret Plum had kept from me. While my life had been hanging by a thread, a very close friend of hers had died from the same disease. My friend director Michael Apted, and another friend of hers, would also die from Covid. Since then, a fourth friend has died of the disease.

I felt that I'd been given a second chance, but over 223,000 others in the UK hadn't, and well over five million people worldwide died from Covid. It was only by reading the daily notes Plum had made that I came to fully realise how much she, and the families of all the other Covid patients, had suffered during the pandemic, as she'd waited for the hospital to phone every day, and then been afraid to answer it in case it brought bad news.

There is something selfish about being critically ill in that, although you aren't aware of it at the time, all your thoughts are of yourself. Doctors and nurses do everything they can to take away your pain, but they never let you know that the smile they are wearing at your bedside is most likely masking how they are feeling inside, as they care for other patients who are dying.

Eating had been impossible while I'd been in a coma, and for nearly six months I'd been fed through a tube into my stomach. So, when I got home a rig that was still plugged into me just above my bellybutton had to be removed, and we took a taxi back to the Chelsea and Westminster Hospital. After a few steps on crutches into the building, however, I knew that I couldn't walk any further and had to sit down while Plum fetched me a wheelchair.

The world looks different from a wheelchair, as I watched bright young people in their masks and white gym shoes hurrying past, and I found myself apologising for being in the way. That's what old people do, I thought. I'd never considered myself old before Covid.

I had no recollection of the rig having been put into my stomach, but, in my mind, it was like a tap, with maybe just an inch projecting inside me. It was nothing like that. There was no pain, but I watched in alarm as a snake-like tube, about eighteen inches long, was withdrawn from my intestines.

For the first month at home, I hobbled about the house with a Zimmer frame, but soon a physio encouraged me to walk with a stick, eventually even going with me to the local shop to buy my newspapers. When she stopped coming, Plum would take me. It was on our first outing when I heard a voice calling my name, and a very pretty, blonde, young woman came rushing towards us. I had no idea who she was.

'It's Hannah,' Plum explained. 'Don't you remember, she nursed you for months.'

I shook my head.

'Don't worry,' Hannah smiled. 'After what we had to do to you, it's probably better you don't remember. I just can't believe I'm seeing you like this, walking in the street.'

'You helped save my life,' I told her. 'Thank you.'

'I just wish we could have saved all the other lives, too,' Hannah replied, tears in her eyes. Then she had to hurry off to start her shift.

A few weeks later, I decided to go out alone for the first time and was just reaching the corner when... Bang! My face hit the pavement. The walking stick went flying.

My face was a mess of blood. The no-clotting pills, that were now part of my 11 pills a day regime, were doing their job too well.

When the paramedics arrived, they asked: 'Have you had a fall?'

'No,' I said. 'I tripped up.'

That wasn't how they saw it. A 79-year-old man has a fall, not a trip.

There was no waiting in the A and E department, my Covid history at the same hospital pushing me to the head of the queue. But it took hours for the bleeding to stop, during which I was given X-rays and a brain scan before it was decided that the only real damage was to my self-esteem.

For the next several months I never went out alone again, and every night Plum and I would watch the Covid reports on TV. There was a very good one about Michael Rosen, the children's author, who'd been in intensive care with Covid at the same time that I was, although in a different hospital. I don't know him, but our shared adversity seemed to make us allies, so I tweeted, telling him how, if things had worked out just a little bit differently, he and I might have met at the Pearly Gates.

To which he replied: 'Yes, Ray, that would have been nice. You could have told me about John, Paul, George and Ringo.'

I was now joking on the phone to friends about my 'brush with the Reaper', until my children stopped me. 'It isn't funny, Dad. You weren't there. You don't know,' one of them chided.

By January 2021, with Plum at my side, I could walk a mile and we went to get my first Covid vaccination. I had to stop and sit down on a park bench on both the way there and back, but it was a big day in my recovery.

Fatigue still swamped me every evening, as it does for many Covid sufferers, but the Zimmer frame, crutches and sticks eventually went, and eventually I began to drive again. Best of all was when I was invited back to the Chelsea and Westminster Hospital, to cut the ribbon, make a speech and declare open their new intensive care unit. To stand with Plum and nurse Hannah Leney and Leigh Paxton, the matron in the intensive care unit, was a great moment. One of the angriest came when I read how Boris Johnson had said 'Let the bodies pile up' during a later Covid wave. Because of the devotion of the NHS, mine hadn't joined his pile of bodies.

All told, it took well over a year after I came home to recover, during which time I wondered why I hadn't died when so many others had. Now I think I know. Continuing hospital tests on my lungs have shown that, by complete chance, they have a 35% better function than the average for my age. I never knew that, nor ever did anything to keep fit. But it would have made a difference when I was hanging on to life. It would also have helped me sixty years ago when I was a schoolboy cross country runner.

Until I was ill, writing was my hobby as much as my job. There was always another project. So, my next project was to write a BBC radio play about Covid from the viewpoint of a patient and his wife. I called it *Devoted*, because that was exactly what Plum and my family were, as were the staff of the NHS, some of whom had risked their own lives to save me and many others. An old friend from my TV series *Honky Tonk Heroes*, Philip Jackson, played me, with Alison Steadman playing Plum. At the time of writing, the full version is still available on BBC Sounds.

While I was recovering in hospital, music was my companion, not just the records that Hannah and her colleagues played to me, but the ones I was listening to in my head. Out in the real world, we are over-entertained, with music accompanying us through life. But there is another music, the one that only the individual can hear, the music that plays in the imagination.

For me the popular classics were sometimes there, but more frequently the tunes were the ones I first listened to at an impressionable age. 'Autumn Leaves' on Pat Boone's album, *Stardust*, was a favourite. It was an old song even when I was 17, but it's become ever more personal the older I've got. Is it about old age and bereavement? I think it is. Another track on that album was 'September Song', which ploughs similar territory, of love in middle and old age. I sang those songs silently to myself for weeks in my head as I waited to restart my life.

When we say, 'They don't write them like that anymore', it's because they rarely do. That's no criticism of contemporary songwriters. The shape of songs was different then, allowing for longer verses with more complexity in the lyrics.

So, what else did I imagine singing? Well, songs that usually painted a picture for me: 'I Want To Be in America' from *West Side Story* was a favourite, then there was Simon and Garfunkel singing 'American Tune', Dire Straits' 'Romeo and Juliet' with that wonderful borrowed line 'My boyfriend's back', Neil Young's 'After The Goldrush', Carly Simon's 'The Carter Family' and the Eagles' 'Take It Easy' with the lyric 'Well I was standing on a corner in Winslow, Arizona, and such a fine sight to see, It's a girl my Lord in a flat-bed Ford slowin' down to take a look at me.'

Then there was Jimmy Webb's lonely song for Glen Campbell 'Wichita Lineman' and its line 'And I need you more than want you, and I want you for all time', Johnny Nash's 'I Can See Clearly Now', Jeff Buckley singing 'Hallelujah', Bruce Springsteen's 'Dancing In The Dark', the Kinks' 'Waterloo Sunset' with Terry meeting Julie at the station every Friday night, and the Bee Gees, with their George Formby voices, harmonising on 'To Love Somebody' and 'In the event of something happening to me' in 'New York Mining Disaster 1941'.

Actually, now that I think of it, the list was endless. My brain had become a private juke box.

33.

'Exactly which psychopath do you mean?'

Nearly six months in a hospital bed gave me a lot of time for reflection, but I was surprised when one memory recurred frequently. It was of a school reunion some years ago when I saw again the boys I'd first met in September 1952, when, as 11-year-olds, about a hundred of us had first put on our new green blazers and made our way for the first time to West Park's Catholic Grammar School in St Helens, Lancashire.

It had been a good reunion, faces from long ago coming ever sharper into focus, as if photographs of today were being placed over negatives of yesterday until they matched. And all around the party, everyone described snapshots of another time. I'd always believed that I'd been invisible at school, but the day I was the only one to swim across Coniston Water while on a school camping holiday had bequeathed me a heritage I didn't know I had.

Back in 1952 we'd been told that we were the New Elizabethans, a term minted to describe the young people of the era who would be growing up alongside the new young Queen, who had just ascended to the throne. But looking around the reunion at my former classmates, it occurred that, in their quiet, industrious way, these men had been a lot more than a catchy Fifties PR phrase. They, and millions of men and women like them, had seen social change and prosperity unthinkable in those post-war days.

The organiser of the reunion, Peter Harvey, once the red-headed captain of England Schoolboys at rugby, before becoming a famous Saints Rugby League star, and later a headmaster, put it best. 'My parents hung my school uniform in the sitting room before I went to the grammar school,' he recounted. 'My dad said, "that uniform tells me you'll never have to go down the pit".'

Looking at old school photographs, it was noticed and remembered that another boy always came to school in his wellies. At the time, it had gone unremarked upon, but its reason was now obvious. His parents would have saved up to buy him his smart new uniform, but they hadn't been able to afford a pair of new black shoes to go with it.

But, how well those boys had done. There was one who had become a civil engineer and had helped bring irrigation to a stretch of the Sudan, massively improving the lot of the people there; while more quietly burying a complete steam train which fell off the tracks in the desert, he admitted. 'We couldn't think what else to do with it.'

Another had left school after O-levels, but later worked in the diplomatic service in Washington, Russia, Nepal and Mozambique. Then there was the old boy who had ended up giving business advice on behalf of the DTI, while another was a consultant to the World Bank on technical education projects. Education, education, education, the great leveller, the choice giver, the door opener, was everywhere at that reunion.

Sadly, the two boys who'd gone on to Oxbridge, a big thing then for that school, one of whom had later become a barrister and another a paediatrician, had both died young. But, as the talk turned to the old boys' children, a picture emerged of a second generation of doctors, lawyers and scientists.

Naturally, despite the years, the paunches, smooth heads, and, in some of the former sporting stars, arthritic joints, it wasn't long before the old schoolboy jokes started, too.

'West Park made me what I am,' said one old boy emotionally, now with the strongest of Antipodean accents following a successful career Down Under.

'You mean an Australian!' quipped a former classmate.

Almost without exception these men relived in still indignant tones the terrors of the Doc, a whippet-thin Belgian fantasist who, during French lessons specialised in daily beatings interspersed with casual torture of a semi-intimate nature. After we had left the school, he was discovered to have had no qualifications and been promptly sacked.

'He wouldn't get away with that now,' averred one chap, still angry after all these years. 'He'd be dead.'

Yet such had been the realisation that we were lucky to be at a grammar school at all, no one had gone running to the police or even complained to the headmaster that a psychopath was on the loose. Considering the number of his staff who wielded a cane as readily as a piece of chalk, the headmaster might reasonably have asked: 'Exactly which psychopath do you mean?'

It was a school, and perhaps a time, too, of moral certainties, three of our year having gone on to be priests. Statistically, there should have been some criminals among us as well, but none of those who made it to the reunion knew of any boys who had fallen foul of the law. Rather the reverse, in fact. They had become the law. John Kenny had served in the Metropolitan Police until he retired, when it was noted that, in a force infamous for absenteeism, he 'hadn't taken a sick day since Lord Lucan disappeared'.

The notion of service must have run like a cable through that school, perhaps that generation, two old boys having taught in approved schools. Although the media had played a part in some careers, two other boys having become national newspaper journalists, virtually no one had gone into the arts. A glance at the landscape of South Lancashire would explain why. While a couple of us might have written novels, of the nine who studied arts in the sixth form, six had become teachers. It was important to be doers, not dreamers.

Few had become entrepreneurs either. Again, perhaps the location explains why. Not many people could have afforded to take risks. A steady white-collar job would have been the aim of the parents of those boys.

This having been a Catholic school, there was, of course, a collection made for masses to be said for the dead among our year. In an overwhelmingly secular world, it was a surprise to see just how much Catholicism still played a part in the lives of so many old boys; because it doesn't in mine.

I can't pretend that I remember my schooldays there with any flicker of fondness. But the boys who went to that school in 1952, were, it seemed to me, a microcosm of all those achievers in post-war Britain, who, in rugby parlance, when tossed the ball of opportunity had run with it.

34.

'Much of what we ate came in tins'

And now, here we are, eight decades since the Second World War, in a world very different from the one into which I was born. Many changes have been for the good since then. Most of us will live longer than our grandparents, and, generally, our bodies are in overwhelmingly better condition than theirs would have been, due to the advances in nutrition, public health provision and medical advances. Think only of antibiotics. Penicillin, the antibiotic pioneer, didn't become available in the UK until 1946. Before then, many people died from infected cuts and wounds, as every war recorded.

When the Salk vaccine against polio was introduced in 1956 it was a huge step forward, to be followed by vaccines against diphtheria, whooping cough, flu, meningitis, shingles, hepatitis B, tuberculosis, tetanus, chicken pox, cervical cancer and now Covid. And, although vaccination against smallpox had been known about in the eighteenth century, the disease wasn't eradicated from the world until 1980. We take our good health for granted, which was something our parents and grandparents could never do.

Then there are our teeth. Photographs from World War 1 reveal a nation with mouths of decayed, broken and missing teeth. False teeth were common in older people when I was little. A hundred and sixty years ago Abraham Lincoln's false teeth were made of wood. Those of us who were war babies were lucky in that, due to rationing, there was little sugar in our diet, which meant fewer cavities later; while our children have benefitted from fluoride in water and toothpaste. Corrective braces became common, initially in America, in the Sixties, when the Beatles ungallantly described American teenage girls as 'ugly' because so many of them had braces on their teeth. It was a rare slip in their romance with America. Soon, however, braces would become common in Britain, too, the happy result being that the teeth of today's young people are so much healthier and straighter than those of their grandparents. Some are also whiter, too, but that's a cosmetic thing.

When I was a child much of the food we ate came in tins. There were tins of spam, corned beef, pineapple chunks, salmon, fruit salad, mandarin oranges and even spaghetti. And, with wartime self-sufficiency still in our habits, seasonal vegetables often came from gardens or allotments, from where new potatoes were an annual treat. Sunday lunch was a roast and two veg, for those who could afford a roast. Fish and chip shops thrived. Nothing was exotic. I never tasted an avocado pear until I was in my twenties, and never regularly had wine with my evening meal until I was 30; while rice was only ever rice pudding. That was fine by me. I've never been a foodie.

But, if, as the Sixties' seers told us, 'We are what we eat', we must be a very different species today from what we were in 1940, because our national diet has been transformed. Most of us now enjoy an astonishment of variety and plenty, with fresh fruits being flown in from other parts of the world all the year round…Brexit allowing. While TV chefs are now as famous as film stars.

Communication satellites began sixty years ago with the launching of Telstar. Now there are over two thousand satellites, showing us what to expect in our weather, telling us where best to avoid traffic jams and taking aerial photographs of continents and war zones. As drones bring us pictures of places that human beings can't physically go, digitally controlled, closed circuit television cameras watch us on the street and show who is standing at our front doors. That we are all willingly connected to each other by mobile phones, emails, texts, WhatsApp, Instagram and Zoom in ways we would, only a short time ago, have believed impossible, we accept without thinking.

So much of our lives is now computerised, from banking, to paying taxes and bus fares, booking airline tickets and holidays, ordering supermarket deliveries, and even writing this book. It almost seems that all human knowledge and services are available at the touch of a keyboard, making 'online' one of the most frequently used words in the English language, although I don't believe it came into popular parlance before the Seventies.

Today's children know no other world, as their fingers learn how to use an iPhone as we once used our hands and toes when we first began to count. Indeed, much of childhood is different from my infancy or that of my parents or grandparents. But parenting is different, too. With more working mothers in the population, fathers, in general, now play a much wider role in family life. That must be good.

Inevitably, however, there are downsides, too. With parents becoming more protective of their offspring, are they now denying their children the freedoms that they themselves once enjoyed? And, while computers, smart TVs and mobile phones continually open young eyes and ears to new and diverse influences, not everything they see or hear is going to be for their benefit.

The greatest change in my life has been associated with gender. When I went to university in 1960 there were far fewer female students than male, with the view still held, in many families, that daughters didn't need to go to university because their destiny was to marry and have and care for children. Today almost 60 per cent of first degree students in British universities are female. That has changed relationships between men and women irrevocably. And, as far more young men and women study into their twenties in the growing range of subjects that will equip them to take up an ever-widening variety of professions, the entire population is better educated than at any other time in history.

Back in 1940, Britain was overwhelmingly white. Today we live in a country that has become a magnet for people of all races, religion and talents, and which, for me, is a universal advertisement for toleration, welcome and inclusivity. Just step inside any NHS hospital and marvel at the array of different nationalities working there, and you'll see what I mean.

Then there's the Pill, and the ability of women to plan when to have children. It became available in Britain in the early Sixties, but attitudes being what they then were, its effects were not immediate, with some doctors being loathe to prescribe it to single women. It's difficult to believe such attitudes existed among professionals so recently, but anything to do with gender and sex has always been a battlefield.

All this happened within my lifetime, and the lifetimes of all the people mentioned in this book. But there's been so much more. The Channel Tunnel had been dreamt about for two hundred years before it was finally completed in 1994; while bicycles, the chariots of my boyhood, which once seemed to be facing obsolescence, have made a complete come-back, the streets of our cities now providing special lanes for cyclists on their journeys to and from school and work.

Once upon a time a glimpse of a photograph of a naked woman in *Health and Efficiency* was a thrilling, possibly furtive, experience for a teenage boy, even with the lady's most secret part painted out. Today we have *Naked Attraction* on Channel 4 and the efficacy of a variety of sex toys regularly compared in *The Times*. Changes in society's sexual norms have forever been a swinging pendulum. Will some of today's attitudes cause astonishment in generations to come? We'll see.

My passage through life has undoubtedly been a blessed journey because so much has been for the good. But I can't be unaware that my generation didn't get everything right. As fast foods now dominate our television commercials, and most of our shopping trolleys are loaded like haycarts, with scooters from Deliveroo and Uber Eats racing to our doors to refuel us, I can't remember there ever being more than one fat boy in my class at my junior school. There were fewer plump grown-ups, too. Today around 30% of all UK adults are classed as being clinically obese, with a third of all children overweight when they finish primary school.

Then there's gambling. Do commercials for betting shops encourage it? Obviously, yes, or the betting industry wouldn't make them. Gambling is addictive. Everyone knows that. But the commercials are still there, excepting for the *Guardian* newspaper which has recently banned it. Encouraging gambling doesn't make sense to me.

Nor does the fact that our beaches and rivers are polluted, that drug wars threaten our streets and young deaths from knife crimes are daily occurrences on the TV news.

There is so much more. The country I was born into was poetically famous for being a green and pleasant land. But it was also well known for its smoke and smog and satanic mills, and our resulting soot-blackened ancient buildings.

Today, as we plant more trees and flowers, and our garden centres are as much a day out in the country as a shopping expedition, our world looks both cleaner and more colourful.
That is, so long as we are away from congested city routes and motorways where lung killers are invisible, and we ignore the fact

that insecticides have bled farmers' fields of what was once their natural diversity.

All around us warnings about the survival of our planet are intensifying. But while some of us look forward to the day that wind turbines reduce the carbon in our air, others see turbines as blots on our landscape. We know that the gas guzzling car has no future, while electrically powered vehicles and solar power do. But we also know, as we step happily on to a plane to a holiday destination, that airline flights are polluting the atmosphere, and that desertification is leading to ever more desperate fleeing populations?

What are we going to do about it? Our children and grandchildren will find out.

When I was young, we didn't foresee the future in the way it has turned out, for good and bad. After World War Two, almost the entire population was poor, but the financial difference between the 'just about managing' and the relatively well-off was narrower, there being so little available in the shops, anyway. To own a television set to watch the Coronation in 1953 was a symbol of some prosperity. Now almost every family will have seen King Charles III crowned on their TV set. But the poor are still with us.

I don't believe I ever saw a beggar on the streets of Britain until the Seventies. Now I pass them every day. Prefabs were built after the Second World War for those who had been bombed out and who were homeless. Today we have an ever-growing number of food banks. We read every day of the housing shortage, but every high street in the country now has empty shops as sales go online or are moved out to shopping malls in the suburbs, leaving empty buildings where famous stores once stood.

Not everyone wants to live in a suburb, so one solution might be for local authorities to buy these empty buildings, often originally Victorian and even Georgian in style, and redesign them as homes, thus turning urban living back into what it was before the retail explosion of the Twentieth Century. But will that ever happen on a large scale? Or will city centres turn into urban deserts of derelict buildings?

I grew up when a general, if sometimes vague, Christianity was the spiritual cathedral upon which the nation's moral code was built, a time when the future promised nothing other than peace and progress, and when most of us looked forward to becoming steadily better off. We thought that in a social democratic country, ever increasing social fairness would go on forever, and that because of man's remorseless ingenuity, progress would never stop.

But it's what we do with that ingenuity that counts, and how equally we share the wealth thus created. Will Artificial Intelligence be a great benefit to the world, or a massive creator of unemployment? Will it help the rich, who control it, get richer, and the poor, who don't, get poorer?

As for peace, we're now remembering that human nature being what it is, peace can still come and go, as wars in the Middle East, Africa and Ukraine have shown.

Undoubtedly my generation's passage through life has been blessed. I believe we really were born at the right time. We have, in general, grown wealthier than our parents, which once seemed to be the natural order of things. But will that be the case for our children and grandchildren?

Will they be as lucky as we have been? There remain inequalities in our educational opportunities, and an ever-widening gulf between the very rich and the poor. There is also a worldwide lethargy in attacking global warming and its extinctions of natural life; while lightweight, sometimes criminal politicians, online disinformation, and dumbed-down celebrity culture sullies and muddles our media.

Will tomorrow's youth be sucked into an amoral lazy swamp, or instead will they choose to build on the achievements of our time and rectify some of our mistakes and disappointments? That is what we must hope for.

We like to think we understand the present and how we got here, and, through a study of history, we interpret the past. But we can never predict the future. All we know is that human nature doesn't change. Tomorrow's people, our children, grandchildren and great- grandchildren, will have the same ambitions and desires as we do, but in a world that is impossible for us to now imagine, as our world would have been impossible for our generation's grandparents to imagine.

Let's keep our fingers crossed for them.

LOVE OUT OF SEASON

'Funny, charming and compassionate. Successfully transposing the conventions of Shakespearian comedy to the 21st Century' - *Mail on Sunday*****

'The perfect book to give someone who's a bit down… Funny, fun and fundamentally wise, this is a cracker of a book' - *Dublin Evening Herald*

KILL FOR LOVE

A picnic for a couple of teenagers ends in a double tragedy. Why? A loving mother poisons her husband and children? Why? Meanwhile a TV reporter finds herself intrigued by a singer-songwriter…

A thriller set in the world of TV news, social networking…and music…

BEING JOHN LENNON – A RESTLESS LIFE

'Excellent…Connolly draws on his archive conversations with the Beatles to give a superb portrait of a dissatisfied star who couldn't stop reinventing himself' – *Daily Telegraph*

'This careful, thoughtful biography… For Connolly, it is Lennon's insecurities that are ultimately most revealing' – *Sunday Times*

'Brisk and eminently readable' – *The Times*

BEING ELVIS - A LONELY LIFE

'Connolly carefully and sympathetically paints the many faces of Presley, faces eventually shrouded in despair' – *Kirkus Reviews*

'A sympathetic and exceptionally well written account' – *USA Today*

'SORRY, BOYS, YOU FAILED THE AUDITION'

On January 30th, 1969, John Lennon ended the Beatles' filmed concert on the roof of their Apple headquarters in London by joking: 'Thank you very much. We hope we passed the audition.' It was the last time the four would be seen playing together.

But what would have happened if in the summer of 1962, the Beatles hadn't impressed at their last chance to sign a record deal? What would the future have held for John, Paul, George and Ringo if producer George Martin had said 'No'?

Sorry, Boys, You Failed the Audition – an alternative history. *Adapted from Ray Connolly's BBC radio play* .

Printed in Great Britain
by Amazon